EDEXCEL A-LEVEL RELIGIOUS STUDI

PAPER 3 NEW TESTAMENT STUDIE

COMPLETE A-LEVEL YEAR 2 STUDY GUIDE

Published independently by Tinderspark Press
© Jonathan Rowe 2018
www.philosophydungeon.weebly.com

CONTENTS

ABOUT THIS BOOK

This book offers advice for teachers and students approaching Edexcel A-Level Religious Studies, Paper 3 (New Testament Studies). It brings together material from three study guides covering these Topics:

4   **Ways of interpreting the scripture**

5   **Texts and interpretation: the Kingdom of God, conflict, the death and resurrection of Jesus**

6   **Scientific and historical-critical challenges, ethical living and the works of scholars**

These three study guides are summarised in note format in **Revision Guide 2**, which also includes revision exercises, quizzes and exam-style questions for the A-Level but doesn't have the sort of detailed explanations that are in this study guide. The remaining books cover the topics in Year 1 of the A-Level and can be purchased separately.

1   **Social, historical and religious context of the New Testament**

2   **Texts and interpretation of the Person of Jesus**

3   **Interpreting the text and issues of relationship, purpose and authorship**

The **New Testament AS/Year 1 Study Guide** brings all 3 of these books together in one volume similar to this book. This material is also summarised in note format in **Revision Guide 1**, but there is also **Revision Guide 3** which covers all 6 study guides in note format and has exam questions for the entire A-Level.

Text that is indented and shaded like this is a quotation from a scholar or from the Bible. Candidates should use some of these quotations in their exam responses.

Text in this typeface and boxed represents the author's comments, observations and reflections. Such texts are not intended to guide candidates in writing exam answers.

TOPIC 4: WAYS OF INTERPRETING THE SCRIPTURE

Ways of interpreting Scripture

- The Bible as inspired: literal, allegorical and moral senses of scripture

- Modern scholarship on the value of scripture including Barth on scripture as the 'story of God', Bultmann on demythologising the text and an overview of the four main approaches to post-Enlightenment biblical interpretation of rational, historical, sociological and literary.

- The contexts, strengths and weaknesses of these positions and the significance of these models of interpretation for understanding the text today and its relevance for the modern world.

WAYS OF INTERPRETING THE SCRIPTURE

What's this topic about?

How did the New Testament Gospels come to be written? Who wrote them and who was the intended audience? What were they originally trying to say? These questions are addressed in this topic.

WAYS OF INTERPRETING SCRIPTURE

This topic looks at the idea of **Scripture as inspired by God** and ways of interpreting Scripture **literally**, **allegorically** and **morally**; the **debate** between **Barth**'s interpretation of 'The Story of God' and **Bultmann** on de-mythologizing the Bible; **post-Enlightenment approaches** to Biblical interpretation: **rational**, **historical**, **sociological** and **literary**. There are no **Key Scholars** in this Topic (although Karl Barth and Rudolf Bultmann take the place of Key Scholars).

Before you go any further...

... there are some things you need to know.

HERMENEUTICS

Hermeneutics is the technique for interpreting things. **Source**, **Form** and **Redaction Criticism** (which you studied in **Topic 3**) are all hermeneutic approaches – they are ways of interpreting how texts come to be composed and what they originally meant. **William Wrede**'s theory of the **Messianic Secret in Mark's Gospel** (from **Topic 1**) is a hermeneutic theory: it claims to interpret the true meaning of Mark.

Of course, there is no agreement about the best hermeneutic approach to the Bible. Should Biblical passages be taken **literally** or **symbolically**? Should prophecies be interpreted in a **preterist** sense (referring to events going on in the prophet's own time) or a **futurist** sense (predicting events that happen centuries later or on Judgement Day)?

- **Catholic Hermeneutics:** The Catholic Church bases its teachings on TRADITION. This means that Catholic hermeneutics are free to reinterpret the Bible in new ways, so long as they stay within the traditional teachings of the Church. An example of this would be the way **Raymond E. Brown** (a Catholic priest) interprets the Fourth Gospel as an allegory for the **Johannine Community**'s expulsion from the Synagogues (*c.f.* **Topic 3**).
- **Traditional (Protestant) Hermeneutics:** Protestant Churches base their teachings on "*Sola Scriptura*" ('Only Scripture'), which means the word of the Bible rather than traditions. Because of this, Protestant interpreters are more likely to treat the Bible literally and regard the four Gospel-writers as independent eyewitnesses, rather than redactors. An example of this would be **Morna Hooker**'s rejection of Wrede's theory of the **Messianic Secret in Mark**.

- **Liberal Hermeneutics:** Liberal Christians (often from the Protestant tradition) are sceptical about the supernatural elements in the Bible and interpret miracles naturalistically. They are less like to view the Gospel-writers as eyewitnesses and more likely to view them as **redactors** who have brought together different sources or constructed a narrative out of *pericopae* (textual units) from an earlier oral tradition. An example of this would be **Rudolf Bultmann**'s idea (p33) that the Bible should be **demythologized** (stripped of its supernatural elements) to reveal its real teaching.

Take an example: **Jesus feeding the 5000** (a miraculous Sign explored in **Topic 2**)

- Catholic hermeneutics would argue this Sign symbolises the mystery of the **EUCHARIST** (which supports Catholic traditions about the importance of going to Mass) and might agree with liberal hermeneutics that the miracle didn't actually happen and that it's the **symbolism** that counts.
- Traditional hermeneutics might agree with the symbolism but insist that the miracle really happened as the Bible describes it.

In another example, Catholic hermeneutics will defend the perpetual virginity of Mary (because that's part of Catholic tradition), but might agree with **Raymond E. Brown** that **Matthew's birth narrative** (*c.f.* **Topic 1**) is just "*an attractive drama that catches the imagination*". Liberal hermeneutics might treat the whole birth narrative as a set of *pericopae* that support Matthew's beliefs about the 'Christ of faith' but have no basis in the 'Jesus of history'. Traditional hermeneutics will insist that the Virgin Birth occurred as Matthew describes it, not because of Catholic tradition (which Protestants reject) but because that's the **literal sense** of the Bible; Matthew presumably learned the story from Jesus' own family.

> *Because it can be pretty free with the Bible, Catholic hermeneutics can sometimes sound like liberal hermeneutics. From the Bible-based viewpoint of traditional/Protestant hermeneutics, both groups can sometimes sound like atheists*

The Four Principles of Hermeneutics

For traditional Christians, hermeneutics follows well-established principles, known as the HISTORICAL-GRAMMATICAL METHOD. This consists of 4 principles:

- **The Literal Principle:** Unless the Bible's text is clearly meant to be a figure of speech or a poetic metaphor, it should be taken **literally** (p16). This principle opposes the tendency of liberal critics to 'spiritualize' the text by claiming it is **allegorical** (p19) or **moral** (p23) rather than literal.

> *In contrast, **Form Criticism** is entirely about identifying passages from the Bible as being legends or myths. Liberal critics often 'spiritualize' the miracles by focusing on their meaning rather than taking them literally. The fact that the Fourth Gospel calls its miracles 'Signs' does support this approach.*

- **The Historical Principle:** Some Bible passages need an understanding of the historical context they take place in. For example, Jesus' confrontations with the Pharisees and Sadducees require a historical understanding of who these groups were and what they believed.

*This is not the same as the 'Sitz im Leben' explored by **Form Critics** in **Topic 3**, which focuses on the situation of the Christians who first told these stories, not the situation of Jesus himself.*

- **The Grammatical Principle:** Some Bible passages require an understanding of the languages they were originally written in (Greek for the New Testament) or which Jesus and his Disciples spoke (Aramaic). For example, 'Christ' is the Greek translation for 'Messiah' but 'Logos' is a term from Hellenic philosophy.

*Liberal critics would agree but they would go further. **Redaction Criticism** (also in **Topic 3**) points out that the beliefs and purposes of the redactors (editors) of the Gospels can be revealed by the words they use.*

- **The Synthetic Principle:** The Bible is best viewed as consistent and passages should be explained by reference to other passages. Traditional critics try to HARMONISE the Bible, treating the Gospels as if they were independent eyewitnesses describing the same events from different perspectives. For example, the **birth-narratives in Matthew** and in **Luke** are combined together to form a single birth-narrative (with visiting magi *and* shepherds seeing angels).

***Source Criticism** (**Topic 3** again) challenges this by focusing on how contradictions in the Bible help identify the different sources that went into composing it - such as the solutions to the **Synoptic Problem**.*

These four principles of the historical-grammatical method work together to make sense of the Bible in a way with which traditional believers are happy. It harmonises the four Gospels into one complete narrative; it explains apparent contradictions; it draws upon enough historical scholarship to illuminate the text, but not so much that basic assumptions about Christian beliefs get called into question. It doesn't chop the Bible up into different sources that contradict each other; it doesn't dismiss parts of the Bible as legends or myths; it embraces the idea that miracles really happen.

When **Morna Hooker** criticises William Wrede's theory of the **Messianic Secret (Topic 1)**, she employs the historical-grammatical method. She points out all sorts of practical reasons why Jesus might have asked people to keep his identity secret, drawing on the **literal principle** (Jesus really did cure lepers and other miracles), the **historical principle** (understanding the Roman occupation and the way claiming to be the Messiah would have been misunderstood as a political revolt) and the **synthetic principle** (that Matthew and Luke knew about Jesus' secretiveness but didn't bother mentioning it because it seemed less important after the Jewish Revolt of 67-73 CE).

Exegesis (and Eisegesis)

Exegesis comes from the Greek for 'taking out'. It's sometimes used to mean the same thing as hermeneutic: a technique for interpreting the Bible. However it also has a more specific meaning: the technique for exploring the meaning of a particular Biblical text.

> *So if hermeneutics refers to the general approach to interpreting the Bible, exegesis is the specific act of interpreting a particular passage. Exegesis is putting hermeneutic theory into practice.*

Someone who does exegesis is an EXEGETE. The Edexcel Exam expects you to be an exegete when Section B asks you to "*clarify the ideas illustrated in a passage from the Anthology*".

The opposite of exegesis is **'eisegesis'** (meaning 'drawing in'). Eisegesis means imposing your own personal views on a Bible text rather than drawing out the text's intended meaning. It's usually a negative term of disapproval. From the viewpoint of traditional hermeneutics, liberal critics are involved in eisegesis when they reinterpret Bible passages using techniques like Form Criticism.

For example, **William Wrede** carries out exegesis on the **Parable of the Sower** (p81) and **Mark 4: 11**. He concludes that Jesus deliberately keeps his Messiah-ship a secret and builds his hermeneutical theory of the **Messianic Secret** on this (*c.f.* **Topic 1**). **Morna Hooker** criticises Wrede's conclusions, saying that there are more straightforward reasons for Jesus to say these things and that Wrede is really engaged in **eisegesis**: he is 'reading too much' into the passage.

However, sometimes the liberal theologians accuse the traditional Christians of eisegesis when they interpret a passage from the Bible by ignoring its historical context – its *Sitz im Leben*.

For example, many passages in the Old Testament that are interpreted as predictions about Jesus Christ have a more plausible **preterist** interpretation based on the prophet's own lifetime, but traditionalists often ignore this..

> *Later in this Topic you will learn about the debate between **Rudolf Bultmann** (p33) and **Karl Barth** (p26). Both critics accuse each other of eisegesis, but they are often viewed as eisegetes themselves by more traditional Christians. Basically, accusing someone of eisegesis means telling them they're interpreting the Bible wrongly!*

TOPIC 4 WAYS OF INTERPRETING THE SCRIPTURE

When people speak of the Bible as inspired, they usually mean that God influenced the human authors of the Scriptures to ensure that what they wrote was the true Word of God. The word "inspiration" means "God-breathed":

> All Scripture is God-breathed and is useful for teaching, rebuking, correcting and training in righteousness – **2 Timothy 3: 16**

God's breath features throughout the Bible, for example when God 'breathes' into Adam to give him life in **Genesis 2: 7** or when the Risen Christ 'breathes' on his Disciples to pass on his Holy Spirit onto them in **John 20: 22**. The breath of God brings with it God's divine **Life** and with it some of God's wisdom and guidance.

How is the Bible 'Inspired'?

When people call the Bible 'inspired', they can mean different things. Inspiration can be natural, conceptual or dictation.

- **Natural inspiration:** This is the ordinary use of the word 'inspired' with no supernatural overtones. The Bible writers were great men caught up in a pivotal moment in history. They wrote with deep insight into things. However, they were 'only human' and occasionally made mistakes. Sometimes they were 'men of their time' and expressed attitudes that many people reject today. Moreover, the Bible is not uniquely inspired: other sacred texts from other religions can be inspired in the same way (such as the Jewish **Torah**, the Islamic **Qur'an** or the **Tripitaka** of Buddhism).

> The **anti-Semitic attitudes in John's Gospel** or the mistakes in the genealogy of Jesus in **Matthew's birth narrative** could be examples of the Gospel-writers being 'men of their time' or making mistakes. **Form Criticism** often takes this assumption.

- **Conceptual inspiration:** The thoughts of the Gospel-writers were supernaturally influenced: they had religious experiences and received **non-propositional revelation**. However, they wrote these divinely inspired thoughts down in a normal human way, adding in normal human errors, biases and misunderstandings. As a result, there is **great moral wisdom** in the Bible, but also factual and scientific error and some truths may be expressed **allegorically** (p19).

> This is the basis for a lot of Catholic and Liberal hermeneutics. The job of the exegete is to separate the authentic revelation in Scripture from the human material - or to 'get behind' the way Scripture is written to understand the divine message that may be expressed in a coded or disguised way. **Redaction Criticism** often takes this assumption.

- **Dictation theory of inspiration:** The entire writing process of Scripture was controlled by God, who dictated the exact wording, down to the very letter. The writers passively recorded God's words without including their own styles or expressing their own personalities. This means the Bible should be understood in a plain sense way with **literal meanings**. However, when the original text is copied or translated into other languages, errors may creep in, so the **Historical-Grammatical Method** of hermeneutics (p9) is needed to sort out the true meaning at times.

> This is the basis for a lot of traditional/Protestant hermeneutics and it usually implies that Scripture is **literally true**. However, it does ignore the clear difference in STYLE between different books of the Bible, like **Mark**'s sloppy grammar and Aramaic phrases compared to **John**'s simple, precise sentences.

Dealing with errors and contradictions

Dictation Theory is linked to the idea that Scripture is **INERRANT** – there are no mistakes or contradictions in it. If there *seem* to be mistakes or contradictions in Scripture, then you are reading it wrong or the text has been corrupted or mistranslated.

An example of these apparent errors and contradictions would be in the **birth-narratives in Matthew** and **Luke**, which you studied as part of **Topic 1 (Context of the New Testament)**.

- The genealogies provided by **Matthew** and **Luke** do not match up with each other or the list of kings in the Old Testament.
- **Luke** describes Mary and Joseph going home to Nazareth straight after Jesus is born but **Matthew** describes them going to live in Egypt as refugees until after King Herod's death.

King Herod died in 4 BCE but Luke describes Jesus being born "*while Quirinius was governor in Syria*" (**Luke 2: 2**) and we know Quirinius only took up this post in 6 CE after Herod's son Archelaus was deposed. Therefore, Jesus could not have been born while Herod was alive **and** Quirinius was governor of Syria.

Traditional hermeneutics employs its four principles to defend the inspiration of the text. For example, Luke's genealogy is claimed to be that of Mary's family rather than Joseph's; the two birth-narratives are **HARMONISED** to describe Joseph and Mary fleeing to Egypt **then** going home to Nazareth; the translation is challenged and altered to "*before Quirinius was governor in Syria*" or else it is supposed that Quirinius had been governor of Syria on a previous occasion.

> Of course, critics have more questions: why does Matthew describe Joseph and Mary intending to return to Bethlehem then changing their mind and going to Nazareth? why does Luke refer to the genealogy as Joseph's family? why do almost all translations agree with the dating being *during* Quirinius' governorship?

These problems become less important if Scripture is conceptually or naturally inspired. **Form Critics** see the birth-narratives as legends rather than history. Catholic scholar **Raymond E. Brown** calls them "*an attractive drama that catches the imagination*". If the stories are only symbolic, then contradictions and historical errors don't matter.

In **Topic 6** (p172), you will focus on the contradictions between the different Gospels' accounts of the Resurrection of Jesus.

Implications of Inspired Scripture

Inspiration is important because it affects the authority of the Bible. If the Bible is only naturally inspired, it has no more authority than any other wise or insightful book from the past. This means its views on morality, worship and equality can be ignored when solving the problems of life in the 21st century. For example, many liberal Christians discount the Bible's views on homosexuality and the role of women.

> *There are non-religious texts that are naturally inspired too. Many Americans look to their Constitution as a document of immense political and social wisdom, written by great minds. However, most of them don't think it is a supernatural document. Other people find in the plays of Shakespeare an incredible insight into the human condition, yet Shakespeare's views on monarchy, women and witchcraft are very much 'of their time'.*

If the Bible is conceptually inspired then its views need to be taken more seriously, but can still be set aside as ideas that were 'of their time'. Techniques like **Source**, **Form** and **Redaction Criticism** are needed to 'get behind' the words of Scripture to understand the religious experience it is describing.

If the Bible is dictated by God, then it contains **moral truths** about life that are relevant in every society and in every century. The Bible becomes a platform from which the changing morals and values of society can be criticised: a sort of unchanging yardstick against which values can be measured.

Many traditional Christians would conclude that, by endorsing premarital sex and homosexuality, society is going against the Bible. They would resist attempts to 'explain away' these Biblical morals as **eisegesis** (critics reading into the Bible the things they would like to find there, rather than what actually is there).

However, we don't have the original versions of any of the texts of the Bible. The earliest manuscripts that have come down to us (like **Rylands Papyrus P52**, a fragment of John's Gospel) are still only copies of copies of copies.

A modern Bible has to be translated from dead languages like *koine* Greek and there is no agreement on which is the best translation to use.

Many traditional Protestants regard the King James Version (KJV) of the Bible as the English translation that is closest to the authentic Word of God. This Bible was first produced in 1611. However, the Edexcel Exam Board uses the New International Version (NIV) in its Anthology. This was originally published in 1978 but was updated in 2011 using the latest scholarship. Nonetheless, traditionalists distrust the NIV translation.

Should scripture be interpreted as inspired by God?

YES	NO
The Bible is the inspired Word of God; it is "*God-breathed*" which means it is transmitted from God into the minds of human writers who set it down exactly as God wants it to be. Exegetes needs to remember the coherence and consistency of the Bible, focusing on its **literal meaning** and assuming that any apparent contradictions are really errors in translation.	The Bible is clearly not 'dictated' by God. The different Bible writers have their own recognisable styles: Mark's Greek is sloppy and he uses Aramaic phrases, Matthew and Luke are more precise, John favours simple vocabulary but Paul writes in long, complicated sentences. This is how we can recognise different 'sources' at work in the Synoptic Gospels.
The Bible's inspiration makes it a timeless text that can never be out of date. It is a fixed standard of morality which can be used to judge what is going on in society; whether social changes are moving towards or away from Biblical values. Christians need to be true to the Bible's eternal values and resist the pressure to 'move with the times'.	The Bible is a historical document, written by men living in a particular *Sitz im Leben* or life setting. Some of its attitudes towards women and sexuality are very much 'of its time' and should be rejected today. If there is timeless wisdom in the Bible, it needs critical techniques to 'rescue' it from the mythological beliefs of its writers in the 1st century CE.

LITERAL INTERPRETATION OF SCRIPTURE

Interpreting something **literally** means interpreting it according to the plain or everyday meaning of words. It is the opposite of looking for symbolism or allegorical meaning in passages. This usually involves reading the Bible as a historical account full of physical and scientific facts, rather than as a code or a story with hidden meanings.

Literal interpretation of the New Testament involves accepting these facts:

- The events of Jesus' life happened as described, including the Virgin Birth, Jesus' ministry in Galilee and Judea, his trial and crucifixion and his Resurrection
- Jesus' teachings are to be taken at their straightforward meaning: e.g. there is Judgment after death and some people will be punished in Hell forever for their sins; Hell and Heaven are physical places, not states of mind or experiences in this life
- The miracles happened as described; e.g. Jesus really did walk on water

There are several reasons for interpreting the Bible in this literal way:

- Jesus himself seems to interpret the Old Testament in this way; e.g. when Jesus is tempted by the Devil, he refers to Old Testament verses that tell people to avoid temptation and worship only God
- Jesus' Disciples seem to interpret Jesus in this way; e.g. when Jesus gives them the 'Great Commission' (**Matthew 28: 16-20**) to go out and convert people all over the world, they obey this instruction in a literal way
- The Gospel-writers seem to interpret Old Testament prophecies this way; e.g. Matthew's proof-texts and John's Gospel both regard Jesus as fulfilling Scripture in an unexpected but literal ways (for example **Psalm 22: 16** says "*they pierce my hands and my feet*" and this is literally what is done to Jesus)

However, literalists are not committed to treating *every* passage in the Bible in this way: they accept that there are different **genres** of writing in the Bible and that there are figures of speech. For example, when Jesus says "*I am the Bread of Life*" (**John 6: 35**), he is not saying he is literally made of bread: he is saying he is the source of spiritual nourishment.

Literalists will use the **Grammatical Principle** (p10) to identify figurative language; however, when language is not clearly figurative, it should be interpreted literally. For example, when Jesus says "*whoever hears my words and believes in him who sent me has eternal life*" (**John 5: 24**), that is not a figure of speech or poetic language but a literal offer of everlasting life.

Literalists are very suspicious of attempts to "spiritualize" the Bible by downplaying the literal meaning of passages in favour of a hidden spiritual meaning. They think God intends the Bible to be understood in plain English. However, they accept that passages can have a spiritual meaning *as well as* being literally true.

Implications of Literalism

Literalism opposes most of the interpretations you learned about in **Topic 3**. For example, literalists would oppose **C.H. Dodd**'s idea of REALISED ESCHATOLOGY. Dodd thinks that Jesus' references to **Eternal Life** and Judgment describe experiences in the present, not in the future, at the end of time or after death. However, literalists argue that the plain meaning of the text is that Jesus is talking about the future.

Form Criticism argues that many passages in the New Testament are really myths or legends or fantastical tales to entertain, not actual historical events. However, literalists argue that passages like the Virgin Birth or Jesus being tempted by the Devil literally happened they way the Bible describes them.

Sometimes passages in the Bible contradict geography, historical knowledge or scientific facts. Here are some examples:

- **Geography: Mark** (who makes a lot of these mistakes) describes Jesus traveling from Tyre through Sidon to get to Galilee and the Decapolis – but this route is impossible, since Sidon is to the north but Galilee is to the south with a mountain range in between.

- **History: Luke** describes Jesus being born when Herod is King of Judea and Quirinius is Governor of Syria – but Herod died in 4 BCE and Quirinius didn't become Governor until 6 CE

- **Science:** Obviously, miracles go against the laws of science. The Synoptic Gospels describe people with mental illnesses caused by demons, which goes against modern Psychology. In one instance, Jesus describes the mustard seed as the smallest of all seeds, which isn't true (the orchid is smaller)

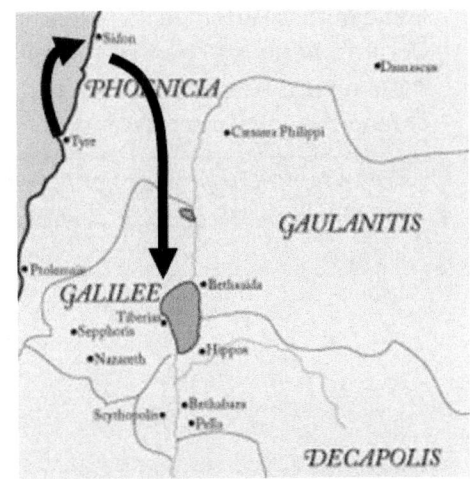

Hugh Anderson says traveling from Tyre to Galilee by way of Sidon is like *"traveling from Cornwall to London via Manchester"*

Literalists can answer these criticisms by speculating that there used to be a route through Sidon to Galilee that no longer exists, or that Quirinius was Governor of Syria on more than one occasion, or that Jesus is speaking **figuratively** about the mustard seed (which is very small even if it's not absolutely the smallest seed) or that it's a mistranslation for a different sort of seed. Literalists will accept miracles and demonic possession as factually true (though they may argue that, since Jesus cast them out, demons no longer cause mental illness in the world today).

Literalism leads to problems when passages in the Bible contradict each other and this is harder to account for. Here are two examples:

- There are discrepancies between **Matthew's birth narrative** and **Luke**'s, with Matthew describing Mary and Joseph fleeing to Egypt but Luke describing them returning to Galilee straight away.
- All four Gospels describe different events at the empty tomb when Jesus is raised from the dead; **Matthew 28: 1-10** has Mary Magdalene discovering the empty tomb then meeting the Risen Christ who tells her to share the news with the Disciples; **John 20: 1-18** has Mary Magdalene running away from the empty tomb in confusion and telling the Disciples that someone has taken Jesus' body away.

Literalists respond by trying to HARMONISE these narratives. For example, Mary and Joseph returned to Galilee with the baby Jesus and then fled to Egypt when Herod found out about the birth of the Messiah. Similarly, Mary Magdalene ran back to the Disciples but then returned to the tomb and met the Risen Christ. These solutions suppose that there are 'gaps' in the narrative that can be filled in by using other parts of the Bible (the **Synthetic Principle** in action, p10).

Some of these attempts to reconcile apparent contradictions can get complicated or improbable. **Occam's Razor** is a rule that tells philosophers to prefer the simpler explanation, which would be that one text is mistaken. However, traditional Christians following the Literal Principle will defend the literal interpretation of Bible passages despite this.

> *Traditional Christians might point out that the 'simpler' explanations offered by **Source**, **Form** and **Redaction Criticism** are just as convoluted and improbable as the literal explanations that they offer.*

Should scripture be interpreted literally?

YES	NO
Jesus gives clear messages to his Disciples that he intends them to follow literally. The whole of the Bible is to be understood in a plain sense, not as a mysterious code to be cracked by critics.	Bible passages contradict what we know about history and geography and – crucially – they contradict each other. It makes more sense to admit that some passages are mistaken or to be understood **allegorically**.
The Four Principles of traditional hermeneutics (**literal, historical, grammatical, synthetic**) enable Christians to reconcile apparent contradictions. The historicity of **miracles** should be accepted by anyone who believes Jesus is truly the **Son of God**. Attempts to 'spiritualize' these passages reveal a lack of faith rather than a deeper understanding.	Attempts to reconcile these contradictions become convoluted and improbable and miss out on the clear spiritual meaning of the text. **John's Gospel** refers to **'Signs'** rather than 'miracles', alerting readers NOT to interpret them literally. There is great **allegorical** and **moral** depth in the Bible if readers get past a shallow literal interpretation.

ALLEGORICAL INTERPRETATION OF SCRIPTURE

As opposed to **literal interpretations** (p16), Scripture can be interpreted as having a secondary or hidden meaning. In an **allegory**, the main characters, events, objects in locations in a story are symbolic and fit together in a systematic way to reveal a deeper meaning that isn't obvious on first reading.

Famous allegories in literature include **George Orwell**'s *Animal Farm* (1945), where the animals represent the people caught up in the Communist Revolution in Russia, and **C.S. Lewis'** *The Lion, the Witch & the Wardrobe* (1950), where the story represents Christian beliefs about sin, prophecy, faith, Jesus and the Resurrection. Other stories have allegorical elements in them; for example in **J.B. Priestley**'s *An Inspector Calls* (1946), the character of 'Daisy Renton' represents all the oppressed workers and the Birling family represents the capitalist class that exploits them.

You have already come across allegorical interpretations of the New Testament in **Topic 2** when studying the **7 Signs in John's Gospel**. By calling these miracles *'semeion'* ('Signs'), John's Gospel draws attention to their allegorical meaning.

1. **Turning Water into Wine:** This is an allegory for Christianity replacing Judaism, with the water representing the Jewish religion and wine the new religion of Christianity
2. **Healing the Official's Son:** This is an allegory for faith, with the Official representing the church trusting that God will fulfill his promises
3. **Healing at the Pool:** This is an allegory for Christianity dispensing with the Jewish **Law**, especially Sabbath regulations
4. **Feeding the 5000:** This is an allegory for the Eucharist, where Christians worship by breaking and sharing bread
5. **Walking on Water:** This is another allegory for faith during times of persecution
6. **Healing the Blind Man:** This is a detailed allegory for the spiritual journey of a believer from being spiritually blind to seeing God more clearly
7. **Raising Lazarus from the Dead:** This is an allegory for the Resurrection, for the Christian believers receiving **Eternal Life** and perhaps for the history of the Johannine Community that **composed the Fourth Gospel**

> *These Signs and other Bible passages don't just have one single allegorical interpretation: they can be interpreted in lots of different ways, with layers upon layers of meaning.*

In the Synoptic Gospels (and especially in **Luke**), Jesus teaches through Parables, which are stories with a hidden meaning to them. For example, the **Parable of the Good Samaritan (Luke 10: 30-35** but also featuring in **Anthology Extract #9** and p225) can be interpreted as follows:

[30] In reply Jesus said: "A man was going down from Jerusalem to Jericho, when he was attacked by robbers. They stripped him of his clothes, beat him and went away, leaving him half dead. [31] A priest happened to be going down the same road, and when he saw the man, he passed by on the other side. [32] So too, a Levite, when he came to the place and saw him, passed by on the other side. [33] But a Samaritan, as he travelled, came where the man was; and when he saw him, he took pity on him. [34] He went to him and bandaged his wounds, pouring on oil and wine. Then he put the man on his own donkey, brought him to an inn and took care of him. [35] The next day he took out two denarii and gave them to the innkeeper. 'Look after him,' he said, 'and when I return, I will reimburse you for any extra expense you may have.'

On a simple level, the man represents any human being, the journey to Jericho is the journey through life and the robbers are misfortunes that happen to people.

- The priest and the Levite represent all the successful people in the world who care more about their own safety and respectability than helping others.
- The Samaritan is a good Christian who loves his neighbour.

A more detailed interpretation would be this:

- The man is Adam (and us, his descendants) and the journey from Jerusalem to Jericho is the journey out of the Garden of Eden towards death.
- The robbers represent the Devil.
- The priest and the Levite represent the Jewish religion and the Law of Moses, which are ineffective in helping.
- The Samaritan represents Christ who comes to the rescue. He bandages the wounds, which represent mankind's sins. The donkey represents Christ's body, which bears the burden of carrying humanity's sins on the Cross.
- The inn represents the Church where sinners are welcome.
- The Samaritan's promise to return represents the Second Coming of Christ on Judgement Day.

Allegorical interpretations like this can be surprising and imaginative. Once they've been explained to you, you re-read the passage and find now that you 'can't not see it' - it seems obvious but before it was hidden.

Some particular types of allegory can be distinguished:

- **Sacramental meaning:** In **Topic 2 (The Person of Jesus)**, **Raymond E. Brown** finds allegory for the **Eucharist** in the **Sign of Turning Water into Wine** and the **Feeding of the 5000**. The Good Samaritan pouring wine on the man's wounds may also represent the Eucharist.
- **Anagogical meaning:** Allegories may refer to the *Eschaton* – the end of the world and Christ's Second Coming. For example, the **wedding party at Cana** can represent heaven and **Lazarus raised from the dead** may represent Judgement Day. These allegories are also prophecies.
- **Moral meaning:** Allegories may represent instructions on how to live. For example, the **Parable of the Good Samaritan** tells us to love our neighbours.

Implications of Allegory

Allegorical interpretation is not new. The early Christian scholar **Origen** (184-253 CE) argues that the Bible should be interpreted at three levels: "flesh" (**literal**), "soul" (**moral**) and "spirit" (**allegorical**). Origin argues that if Biblical passages are only interpreted in the fleshly (literal) sense then they are often impossible or nonsensical. They must be interpreted morally and allegorically to be understood.

> *The reader must endeavor to grasp the entire meaning, connecting by an intellectual process the account of what is literally impossible with the parts that are not impossible but historically true* **– Origen**

This allegorical method was used all the way through the Middle Ages. Scholars did not think they were 'reading too much into' Scripture (**eisegesis**) because, if the text is truly **inspired** (p12), you would *expect* multiple levels of meaning to be there.

> *The literal sense is that which the author intends, but God being the Author, we may expect to find in Scripture a wealth of meaning* **– Thomas Aquinas**

Thomas Aquinas has a few concerns about excessive allegorizing: it can easily lead to confusion or self-deception, where critics project their own imagination onto the text, reading things into it that just aren't there.

The Protestant Reformation brought a backlash against allegorizing and many Protestant churches are suspicious of allegorical interpretation to this day. Many of these Christians uphold the Literal Principle of hermeneutics and feel that allegorizing downplays the historical truth of the Bible in favour of a non-historical 'spiritual' truth.

They also complain that the 'spiritual' truths allegorizers claim to find in the Bible often go against Christian teachings in various ways. For example, **Form Criticism** and **Redaction Criticism** tend to lock the meaning of a New Testament passage to its *Sitz im Leben* in the 1st century, making it irrelevant to life in the 21st century (for example, the way **Raymond E. Brown** allegorizes the **Signs** in the Fourth Gospel so that they represent the Johannine Community).

> People who oppose allegory are not against a spiritual meaning to the Bible - but they are opposed to treating everything in the Bible as figurative or symbolic. This debate goes back to the 2ⁿᵈ century CE when the **Gnostics** in the Johannine Churches interpreted the Fourth Gospel entirely symbolically.

Should scripture be interpreted allegorically?

YES

NO

Treating Scripture symbolically goes right back to the beginning of Christianity. **John's Gospel** positively invites readers to treat its miracles as allegorical 'Signs'. The spiritual meaning behind the Bible text reveals the identity of Jesus and beliefs about the afterlife.

Allegory has been misused by interpreters who read their own meanings into the text (**eisegesis**). The Literal Principle says that, as far as possible, readers should attend to the plain meaning of Scripture and not attempt to decode it for hidden meanings.

As Origen pointed out, many passages in the Bible are either impossible or silly if treated literally. Signs like **Feeding the 5000** are just magic tricks unless they are taken allegorically. Bible critics need to explore the deeper meaning of the Bible to relate it to problems people experience today.

Exploring 'deeper meanings' often means undermining traditional beliefs, such as denying that miracles happened or that Jesus ministry was historical. This does not guide people in how to live; it just leads to confusion and atheism.

MORAL INTERPRETATION OF SCRIPTURE

Jesus was a moral teacher who preached a message (*kerygma*) of love and forgiveness. Even when he was performing miracles or telling Parables, he was still driving home his moral message. Many Christians believe Scripture can be interpreted in a moral sense, looking for ethical guidance. This is similar to the allegorical approach to interpretation, but the results are more practical. It is also known a *telic* or **tropological** interpretation.

This approach to interpreting the Bible begins with Judaism, where it is known as *midrash*. Jews believe that the Laws, poems and stories in the Old Testament all contain layers of meaning, but especially moral meanings.

Paul's **epistles** (letters) explain his view that the Old Testament contains teachings for Christians:

everything that was written in the past was written to teach us – **Romans 15: 4**

You have come across moral interpretation of Scripture in **Topic 2 (Person of Jesus)**, while studying the **Sign of Feeding the 5000**. Rather than a miracle of multiplying food, this can be interpreted as a non-supernatural miracle of sharing: when we all share the little we have, we find that collectively we have enough for everyone. This moral interpretation has been championed by **Rudolf Bultmann** (p33) and, more recently, by **Pope Francis**:

This is the miracle: rather than a multiplication it is a sharing, inspired by faith and prayer. Everyone eats and some is left over – **Pope Francis**

Moral interpretations can be more ingenious than this. The **Epistle** (letter) **of Barnabas** is a non-canonical New Testament text from the 2nd century CE. The author explains the real moral meaning behind the Jewish food laws which (he thinks) the Jews have misunderstood. According to Barnabas, God does not want worshipers to avoid certain types of food but to avoid behaviour associated with these animals:

- Pork is banned because pigs grunt when they are hungry but are silent when full – this represents people who only pray to God when they need help, so the ban on 'pork' REALLY means not ignoring God during the good times
- Rabbit is banned because rabbits breed quickly – this represents people who are sexually promiscuous, so the ban on rabbit REALLY means not having sex outside of marriage

Barnabas never made it into the New Testament Canon, which is good because it's intensely antisemitic and frankly a bit weird. Barnabas thinks the Jewish ban on eating weasels is really a ban on having oral sex, for instance!

The interesting thing about this moral or tropological way of interpreting the Bible is that it is often applied to passages that, in their original context, have no obvious moral content at all. For example, **Mark's Gospel** describes a miracle where Jesus heals Jairus' daughter. He goes to the dying girl's bedside, takes her hand and says:

"Talitha koum!" (which means "Little girl, I say to you, get up!") – **Mark 5: 41**

> Talitha koum *(or* talitha cumi*) is one of those expressions in the original Aramaic language which persuade many scholars that Mark is the earliest Gospel.*

Talitha koum used to be translated as "*Maiden, arise*!" and became the slogan for campaigners for Women's Suffrage in the 20th century and several girls' schools and women's colleges aimed at helping women become more equal in society. No one in the 1st century CE could have thought this phrase would one day be associated with women's rights.

Other New Testament passages have been interpreted to oppose slavery, such as:

> *For freedom, Christ has set us free; stand firm therefore and do not submit again to the yoke of slavery* **– Galatians 5: 1**

In its original context, this passage is talking about being enslaved to sin – but Christian abolitionists used to it oppose slavery in the USA in the 19th century.

A final example would be Jesus healing the Centurion's servant in **Matthew 8: 5-13**. Matthew uses the word *pais* to describe the sick servant which, according to **James Neill**, is a term that indicates a homosexual lover rather than a 'servant'. A tropological interpretation of this passage would be that, by healing the servant without commenting on the relationship, Jesus is showing tacit approval of same-sex relationships. Since Christian churches condemned homosexual sex as sinful, this is an interpretation that would probably **not** have been intended by the Gospel-writer.

Implications of Tropology

The moral interpretation of Scripture raises many of the same issues as the more general **allegorical interpretation** of Scripture (p19). On a positive side, it can reveal new depths to Christian ethical teachings in new situations. For example, in the 20th and 21st century, people look for guidance on ethical issues like racism, gender identity, sexuality and the environment – topics that the Bible either doesn't address directly or takes a position of severe condemnation. Tropological interpretation offers a justification for Christians holding to a more tolerant or progressive view than in the past.

On the other hand, it's clear that moral ideas that seem quite alien to the minds of the Gospel-writers and Jesus' disciples can be read into the Bible this way. Interpretations that show the New Testament supporting women's equality or homosexual relationships or opposing slavery are probably in this category, because the culture of the 1st century CE did not promote these things in general.

However, if Scripture is truly **inspired by God** (p12), it may contain moral messages for all ages, some of which won't become apparent for many centuries. Women were second class citizens and slavery was taken for granted in the 1st century CE and for many centuries after; although **Hellenic (Greek) culture** accepted same-sex relationships, Jewish and Christian communities did not (and still do not for the most part). Nevertheless, if God opposes such prejudices, he might inspire such passages in the Bible, for them to be recognised and correctly interpreted later.

For traditional Christians, such radical interpretations are **eisegesis** - imposing un-Biblical modern values onto the Bible rather than accepting the Bible's plain teaching on women and sexuality. In the 19th century, Christian slave-owners argued the same way against people who tried to use the Bible to show that slavery was wrong.

Should scripture be interpreted in a moral sense?

YES	NO
Jesus' are very broad (such as the GOLDEN RULE) and require guidance in how to apply them. Much of the Bible is 'of its time' and doesn't comment favourably on women, slavery or homosexuality. Tropological interpretation reveals more tolerant teachings for the 21st century.	The Bible's teachings on gender roles and sexuality are very clear. Scholars who apply tropological interpretation to come up with a different moral code are guilty of **eisegesis**: projecting their own wishes into the Bible rather than allowing the Bible to teach them about morality.
Slave-owners in the 19th century opposed tropological analysis of the Bible because they wanted to justify owning slaves. With hindsight, we can see that the campaigners who interpreted passages as condemning slavery were in the right and were actually more faithful to the spirit of Jesus' teachings. This supports continuing to interpret the Bible in a moral sense.	This sort of tropological analysis assumes that modern readers can teach the Bible about right and wrong rather than learning from the Bible about morality. It assumes that the Bible is not **inspired by God** and is a document 'of its time'. It also goes against the **Literal Principle**, which is a plain sense reading of Scripture rather than searching for hidden messages.

KARL BARTH: the 'Story of God'

Karl Barth (1886-1968) is a Swiss theologian and a towering figure in 20th century Bible scholarship – in spite of the fact (or perhaps because of the fact) that people still can't quite agree on where he stood on many matters.

Barth studied at the best universities in Germany where liberal or 'modernist' Christianity was being developed. This sort of Christian thought was sceptical about miracles and the supernatural, downplayed literal concepts like Heaven and Hell and interpreted the Bible as a human document full of errors – but emphasised instead the goodness of God as a loving Father, the brotherhood of man and the **allegorical** (p19) and **moral** (p23) message of the Bible.

Barth became disillusioned with this sort of Christianity during the First World War. He noticed that many liberal Christians supported German military aggression.

Barth is pronounced 'Bart' - as in 'Simpson'

This disturbed him because they were interpreting the Bible based around the values of their society and this meant the Bible was unable to help them challenge their society when it went wrong. After the War, he wrote his *Commentary on the Epistle to the Romans* (1919), which was a warning to liberal theology that it had become complacent about God. Barth warned that the world was in a "*time of Crisis*" and being judged by God.

Barth's greatest work was his *Church Dogmatics* (1931), which grew year on year until it filled four volumes with thousands of pages. In the 1930s, Barth campaigned against the Nazis and their project to distort Christianity to their own ends. Barth helped found the German Confessing Church to oppose Nazi ideology. He drafted the *Barmen Declaration* (1934), which declared that true Christianity was always separate from the State and did not follow any earthly leader; Christians would have to choose between Jesus Christ and Adolf Hitler as their Lord.

After the War, Barth worked as a prison chaplain and delivered widely-read sermons to the prisoners. He became a world famous theologian, admired for his evangelical passion and his concern for social justice. His views remained difficult to pin down and he frequently expressed himself in PARADOXES (statements which seem to be contradictory). When asked to summarise his beliefs, he famously replied:

Jesus loves me. This I know, because the Bible tells me so **– Karl Barth**

This is a children's nursery rhyme that was made into a popular hymn. Is Barth mocking the interviewer for asking such a simplistic question? Or is he saying that a childlike faith is more important than a complicated theological system?

The Rejection of Idolatry (and "No!" to natural theology)

Idolatry is the sin of worshiping something else instead of God. It is forbidden in the Ten Commandments (**Exodus 20: 1-17**): the 1st Commandment forbids having other gods before God and the 2nd forbids worshiping "*graven images*" (i.e. things humans have created themselves).

Originally 'idols' were statues of pagan gods. However, Jewish and Christian thought extended the idea of idolatry to worshiping anything instead of God: this included **worshiping the Roman Emperor**. Eventually, idolatry was understood to mean placing anything other than God at the centre of your life. This means that your hobby, your girlfriend or boyfriend, your bank account or your career could be 'idolatry' if those things take the place of God in your life.

Barth takes the idea of idolatry in an unusual direction. He links NATURAL THEOLOGY with idolatry. Natural theology means the attempt to find out what God is like through using reason and observation. This includes the classical arguments for the existence of God: the **Design Argument**, the **Cosmological Argument** and the **Ontological Argument**. It also includes the 'Quest for the Historical Jesus' and various attempts to reconstruct "what really happened" using **Source**, **Form** and **Redaction Criticism**.

Barth sums up his "*No!*" to this sort of theology by saying:

> One can not *speak of God simply by speaking of man in a loud voice* – **Karl Barth**

Barth means that the God we discover through natural theology is a human construct; it's something we have made, not with our hands but with our minds. The 'God' of the various classical arguments or the 'Jesus' we arrive at through historical investigations just turns out to be a product of our imagination – which we then worship as if it was the real God. We think we are saying things about God, but really we are saying things about ourselves and our own cleverness 'in a loud voice', meaning in exalted or spiritual tones.

> *Barth proposed his famous "No!" in 1934, in response to German scholars who were arguing that God approved of Nazi racism and antisemitism. Barth accused such scholars of replacing the true God with an idol they had created in their minds.*

Barth was not the first person to suggest that all **religious language** has a purely human origin and content. **Ludwig Feuerbach** suggests that the idea of God is a 'projection' of our deepest fears and aspirations onto a universe that doesn't care; **Sigmund Freud** argued that God is also a 'wish fulfillment' of our unconscious desires; **Karl Marx** suggests that religion is an "*opiate*" to help humans cope with living in a cruel world. However, all these thinkers were atheists. Karl Barth believed in God.

If we cannot know God through using reason, observation and our own intellects, how can we ever know God? Barth has the answer:

> *It is by the grace of God that God is knowable to us* – **Karl Barth**

The Importance of Grace & Revelation

In **Topic 2 (Person of Jesus)**, you explored the concept of **Grace** as part of **John's Prologue**, where it refers to God's generosity in giving his Word to the world. In Christian thought, 'Grace' similarly refers to anything God gives to humans without them asking for it or earning it:

- If humans receive things because they demand them, that would give humans power over God, but God is omnipotent, so anything he gives he must give freely
- If humans receive things because they earn them, that would mean humans have a value and importance of their own, but humans are only important insofar as God loves and values them, therefore humans can earn nothing from God

Ultimately, the existence of the entire universe is by the Grace of God: God didn't have to create the world or humans, nothing could make him do it, it didn't deserve to be created: it is by God's Grace that we even exist at all. This leads Barth to conclude:

> *The fact that we know God is His work and not ours* – **Karl Barth**

> Barth is arguing for CONTINGENCY: the idea that humans depend utterly on God. This is central to a lot of **religious experience**, especially **Rudolf Otto's idea of the Numinous**. Barth follows the logic of human contingency through into theology and concludes we can know nothing about God through our own powers of understanding.

If humans can't 'figure God out' without falling into idolatry and confusion, they need God to **reveal** himself to them. Barth believes God reveals himself to us in Jesus Christ. He argues there is no revelation outside of Jesus Christ: for Barth, it is either learning about God through Jesus or learning nothing about God. The revealing is something God does. We don't reveal God in Jesus through our research and interpretation: God reveals himself in Jesus for us through Grace, as Jesus himself explains:

> *No one knows who the Son is except the Father, and no one knows who the Father is except the Son and those to whom the Son chooses to reveal him* – **Luke 10: 22**

The problem is, that Jesus lived 2000 years ago in Palestine. People back then had the chance to meet Jesus personally, hear him preach and come to a knowledge of God through knowing him. This sort of direct knowledge of God is called an **EPIPHANY** and several of Jesus' followers have these epiphanies when they suddenly realise who Jesus is and understand God properly:

- In all the Synoptic Gospels, **Peter** is the first to realise that Jesus is the Son of God (e.g. **Matthew 16: 16**)
- In **John's Gospel**, **John the Baptist** recognises that Jesus is "*the Lamb of God who takes away the sins of the world*" (**John 1: 29**)
- Also in John's Gospel, **Andrew** is the first to realise Jesus is the **Messiah (John 1: 41)**, **Martha** recognises Jesus is the **Son of God (John 11: 27)** and **Thomas** calls the Risen Christ "*my Lord and my God*" (**John 20: 28**)

But what are modern people in today's world supposed to do? We can't go back in time and meet Jesus – and according to Barth we can't use our critical abilities to reconstruct a 'historical Jesus' either, because that's idolatry.

That only leaves us with what Barth calls "*God without Jesus*" but unfortunately such a God is:

a ghost, a phantom and a delusion, a far-away and unapproachable God – **Karl Barth**

Fortunately, God will not let the matter rest there. Barth titled one of his collections of sermons *God's Search for Man* (1935) and this title sums up his view on Grace: we are not searching for God, God is searching for us. Our job is not to seek, but to allow ourselves to be found – and God finds us when we read the Bible.

The Value of Scripture: a Witness not Revelation

God searches for humans through the Bible and the Church. These are two institutions that trace their existence back to Jesus Christ and are in the world today. Once again, Barth warns against turning either the Bible or the Church into an idol:

- Some **fundamentalist Christians** treat the Bible as a **revelation** in its own right, but for Barth the only revelation of God is through Jesus Christ, so putting the Bible on a pedestal like this is idolatry
- Some **Roman Catholic Christians** treat the Church as a **revelation** in its own right, but Barth regards this too as setting up something that humans have created in place of Jesus Christ

Barth regards the Bible as a WITNESS to Jesus Christ and the Church as the PROCLAMATION of Jesus Christ to the world. They are both human institutions and therefore have the "*capacity for error*". They are not revelations in and of themselves. However, they can become a vehicle or medium for revelation.

The Bible is God's Word to the extent that God causes it to be His Word – **Karl Barth**

Karl Barth is saying that the Bible is a human document and therefore flawed and limited to the situation and context it was written in. However, it is a witness to God's revelation in Jesus Christ and therefore it can **become** a revelation too when it is read. It becomes a medium through which God reveals himself. This doesn't happen automatically: the words of Scripture are ordinary human words until the moment God chooses to speak through them to the reader, then they temporarily transform. Barth views this as a sort of **miracle**.

Barth distinguishes two opposing mistakes we can make regarding Scripture, which he names after two ancient Christian heresies:

- **Ebionitism** was the belief that Jesus was only human and not at all divine
- **Docetism** was the belief that Jesus was purely divine and not at all human

Liberal Christians are like the Ebionites: they treat the Bible as an entirely human book without any divinity to it. Traditional Christians are like the Docetists, treating the Bible as a divine book that is INERRANT (without flaw) but ignoring its human construction.

Barth argues that we need to allow the Bible to **become** the Word of God for us when we read it, rather than turning it into an idol that can only teach us things we already know. For Barth, good **exegesis** (as opposed to bad **eisegesis**) should be:

> *a strenuous and disciplined attempt to lay ourselves open to hear the Word of God speaking to us, to read what the Word of God intends ... and to refrain from interrupting it or confusing it with our own speaking* – **Karl Barth**

The Story of God

To sum up: Barth argues that revelation comes only through God's Grace, which is in Jesus Christ. Attempts to know God in other ways turn into idolatry. The Bible is a witness to Jesus Christ:

> *Scripture does indeed bear witness to revelation, but it is not revelation itself* – **Karl Barth**

Barth warns that, if we treat the Bible as a revelation in its own right, it becomes a *"paper Pope"* - a human authority mistaken for a divine one and blindly obeyed.

Barth compares the Bible to the Pool of Bethesda in the **Sign of Healing at the Pool** (*c.f.* **Topic 2**). In this Sign, the crippled man wants to bathe in the pool because he believes it has healing powers, but Jesus arrives and heals him with a word. The real power is in Jesus, not the Pool, although the man would never have met Jesus and been healed if he hadn't first come to the Pool. In the same way, the Bible is a place where the reader can 'meet' Jesus Christ – but it has no power of its own.

Barth calls Scripture the **'Story of God'** and argues it should be read as a story rather than as a set of facts or as history. If the Bible is read as a story, you can encounter God within the story. If it is read as a set of beliefs, a history lesson or a code for living, the reader will only encounter their own thoughts and reflections.

Even though he acknowledges that the Bible has errors, Barth refuses to identify them. He warns readers not to make assumptions that the most 'human' parts of the Bible are the least true. For example, the **birth-narrative in Matthew** (*c.f.* **Topic 1**) *seems* a very 'human' episode in the Bible: it contains factual mistakes, it contradicts **Luke**, it seems to mistranslate **Isaiah**'s prophecies. However, in the story of the *magi* visiting the Jesus Christ, the Word of God can speak to readers. Instead of treating passages like this as 'un-historical' and passages like Jesus' trial and crucifixion as 'historical', Barth advises readers to reserve their judgement and read the story receptively.

> *The Bible witnesses speak as men and not as angels or gods* – **Karl Barth**

Barth claims there are two events in history which are *"unhistorical history"* and they are the creation of the universe and the Resurrection of Christ. No one was there to see these things happen and they are unimaginable, so they are not like normal history – yet Barth says they nonetheless happened.

He concludes that Christians can do what Scripture does: they can bear witness to the Resurrection of Christ in their lives by the way that they live, but they can never hope to describe the Resurrection or explain it. It is beyond human words.

Implications of Barth for Modern Scholarship

Karl Barth writes largely to correct the errors of Liberal/Modernist Christianity. He argues that attempts to reconstruct a 'historical Jesus' have no religious value and that Christians can only know God through encountering the Word of God in the Bible, not through trying to re-interpret the Bible in new ways. The fact that his insights gave him the wisdom and the courage to oppose Nazism (when many in the German churches did not) suggests that his ideas have great value.

However, traditional/conservative Christians remain suspicious of Barth because of his views on Scripture. Shortly after Barth died, various Protestant churches issued the **Chicago Statement** which affirmed that, as far as they were concerned, the Bible was INERRANT (without error):

> *Being wholly and verbally God-given, Scripture is without error or fault in all its teaching –* **Chicago Statement (1978)**

Barth would have opposed this interpretation of Scripture, but traditional/Protestant churches have largely ignored Barth's views.

Maybe Barth's views on the Bible were too nuanced and subtle for ordinary readers to appreciate. A lot of people look for clear answers and cut-and-dried advice from the Bible, especially on controversial issues like sexuality and abortion.

Liberal Christians often admire Barth's imagination and emphasis on reading Scripture for yourself – they agree with him that Scripture contains human flaws but they are much more willing to state exactly what they think those flaws are! Barth's ideas about listening to God speaking **through** Scripture strikes many people as mystical; it seems to go against rational analysis and logical thought and encourages readers to accept traditional interpretations and not challenge them. They therefore see Barth as a conservative opposed to new interpretations of the Bible and Christian ethics.

But given that the last time a brand new interpretation of the Bible and Christian ethics was offered it turned out to be Nazism, maybe Barth is right to hold to a conservative position

A bigger question is whether Barth was right to reject the role of human reason in knowing God. Clearly *some* theology can be 'idolatry' if it replaces God with human concerns; Barth is probably right that many Christians have become more concerned with getting Christianity to fit into society than getting society to fit Christianity. However, making theology a matter of pure faith has meant that Barth's teachings haven't really led anywhere: liberals and traditionalists have tended to ignore him in favour of theological positions that give human reasoning something to *do* (such as reconstructing the 'historical Jesus' or reconciling apparent contradictions in the Bible).

Has Karl Barth made an important contribution to Bible scholarship?

YES

Karl Barth recalled liberal Christian scholarship from a route that was heading into atheism and worldliness. The fact that he recognised and rejected Nazism clearly shows his insight into the true nature of the Word of God. His ideas act as a warning to keep Jesus Christ at the centre of interpreting Scripture.

Barth is equally critical of conservative Christianity. His view of Scripture as a witness and as the 'Story of God' challenges the traditional view that Scripture is inerrant and must only be read **literally**. He encourages these Christians to think more carefully about what the Bible means.

NO

Barth's integrity is great but his ideas are very conservative. He asks Christians to suspend their rational and critical faculties and read the Bible in a childlike way, receptive only to traditional ideas and values rather than criticising and challenging old interpretations. His views are too **mystical** to be useful for applying the Bible to the modern world.

Barth's thinking has become a theological dead-end. By rejecting the idea of knowing God through reasoning and replacing that with faith, there's no further development for this type of thinking. The idea that humans can know **nothing** about God without Grace leads to a loss of faith in theology itself.

RUDOLF BULTMANN: De-mythologizing Scripture

Rudolf Bultmann (1884-1976) is a deeply influential figure in liberal Christian theology whose views shaped the teaching of Christian beliefs well beyond his own lifetime.

He is praised by some with 'rescuing' Christianity from atheism and condemned by others for being practically an atheist himself!

Bultmann established his fame by publishing *The History of the Synoptic Tradition* (1921), which was a key work in the development of **Form Criticism** (*c.f.* **Topic 3**).

Bultmann's name is strongly linked to Form Criticism, especially in *The Gospel of John: A Commentary* (1941), in which he identifies the 'Sign Source' used by the Fourth Gospel.

Bultmann spent most of his career lecturing at the University of Marburg in Germany. During the Second World War, he was a member of the **Confessing Church** that opposed Nazism. Bultmann spoke out against the Nazis but less boldly than **Karl Barth** (p26), which is why he kept his job (unlike Barth, who moved to Switzerland). Bultmann's beliefs were strongly influenced by the existentialist philosophy of his friend **Martin Heidegger** (who was, for a time, a Nazi supporter).

After the War, Bultmann became internationally famous. In the 1950s he gave lecture tours in Britain and the USA that were turned into influential books (notably *Jesus Christ & Mythology*, 1958). Bultmann was also an inspirational teacher and his students carried on his philosophy, forming a group of scholars with similar views called the 'Bultmann School'

Bultmann's thought is complex and needs to be unpacked in steps.

The Mythological World View

Bultmann argues that Jesus and the early Christians had a MYTHOLOGICAL WORLD VIEW whereas modern people have a SCIENTIFIC WORLD VIEW. Bultmann gives examples of the mythological thinking in the Bible:

- The world has 'three storeys', with Heaven up above, Earth in the middle and Hell down below (the 'triple-decker' universe)
- Supernatural powers intervene in life, causing miracles
- The world is ruled by the devil, Satan, and demons cause evil and disease
- The world is coming to an end (APOCALYPTICISM) and will be replaced with a supernatural world

There is evidence of this mythological worldview in **Topic 5**, *especially the idea of the Apocalypse and Jesus' parables about demons (p83) as well as Jesus' Ascension (p152)*

Bultmann claims that this sort of thinking is completely opposed to the way modern people view the world, which is based on science:

> *We cannot use electric lights and radios and, in the event of illness, avail ourselves of modern medical and clinical means and at the same time believe in the spirit and wonder world of the New Testament* – **Rudolf Bultmann**

Bultmann points out that modern historians do not explain events in history by referring to God or the Devil: they explain events by referring to people's choices, political decisions or just luck. In the same way, newspapers do not explain events as being due to miracles or evil spirits, but instead due to economics, nature or human decision-making.

Similarly, ordinary people look for rational and natural explanations for things in their life, not supernatural ones. This type of thinking, Bultmann claims, goes back to the Ancient Greeks. The Greeks had supernatural beliefs too, but they first came up with a non-mythological view of the world that developed into modern science.

Bultmann thinks that, for modern people, the mythological view of the world is "*over and done with*". There's no going back to it. Even trying to view the world that way is a *sacrificium intellectus* (sacrificing your understanding – becoming deliberately foolish).

> *Can the Christian proclamation today expect men and women to acknowledge the mythical world picture as true? To do so would be both pointless and impossible* – **Rudolf Bultmann**

Forcing yourself to believe in the mythological world view is "*pointless*" because it's not even a specifically Christian view – the world of spirits and miracles is a view that everybody in the pre-scientific past held but which has been overtaken by scientific progress.

It's "*impossible*" because you can't hold these views sincerely – when you flick a light switch or turn on the TV you *know* the world is operating according to scientific principles; the moment you or a loved one falls ill, you will go to a doctor for scientific medicine because you *know* that the real causes of illness are not supernatural.

However, the Bible does not just contain mythological material. Bultmann thinks there are philosophical teachings and stories in the Bible which modern people can accept without sacrificing their understanding:

> *Jesus demands truthfulness and purity, readiness to sacrifice and to love* – **Rudolf Bultmann**

*You first came across Bultmann in **Topic 3** as a founding figure in **Form Criticism**. Can you see how Form Criticism's concerns with genre (tales, legends, paradigms) could lead to Bultmann's view of Christianity as a mythological world view?*

Existentialism & Christianity

Inspired by **Martin Heidegger**, Bultmann outlines a view of Christianity based on **existentialism**. Existentialism is a philosophy which sees human beings as 'thrown into the world' without choosing to be here. As humans, we are self-aware: we can foresee our inevitable death and we are forced to make choices and live without any supernatural guidance. Existing in this way is confusing and frightening, so many people hide from the truth about life. They live in a very shallow way, allowing themselves to be defined by things they haven't chosen, such as their family, their job, their race or age or gender, even their interests or religion. Existentialists regard this sort of living as INAUTHENTIC - it's dishonest and fake.

Bultmann thinks that the scientific world view that has cut us off from the old mythological world view has also made our existence even more distressing. Scientific thinking teaches us to expect to be able to control everything, but in fact we can't control our lives. Our ancestors could take comfort in mythological beliefs about life after death, miracles and guardian angels, but modern scientific people can't enjoy this sort of consolation. Instead, we look for security in a frightening world and we settle for things like money, material comfort and selfishness.

> By means of science men try to take possession of the world, but in fact the world gets possession of men – **Rudolf Bultmann**

> In a nutshell, Bultmann is saying that progress has not made us happy. Our lives are comfortable but lack meaning.

This leaves people trapped. Because we are limited and contingent creatures, we are doomed to feel *"sorrow and anxiety"*. The only alternative is to bury yourself in inauthentic ways of living that offer bogus solutions to life, such as throwing yourself into your job or hobby, living for your family or social respectability – or sacrificing your understanding by believing in the mythological world of religion.

However, Bultmann thinks there is another option offered by Christianity which can free people from the choice of either anxiety or inauthenticity.

> Bultmann isn't the first Christian Existentialist - that would probably be **Søren Kierkegaard** (1813-1855), who argued that people need to take a "leap of faith" *rather than trust in reason all the time*

Bultmann believes there is a Christian way of living that is free from anxiety because it does not fear death. Living in this way involves letting go of selfish desires and no longer clinging to things like money or power or popularity. He thinks the New Testament describes a programme for living life in this way. Bultmann calls this the *'Word of God'*.

> There's nothing SUPERNATURAL about Bultmann's use of 'Word of God'. It's very different from the way the phrase is used in **John's Prologue** or by **Karl Barth**. Bultmann's 'Word of God' is a way of life based around fearlessness, love and honesty. It's a psychologically healthy frame of mind.

According to Bultmann, a lot of people – even religious people (perhaps *especially* religious people) – don't understand this 'Word of God'. Atheists just dismiss the Bible as irrelevant to them and Christians focus on all the wrong things in it. Bultmann wants to draw everyone's attention to the REAL 'Word of God' in the Bible, which offers the solution to modern life. However, first we need to disentangle the 'Word of God' from the mythology surrounding it.

De-mythologizing the Bible

Bultmann doesn't seem to like the word 'de-mythologizing' either and apologizes for it. In German it's Entmythologisierung, *which isn't any prettier. It's a provocative word that attracted a lot of hostility at the time (and still does)*

De-mythologizing means **discarding the mythological elements of a story to make the underlying meaning clearer**. Bultmann doesn't regard myths as fairy tales or nonsense. He thinks that they contain deep wisdom about the meaning of life.

> *Myths express the knowledge that man is not master of the world and his life, that the world within which he lives is full of riddles and mysteries and that human life also is full of riddles and mysteries* – **Rudolf Bultmann**

Since we no longer have a mythological world view, people can't understand myths any more. They either treat them **literally** (which Bultmann thinks misses the point) or else dismiss them as silly. That's why Bultmann argues for de-mythologizing the Bible: focusing on the meaning *behind* the myths. This meaning Bultmann calls the *kerygma* (the Greek word for 'preaching').

Bultmann claims that the earliest Christians created myths about the historical Jesus (crediting him with super powers) and these get in the way of understanding Jesus' *kerygma*. However, he also thinks that the Christians were the first de-mythologizers too. He points out that in the earliest Bible episodes there is a strong APOCALYPTIC belief in the imminent end of the world; this belief gets weaker with Paul's epistles (letters) in the 50s CE (Paul allows his converts to marry, which shows that they weren't expecting the world to end at any moment) and by the time of **John's Gospel** in the 90s CE the end of the world has largely been replaced by the idea of **Eternal Life**. Later Christian churches downplayed the end of the world even more.

> *De-mythologizing has its beginning in the New Testament itself, and therefore our task of de-mythologizing today is justified* – **Rudolf Bultmann**

Bultmann argues that episodes like the Virgin Birth and other miracles are mythological and should **not be taken literally**. Even the Resurrection of Christ is a myth: Bultmann urges people to live *as if* the stories in the Bible were true, rather than trying to convince themselves that they actually happened historically.

This last point is important. Bultmann is *not* arguing that the Bible is just a collection of **moral messages**. He thinks the *kerygma* of the Bible is more than just ethics: it's a total way of life. For example, Bultmann de-mythologizes the story of Adam and Eve and explains that Adam's 'sin' was not living authentically – when Adam and Eve eat the fruit of the Tree of Knowledge of Good & Evil, their 'sin' is seeking false security. Their punishment is to leave the Garden of Eden, which means entering a life of sorrow and anxiety. Adam and Eve symbolise *us*. The Resurrection is *not a literal event*: Jesus rises from the dead in the faith of his followers, but not in history. The *kerygma* of the Bible is about living your life like Jesus lives his and being free from false security, fear and anxiety.

It's also important to note that Bultmann is *not* an atheist. He believes in God and he believes that Jesus uniquely reveals the 'Word of God'. However, he doesn't accept the mythological view of God as a super-powerful being who inhabits Heaven overhead or the mythological view of Jesus performing miracles and coming back to life.

Implications of Bultmann for Modern Scholarship

Bultmann was influenced by **Karl Barth**'s criticisms of liberal theology (p26). Bultmann agreed that reducing Scripture to a set of **moral allegories** (p23) was sterile and shallow. However, he could not agree with Barth's focus on God's revelation in Christ. For Bultmann, there just wasn't enough historical information about Jesus Christ to build a picture of what he was like. The New Testament could only be read as myth, not as history. However, Bultmann wanted to rescue liberal theology because he was convinced that the essential Christian *kerygma* (preaching) still had value. So he set about interpreting the Scriptures as myth-with-a-meaning.

> *What is the importance of the preaching of Jesus and of the preaching of the New Testament as a whole for modern man?* – **Rudolf Bultmann**

Bultmann's argument that modern, scientifically-minded people need to interpret the Bible in a new way proved incredibly popular. His ideas dominated New Testament studies in the '50s and '60s and the 'Bultmann School' continued this influence to the end of the 20th century.

Because he stated his views rather provocatively, Bultmann was (and is) often misunderstood as someone who simply wanted to 'de-bunk' Christianity. This misunderstanding was based on the fact that, for a lot of people, 'myth' just means "an untrue story" whereas for Bultmann a 'myth' was a story containing a much deeper truth. Bultmann was trying to make Christianity MEANINGFUL to modern people because he thought that the way it was being interpreted made it increasingly out-of-touch with modern life.

Bultmann might be out-of-touch in his view of how scientific modern people are. A **2013 YouGov poll** shows 68% of Americans believe in the literal existence of the Devil and, in **2017** according to **Gallup**, 38% believe God created the world less than 10,000 years ago. These beliefs continue to exist in the most scientifically advanced country on Earth. This clearly shows that people are capable of holding beliefs that Bultmann would regard as incompatible.

A stronger criticism is that Bultmann exaggerates how little we can know about the historical Jesus. Many of Bultmann's own students in the 'Bultmann School' went against him on this and there is a renewed confidence today that we can know things about Jesus' life and preaching.

Bultmann was criticised for not following his de-mythologizing project through to its logical conclusions: why treat everything in the Bible as a myth *except* the life and *kerygma* of Jesus? Why not regard that as a myth too and allow that modern people can get their meaningful myths from the Buddha or Socrates.

> *Or* Star Wars, Buffy the Vampire Slayer *or* Lord of the Rings*!!! Bultmann's existentialist code for living could just as easily be based on a popular novel, film or TV show. Bultmann's attachment to Christianity prevented him from seeing that, if the Bible didn't need to be historically true, you could just as easily base your life on Shakespeare plays,* Dungeons & Dragons *or* Harry Potter.

Bultmann's existentialist philosophy is no longer as popular as it was in the '50s and '60s and his attempts to interpret Christ in the light of this philosophy now seem, with hindsight, more like **eisegesis** than exegesis. Despite this, Bultmann's idea that the Bible should be interpreted to provide a living message relevant to modern society remains influential.

Has Rudolf Bultmann made an important contribution to Bible scholarship?

YES	NO
Bultmann saved liberal theology, which was heading down a dead end road of presenting a purely 'social Gospel' in which Jesus appears to be recommending popular political policies. He restored the idea that the Bible is personally meaningful and leads you to change your life.	Bultmann probably did more harm than good. His idea of 'de-mythologizing' was widely misunderstood as treating all of Christianity as a fairy tale. He was too extreme in claiming we can know nothing about the historical Jesus nor relate to the world view of the first Christians.
When Bultmann says the Bible contains 'myths', he means that it is meaningful and telling us important truths. He was only trying to reinterpret the LANGUAGE of the Bible to make it relevant to modern people. This is still the goal of liberal theology today.	Bultmann's existentialist ethics now look very dated and his interpretation of the *kerygma* preached by Jesus and the first Disciples doesn't look plausible. Modern scholarship is more interested in reconstructing a historical Jesus than Bultmann was.

The Barth-Bultmann Debate

Before you read this page, you need to be familiar with the different positions proposed by these two giants of 20th century scholarship on how the Bible should be interpreted.

The Whale & the Elephant

Karl Barth (p26) and **Rudolf Bultmann** (p33) became friends when they met in Marburg in 1908. Bultmann was strongly influenced by Barth's criticism of liberal theology. However, the different directions they took in their interpretation of the Bible drove them apart. Their 'debate' lasted for years, being conducted in published articles, lectures and letters. Barth in particular grew frustrated and their friendship suffered. Barth describes their relationship like this, in a letter from Christmas 1952:

> *It seems to me that we are like a whale . . . and an elephant, who have met in boundless astonishment on some oceanic shore. . . . They lack a common key to what each would obviously so much like to say to the other according to its own element and in its language* – **Karl Barth**

Barth is comparing them both to two creatures from different worlds. How can the whale understand what it must be like for the elephant on land? How can the elephant understand the whale's life under the water? This is how Barth feels trying to get his views across to Bultmann and trying to understand Bultmann's replies.

Barth and Bultmann exchanged letters from the 1920s through to the 1960s, although the 'Christmas Correspondence' of 1952 particularly interests their fans and critics. Most critics view Bultmann as the more consistent of the two, with Barth's views changing significantly during the course of his life.

Implications of the Barth-Bultmann Debate

It's become so common to represent Barth and Bultmann as opposites that it's worth focusing on what they have in common:

- Both come from the **liberal hermeneutic approach** to Scripture
- Both criticise 20th century liberal theology as flawed and too focused on **morality** and politics
- Both see themselves as 'rescuing' liberal theology from its dead end
- Both reject **literalist interpretations** of the Bible (p16)
- Both reject the idea that the Bible is **inerrant** (without flaws)
- Both reject the idea of life after death in favour of life lived in the present in a better way
- Both believe the Bible contains the 'Word of God'
- Both believe the Bible should be read as a story, not as history

However, they also represent two very different directions Bible scholarship takes. Bultmann's route freely adapts the Bible to fit in with modern modes of thought, treats much of what used to be thought of as historical facts as 'myths' and sometimes sounds more like an atheist than a believer; Barth argues that modern people should alter their thoughts to fit into the Bible's mode of thinking, treats the Bible as a medium through which God can speak to us and sees Jesus Christ as an objective reality, not a myth.

One way of understanding their differences is in their focus on **individualism** or **community**. Bultmann offers the Bible to people who are going to read it as individuals, looking for answers in it to their own individual problems and anxieties. He suggests that treating the Bible stories as myths with deep meaning is a helpful way of doing this. His main concern seems to be that people who might really benefit from the Word of God won't pay any attention to it because its mythological language puts them off.

Barth offers the Bible to pastors (church leaders) or Christian communities - groups of people who already believe in Christianity and are looking for advice in how to put their faith into practice. He suggests that reading the Bible as a witness to Jesus Christ will keep them in touch with the Word of God and stop them from sliding into distorted ways of thinking about their religion. Barth isn't worried about people being put off the Bible; he's more concerned about people complacently thinking they've already got it figured out.

Both scholars are trying to 'jolt' readers into seeing the Bible clearly - as a book from out of which the Word of God speaks directly to them. Bultmann does this with some provocative, even shocking suggestions to get through people's resistance; Barth does this through paradoxes that force you to think in order to make sense of them. Both Barth and Bultmann agree that what they are arguing about is a Mystery: something human minds cannot properly comprehend.

> *It's just a shame these differences outweighed their similarities and ruined their friendship.*

FOUR POST-ENLIGHTENMENT APPROACHES TO BIBLICAL INTERPRETATION

RATIONAL APPROACH	HISTORICAL APPROACH
SOCIOLOGICAL APPROACH	LITERARY APPROACH

If you search online for these "Four Approaches" you'll not find them conveniently listed. Edexcel appears to have taken them from **Alister E. McGrath**'s Christian Theology: An Introduction *(p119). Don't rush out and buy it because (i) it's a big coursebook for undergraduates, (ii) McGrath only writes a summary paragraph on each approach and (iii) you can read this bit FOR FREE on Google Books if you search online.*

The **Enlightenment** is often referred to as the "Age of Reason". This period begins with the ideas of Descartes in the 17th century and ends with the American and French Revolutions in the 18th century. Thinkers in France, Germany and Britain (especially Scotland) rejected many of the beliefs and traditions of previous generations and developed new ways of looking at the world. The Enlightenment had a huge impact on Western culture, changing philosophy, science, and politics in the process.

Several key ideas are essential to understanding the Enlightenment:

Rationalism

René Descartes introduced rationalism into philosophical thought, arguing that the power of reason could and should test all ideas.

Rationalism inspired philosophers to question religion and propose new answers to religious questions. Inconsistencies and contradictions that earlier Christians had accepted as part of the mystery of holy things were now dissected and the traditional explanations were found to be lacking. *Dare to use your reason!* became the slogan of the Enlightenment.

> *SAPERE AUDE! 'Have courage to use your own reason!' - that is the motto of Enlightenment* – **Immanuel Kant**

One of the key developments was **Deism**, a new religious idea of a non-interventionist God who would not do the irrational things described in the Bible.

Empiricism

Empiricism is the idea that all knowledge comes from our experience of the world using the 5 senses. **Francis Bacon** argued for a scientific worldview based on empiricism and this culminated in the work of **Isaac Newton** who created a physical explanation for the workings of the natural world.

In many ways, empiricism opposes rationalism: **John Locke** developed the analogy of the mind as *tabula rasa* ("a blank slate") to describe how all our thoughts come originally from our sense-experiences. Since these explanations accounted for the working of the world without supernatural interference, they added to the appeal of **Deism**, which proposes that God exists but does not intervene in the world.

Scepticism

> *Scepticism with a 'C' - the Americans spell it 'skepticism' with a 'K'*

Scepticism is doubting the truth of all knowledge claims. **David Hume** questioned whether knowledge can be obtained at all, either rationally (from reason) or empirically (from the senses). Scepticism went further than just questioning science – sceptics also questioned the truth-claims of religion. Hume cast doubt on **miracles** and the classical **arguments for the existence of God** and **Voltaire** mocked the behaviour of the churches and exposed religious hypocrisy. This scepticism caused many thinkers to abandon Christianity in favour of **Deism** or outright atheism.

Implications of the Enlightenment for the Bible

Before the Enlightenment, most Biblical interpretation had been DEVOTIONAL. This means that scholars studied the Bible to understand God's will, not to question the text itself. Previous scholars had noticed things like the **Synoptic Problem** or contradictions and inconsistencies between different passages, but had not questioned the Bible itself.

Thomas Hobbes (1651) broke with tradition by questioning whether Moses could really have written the first five books of the Old Testament (the *Pentateuch*). This inspired others to read the Bible sceptically and challenge longstanding beliefs about its perfection and inspired authorship. The Enlightenment introduced Biblical CRITICISM, where the Bible was treated as a book like any other to be analysed and evaluated.

Enlightenment scholars were still held back by a certain amount of respect for Christianity (and perhaps fear of the Church). The first Biblical Criticism was directed at the Old Testament. **Jean Astruc** (1753) used the techniques that scholars had applied to non-religious books from ancient history (notably the works of the Greek poet Homer) and applied them to the Old Testament. He demonstrated that the **Book of Genesis** was not written by one person, but that several different sources had been combined together to form the text.

> *The fact that European scholars were quite willing to dissect the Old Testament and hold parts of it up for ridicule is perhaps an example of their antisemitism - it was OK to attack the Jewish part of the Bible, but not the Christian part.*

Eventually, the same relentless logic that had been applied to the Old Testament was applied to the New Testament too. **Baron D'Holbach** wrote *Christianity Unveiled* (1761) in which he exposes the illogicality of the entire Bible, D'Holbach calls the Old Testament "*a tissue of fables and allegories, incapable of giving any true idea of things*" and uses contradictions between the four Gospels to question whether they really could be **inspired** by God. He concludes that the Bible is more likely to be:

> *the work of a malign spirit, a genius of darkness and falsehood, than of a God desirous to preserve, enlighten and beautify mankind* – **Baron D'Holbach**

D'Holbach wrote under a pseudonym to protect his reputation, but does not hide his atheism. Other critics (like **Immanuel Kant** and **Hermann Reimarus**) still saw some good in the Bible and Christianity, but wanted to 'purge' religion of its irrational and dangerous elements.

There were reasons for this. The period immediately before the Enlightenment was the **European Wars of Religion**, when Catholics and Protestants battled each other over their religious differences. The bloodshed was huge, not just from battles but also from people who were executed for their beliefs. **Merold Westphal** argues that the horror at what had been done in the name of religion was a big motivation for Enlightenment thinkers:

> *they sought above all to define a religion that would foster moral unity rather than immoral hostility within and among human societies* – **Merold Westphal**

Did the Enlightenment add to our understanding of the Bible?

YES	NO
The Enlightenment was about casting the light of reason on the darkness of superstition and ignorance. By being sceptical, focusing on the evidence and drawing rational conclusions, scholars exposed things in the Bible that previous generations had been unable to see.	The real motivation of many Enlightenment scholars was atheism and a hatred of religion. Many scholars like **Hume** and **D'Holbach** were more interested in attacking Christianity than exploring it. They start with the assumption that there is nothing good in the Bible.
Not all the Enlightenment scholars were atheists; some were Christians or **Deists** with a respect for Christian values. What united them was that they put reason ahead of defending their religious position. **Rudolf Bultmann** shows how the Enlightenment made the old mythological world view impossible for modern minds.	**Deism** is a really just atheism without the courage of its convictions, because the God of Deism doesn't *do* anything. The liberal tradition which tries to 'water down' Christianity and the Bible has its roots in the Enlightenment. As **Karl Barth** shows, this sort of Christianity was powerless to oppose militarism and Nazism in the 20th century.

The Rational Approach

The **rational approach** is based on **Deism**, which is a type of religion that became popular in the 18th century. **Merold Westphal** suggests that Deism can be called "*the religion of the Enlightenment*". Here are some famous Deists from the **Enlightenment** up to modern times:

Abraham Lincoln	16th American president
Antony Flew	philosopher and former-atheist
Adam Smith	Enlightenment philosopher and 'father of Economics' (*he's on the £20 banknote!*)
Benjamin Franklin	American founding father (*he's on the $100 bill!*)
Ernest Rutherford	New Zealand physicist who created the periodic table
Gottfried Leibniz	Enlightenment philosopher and mathematician
James Watt	Scottish inventor of the steam engine
John Locke	Enlightenment philosopher
Mark Twain	American author
Maximilian Robespierre	French revolutionary leader
Napoleon Bonaparte	French ruler
Neil Armstrong	the first man on the moon
Thomas Edison	American inventor
Voltaire	Enlightenment philosopher and writer

Deism is the belief in a supreme being ('God') who does not intervene in the word. Deists usually believe that God created the world and usually believe that God is good and wants humans to behave morally; many Deists believe that God will reward or punish people in the afterlife. However, the Deist God does not answer prayers or perform miracles and he does not grant **revelations** to his followers. Therefore, revealed religions (religions that claim to be founded on a revelation from God) are all mistaken and the real God does not favour one religion over another.

For Deists, there is no need for churches or priests. The Deist God isn't interested in being worshiped; he just wants people to lead moral lives. Because of this, conflict between religious groups is unnecessary. They are all worshiping the same Deist God at heart, but have lost sight of this because they place too much emphasis on revelation.

Instead of revelation, Deists think humans can arrive at some knowledge of God through reason and studying nature. The **Design Argument** is a popular proof for the existence of the God of Deism. Because this God does not intervene, Jesus can only be an inspirational moral teacher and the Bible can only be a book of **moral teachings**. Unfortunately, these moral teachings are often obscured by tales of visions and miracles. A Deist approach to the Bible will focus on separating the valuable moral lessons it can teach from the superstitious and illogical supernatural details.

> *These are very similar to **Rudolf Bultmann**'s view (p33) of the central kerygma (preaching) of Christianity needing to be 'rescued' from out-of-date mythology. You could argue that what Bultmann is offering people is not Christianity, but Deism.*

Implications of the rational approach

The rational approach to Biblical interpretation is very hostile to reports of miracles, spirits, visions and other supernatural events. It assumes that the real events of Jesus' life, ministry and death have become distorted or exaggerated – rather like the game of 'Chinese Whispers'. Deists believe that religions should teach general principles of morality and good living which everyone can understand and relate to. This is called **universalist religion**. However, **revealed religions** prioritise believing in supernatural wonders, privilege some groups of people as 'specially chosen' by God and offer stories that not everyone can understand or relate to. Rational criticism therefore involves stripping away the supernatural elements to focus on the underlying rational and universal truths that are positive and good.

> *they seek to separate the rational kernel of religion from the irrational husk* – **Merold Westphal**

> *This is important. The rational approach is still an approach to INTERPRETING the Bible because it thinks there's something positive in there to interpret. Atheists like **Baron D'Holbach** are not interpreting the Bible: they are CHALLENGING it and this is studied further in **Topic 6** (p172)*

However, Deism has declined in popularity since the 18th century. Arguments like the **classical arguments** used to prove the existence of the Deist God were dealt severe blows by **David Hume** and **Immanuel Kant** and the **Design Argument** was further weakened by **Charles Darwin**'s theory of evolution.

Another blow came from Immanuel Kant who attacked the idea reason can tell us about God. Kant makes a distinction between the **Phenomenon** (reality we experience through our senses) and the **Noumenon** (reality as it actually is). God would be part of the Noumenon but, as human beings, we only ever experience Phenomenon. This means we can never draw conclusions about God just from studying the world around us.

In the 21st century, the universality of reason has been attacked by **postmodernism**. These philosophers question whether everyone in the world reasons in the same way. "Universal reason" could mean just the way Western cultures like to think about things. There might not be a single way of reasoning that works for all cultures. This leads **Alister McGrath** to comment on the decline of the rational approach:

> *With the general collapse in confidence in both the universality and the theological competence of reason in more recent times, the attractions of this approach have dwindled* – **Alister McGrath**

Reimarus & the *Wolfenbüttel Fragments*

Hermann Reimarus (1694-1768) was a professor of oriental languages in Hamburg and a dedicated Deist. Reimarus wrote a powerful attack on conventional Christianity called *Apologia or Defence of the Rational Worshipers of God*. The original book was only shared among Reimarus' friends but, after his death, **G. E. Lessing** (another Deist philosopher) published extracts from it that became known as the *Wolfenbüttel Fragments.* These caused a sensation and introduced people to Reimarus' new ideas.

Reimarus distinguishes between what Jesus actually said and did and what his Disciples merely *claimed* he said and did. In other words, Reimarus is one of the first scholars to point out a difference between the 'Jesus of history' and the 'Christ of faith'.

Reimarus argues that Jesus started off as a humble preacher who respected the **Jewish Law** and did not want to abolish it. He didn't see himself as God or try to start a new religion.

> *Reimarus has a striking insight that still inspires Bible critics: to analyse the Gospels you must put yourself in the position of Jesus' original 1st century audience of Palestinian peasants. Any account of Jesus saying or doing things that would make no sense to such an audience should be rejected as un-historical.*

However, Jesus unwisely turned into a political revolutionary. Reimarus thinks this because of the references to the **Kingdom of God** (p75) in the Gospels. Jews in the 1st century CE expected God's Kingdom to be a real kingdom on Earth that would overthrow the **Roman occupation** and Reimarus suggests that Jesus sympathised with the **Zealots** and hoped to set up such a kingdom. Jesus entered Jerusalem intending to trigger a rebellion, but his people deserted him and he was executed by the Romans as an enemy of the state.

> *But surely Jesus told his followers to "Love your neighbour"? Reimarus thinks that Jesus never said these things - they were added in later by the Gospel-writers who 'put words in Jesus' mouth'*

Reimarus concludes that Jesus' fanatical Disciples stole his body from its tomb then made up the story that Jesus had been raised from the dead. They 'reinvented' Jesus as a saviour figure rather than a political leader and preached that he would return again at the end of the world, which they thought would happen soon. Reimarus argues that the fact that the world did not end means that Christianity is entirely mistaken: it's just a hoax that got carried too far.

> *Do you see why Reimarus didn't publish the Wolfenbüttel Fragments while he was still alive?*

Implications of Reimarus' critique

Reimarus tries to demolish Christianity so as to prove Deism true (he also attacks atheism). His rational criticism of the New Testament is extreme but it has some points in its favour. There clearly *was* a suspicion in the 1st century CE that Jesus' Disciples had stolen his body to fake his Resurrection. **Matthew's Gospel** describes the Jewish priests bribing the guards to spread the story that Jesus' body was stolen by the Disciples.

> *You are to say, 'His disciples came during the night and stole him away while we were asleep'* – **Matthew 28: 15**

> *Matthew puts this passage in specifically to deny the rumour that the Disciples stole the body - but the very fact that Matthew has to deny it shows that the rumour was believed by some people at the time*

However, this theory can be opposed on equally rational grounds. The Roman army tortured and executed guards who slept on duty, so the priests would have to have bribed the soldiers a huge amount to get them to tell that sort of lie.

Moreover, **Frank Morison** (p188) explains how unlikely it is that the Disciples would have carried out such a fraud, given that most of them went on to be murdered for the sake of their beliefs. Who would be willing to die for a belief they know to be untrue?

> *no great moral structure like the early church, characterized as it was by lifelong persecution and personal suffering, could have reared its head on a statement that every one of the eleven apostles knew to be a lie* – **Frank Morison**

A more specific criticism is that Jesus' Disciples would have been followers of someone who (according to Reimarus) advocated violence. If they were so devoted to him, why would they turn into pacifists after his death and invent peace-loving teachings for their leader?

The influential Bible scholar **David Strauss** wrote a biography of Reimarus and adapted some of Reimarus' ideas in his own landmark book, *The Life of Jesus Critically Examined* (1836). Strauss does not agree that the Disciples deliberately set out to deceive. He suggests that the miracles in the Gospels are 'myths' that represent the intense hopes and dreams of the early Christians.

> *Again, this is very similar to **Rudolf Bultmann**'s idea that Christ rose from the dead in the faith of his followers but not in history. You will study rationalist challenges to the Resurrection in detail in **Topic 6** (p172)*

Reimarus' Deism is not so popular today and his specific theories about the rational origins of Christianity are not supported by evidence. Reimarus also has a rather black-and-white view of matters and treats all parts of the Bible that he disagrees with as lies and stupidity. However, he was years ahead of his time in trying to write about the historical Jesus, recognising the difference between Jesus' actual teachings and the beliefs of the early churches (an essential idea in **Form Criticism**) and recognising that the world view of the early Christians was APOCALYPTIC (they believed the end of the world was happening soon).

---

*William **Wrede** also argued that Jesus' later followers saw Jesus differently from the way he saw himself. Wrede's theory of the **Messianic Secret** (c.f. **Topic 1**) states that Jesus never claimed to be the Messiah, but that his followers put such claims into his mouth when they wrote the Gospels.*

Is the rational approach helpful in interpreting the Bible?

YES

NO

As **Bultmann** points out, there are important ideas in the New Testament that are hidden by the mythological world view the Gospel-writers share. The rational approach uncovers what *really* happened and promotes universal values instead of **revelations**.

Reimarus' hostile criticisms don't uncover what really happened and don't reveal universal values either. His Deism faded away without arguments to support it but Christianity is still with us. As **Barth** says, the Bible is a witness to the revelation of God in Jesus.

Deism may have dwindled but it's not entirely gone and Deist-inspired interpretations like Bultmann's de-mythologizing are very influential today. The rational approach reminds us there are still important things we can learn from the Bible.

The rational approach uses human reason to define God, which is impossible, as **Kant** shows. It's also an example of what Barth call's 'idolatry' – making an idol out of human reason and worship a God you've created in your mind rather than the God who reveals himself in Jesus Christ.

The Historical Approach

One of the key ideas to come out of the Enlightenment was that traditional ideas about the origins of the Bible texts were not correct. **Thomas Hobbes** argued that Moses did not write the first 5 books of the Old Testament, other scholars criticised the idea that the Gospel-writers really were eyewitnesses to the events of Jesus' life. **Hermann Reimarus** even suggested that the historical Jesus was a completely different sort of person from the character the Gospel-writers invented.

The historical approach tries to identify the true events behind the Bible texts. It differs from the **rational approach** because it's not arguing for a Deist interpretation of religion and it's not *necessarily* ridiculing the supernatural elements in the Bible.

The Higher Criticism

The historical approach used to be known as "Higher Criticism" as opposed to "Lower Criticism" which focuses on the original meanings of words in the earliest versions of Bible texts. The **Synoptic Problem** is a key subject for Higher Criticism and the critical theories you learned about in **Topic 3 (Interpreting the Text) – Source**, **Form** and **Redaction Criticism** – are all examples of Higher Criticism at work. These theories try to get an insight into "*the world **behind** the text*".

*This means that **Rudolf Bultmann** (p33) is using the historical approach to de-mythologize the Bible. It turns out you've covered a LOT of the historical approach in this course so far.*

Higher Criticism begins with **Friedrich Schleiermacher** (1768-1834), a German pastor who is widely considered to be the 'father of hermeneutics'. Schleiermacher argues that, in order to interpret a text, you needed to get into the mind of its author and that involved understanding the author's background, beliefs and experiences and their whole historical situation. If successful, Schleiermacher's technique has as its aim

to understand the text at first as well as and then even better than its author **– Friedrich Schleiermacher**

In order to interpret a text like this, you need to steep yourself in the historical period that produced it. The scholars of Higher Criticism were mostly linguists in German Universities who studied ancient languages (so they could read the Bible in its original form) and for comparison purposes they looked at other texts from the same time period to gain a sense of the beliefs of 1st century Jews, Greeks and Romans. This is called "*the world **of** the text*".

Whereas critics from the **rational approach** (p44) tend to focus on contradictions or inconsistencies to attack the reliability of the Bible, the historical approach focuses on these things because they reveal an author's distinctive viewpoint or bias. For example, **Matthew's birth narrative** describes the arrival of the *magi* guided by the star and Herod murdering the innocent children of Bethlehem but **Luke**'s birth narrative does not mention these things. How could Luke not have heard about such momentous events or thought them not worth including?

Higher Criticism would say this is because Matthew wants to make a specific point about Gentiles understanding who Jesus is but the Jews failing to understand this despite having the prophecies in the Old Testament to guide them. Luke is more interested in Jesus being on the same side as the poor and the lowly, which is why he describes the baby Jesus being placed in a manger and visited by peasant shepherds.

Implications of the Higher Criticism

Most Christians welcome scholars who help them understand better the world that the Bible was written in and how the characters in the Bible texts looked, acted, thought and spoke. This can help prevent ANACHRONISM, which is the problem of assuming people in the past looked, thought or acted in ways which are historically impossible.

For example, a lot of Christian art used to depict Jesus as pale-skinned and fair-haired (which is unlikely) but the historical approach focuses on Jesus' Jewish background in **1ˢᵗ century Palestine**.

Another example of anachronism would be attitudes to slavery. In the 19ᵗʰ century, slave-owning Christians justified their position by pointing out that there is slavery in the Bible. However, historical scholarship shows that Biblical slavery was not like the conditions of African slaves on the American plantations: Roman slaves were not all of one race, they were paid and they could buy their freedom. Therefore Biblical accounts of slaves (like Paul's prison companion Onesimus) do not justify owning slaves in the modern world.

However, Higher Criticism has a tendency to be REVISIONIST – it's always trying to revise or alter our understanding of Jesus and keeps offering more and more surprising and unusual theories about Jesus and the early Christians.

- **Joseph Renan** (1863) presents Jesus as a wise teacher who expected too much from his followers, so they abandoned his ethical teachings in favour of supernatural beliefs
- **Heinrich Holtzman** (1863) presents Jesus as a popular moral teacher whose popularity went to his head, causing him to get delusions about being the Messiah
- **William Wrede** (1901) presents Jesus as no Messiah at all (his later followers invented the **Messianic Secret**)
- **Albert Schweitzer** (1906) presents Jesus as an apocalyptic prophet who thought the world was ending another *"failed messiah"*
- Since then, other critics have suggested Jesus was a Marxist revolutionary ahead of his time, a Cynic philosopher and a Zealot rebel.

Albert Schweitzer (p162) makes a good point that critics have a tendency to present Jesus as embodying the things that **they** care about. In his book *The Quest for the Historical Jesus* (1906), Schweitzer argues that the picture of Jesus as a wandering wise man preaching a simple message of love isn't based on evidence at all; it's based on the ideology of the Enlightenment which promoted such values. He calls this sort of 'historical Jesus'

a figure designed by rationalism, endowed with life by liberalism, and clothed by modern theology in an historical garb - **Albert Schweitzer**

> *Schweitzer's language makes Jesus sound like Frankenstein's Monster - a patchwork person brought to life by a mad boffin! In more technical terms, all the historical scholarship in the world doesn't stop **exegesis** turning into **eisegesis**, which is the tendency to project things onto the text when you think you're drawing things out of the text.*

Higher Criticism has focused too much on the world **behind** the text and the world **of** the text. There's an increasing concern with addressing the world **in front of** the text. This means addressing what the Biblical text could mean for people reading it today, which is a point easily lost by scholars who are obsessed with the 1st century background to the New Testament. **Rudolf Bultmann** (p33) started moving Biblical interpretation in this direction by asking how the mythological world view of the Gospel-writers could be relevant to modern people in a scientific age.

F.C. Baur and the Tübingen School

F.C. Baur (1792-1860) was one of the founders of Higher Criticism. He was strongly influenced by **Schleiermacher** but also the famous philosopher **Hegel**. Baur set up an approach to historical Bible interpretation known as the **Tübingen School** (after the university he worked at).

From Hegel, Baur took the idea of history have a structure of its own and an inevitable progress brought about by the clash of opposing ideas.

Hegel claims that every age was dominated by a defining idea (the ***thesis***) and its opposite number (the ***antithesis***) and these clashing ideas eventually resolve by combining to form a new idea (the ***synthesis***), which immediately becomes a new *thesis* and a new *antithesis* emerges to oppose it.

For example, in the 20th century you could say the conflict was between liberal democracy and totalitarian communism. The conflict between these opposing ideas is ultimately beneficial: it leads to progress.

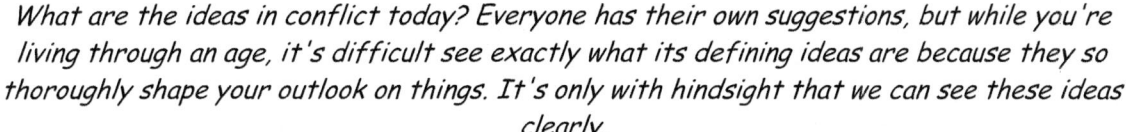

> *What are the ideas in conflict today? Everyone has their own suggestions, but while you're living through an age, it's difficult see exactly what its defining ideas are because they so thoroughly shape your outlook on things. It's only with hindsight that we can see these ideas clearly.*

From a Hegelian perspective, the sudden emergence of Christianity in the 1st century CE must be prompted by the conflict of two opposing ideas. But what is the *thesis/antithesis* behind the Bible?

Baur thinks that the conflict in Christianity was between **particularity** and **universalism**. 'Particularity' means the Jewish roots of Jesus and his Disciples: following the Jewish Law, observing the rules on food and the Sabbath, being circumcised, remaining linked to Jerusalem and the Jewish synagogues. 'Universalism' means becoming a religion for everybody, not tied to a particular race or place but accepting Gentile members and dropping the rules that tend to exclude people (like circumcision). A universal Christianity would break away from the synagogues and no longer see itself as Jewish.

Baur identifies this conflict as revolving around two people: **Peter** and **Paul**. Peter is the head of the Twelve Disciples and represents the Jewish particularistic side of Christianity – Baur calls this **Petrine Christianity**. Paul was never one of Jesus' Disciples but converted to Christianity after seeing a vision of Christ; he campaigns for the Gentile universalistic side of Christianity – Baur calls this **Pauline Christianity**.

- Petrine Christianity is based in Jerusalem. Its members are Jewish Christians who operate out of the synagogues in the Roman Empire.

- Pauline Christianity operates out of 'house churches' in the towns of Turkey and Greece where Paul makes his Gentile converts: Ephesus, Thessalonica and Corinth are the famous ones.

We know quite a lot about Paul's churches because his **epistles** (letters) to them survive in the New Testament; we know a bit less about Petrine Christianity but its views seem to appear in the **Epistle of James** and the **Epistle to the Hebrews**.

Traditionally, Christians have always thought of Peter and Paul as allies who worked together to spread the Christian religion. Baur presents them more as enemies. Baur researched early Christian sects called the **Clementines** and the **Ebionites** who preserved Petrine views and completely rejected Paul as a 'false apostle'. These sects date from the 4th century CE but Baur thinks their views represent what Petrine Christians thought of Paul back in the 1st century CE.

Baur goes through Paul's epistles carefully and reconstructs the conflict. In Antioch in Syria, Paul is humiliated because Peter and the Jewish Christians refuse to eat alongside his new Gentile converts (**Galatians 2: 11-13**). Paul goes to Corinth in Greece and founds a church of his own with Gentile converts. However, the Petrine Christians send messengers with letters of authority, saying that Paul doesn't represent them and isn't a real apostle. Paul argues that his vision of the Risen Christ makes him an apostle too.

> *Am I not an apostle? Have I not seen Jesus our Lord? Are you not the result of my work in the Lord? Even though I may not be an apostle to others, surely I am to you!* **– 1 Corinthians 9: 1-2**

> *One of the great things about Paul as a writer is that he never hides his feelings. You can sense his squirming embarrassment here, having to justify himself to the people he converted when 'proper' Christians show up in Corinth*

Eventually, these two opposing sides made their peace and united in a *synthesis*: the religion we call Christianity today. Both sides compromised. The Petrine Christians accepted the Gentiles as equals and relaxed their attachment to Jewish laws; the Pauline side kept the Old Testament as part of the Scriptures and downplayed their criticism of the Jewish Law. Baur thinks the Pauline side brought numbers to the new religion but the Petrine side provided the brains and the organisation. Most importantly, the new religion was **universalistic** and could appeal to everyone (except the Ebionites, who never gave up the Petrine fight).

Baur thinks the Gospels represent different positions in this *synthesis*. **Matthew's Gospel** (which Baur thinks came first) tries to compromise between both sides, presenting Jesus as belonging to both Jews and Gentiles but giving a lot of prominence to the character of Peter. **Luke** is much more pro-Paul and so is **John** (in John, Peter is sidelined by the "Beloved Disciple" and Jews are the enemy).

> *You can see that Baur's theory is a type of **Redaction Criticism**: he thinks the Gospels have been edited to reflect the views at the time they were written*

Implications of Baur's theory

Baur's theory is strongly rooted in the Hegelian idea of how historical progress happens. **Alister McGrath** notes that:

> *With the waning of Hegelianism, Baur's impact also diminished* – **Alister McGrath**

Splitting everything into a conflict between just two opposing ideas is simplistic. There seem to have been LOTS of competing ideas in early Christianity. For example, there were also the followers of John the Baptist and (according to **Raymond E. Brown**) the Samaritan Christians who joined the **Johannine Community** but had their own traditions about Jesus.

Baur's theory is entirely based on 'reading between the lines' of various New Testament texts and non-Canonical sources. Baur may be twisting the text to fit in with his pre-conceived ideas. For example, **Galatians 2: 12** admits that Peter *used* to eat with the Gentiles, but only stopped when more Jewish Christians arrived from Jerusalem. Maybe he was just hanging out with his friends! In any event, the passage shows that Peter was capable of having moderate views.

Baur doesn't really explain how the Petrine and Pauline Christians compromised their deeply held views to achieve unity. After all, the Ebionites never compromised. They were still hating Paul and rejecting Gentiles way into the 4th century CE.

On the other hand, Baur's influence lives on in other ways. His broad historical approach became the Higher Criticism and is widely used. He proposed a radical idea by suggesting there was a conflict right at the heart of the first Christian community (which was always portrayed as a smiley-happy group of people up until then) and this opened the way for more open-minded investigation into the origins of Christianity. By focusing on the hidden biases and political agendas in the Gospels, he also prepared the way for **Redaction Criticism**.

*You can see the ideas of the historical approach at work in **Raymond E. Brown**'s idea of the Johannine Community (c.f. **Topic 3**) and the idea of a rivalry between Johannine Christians who based their faith on the testimony of the 'Beloved Disciple' and the other Petrine churches.*

Does the historical approach help us to interpret the Bible?

YES	NO
The Bible was written 2000 yeas ago by people living in a very different sort of society and speaking long-dead languages. In order to understand their meaning, we need scholars who can steep themselves in that ancient society and understand how the original authors saw things.	The Bible is intended for readers who are reading it right now, today. Historical interpretations turn the Bible into a historical curiosity, just an old book from long ago that cannot be relevant to the world we live in now. But there is a world in front of the text as well as a world behind the text.
Without historical scholarship there is a danger of **anachronism**. This is where we falsely assume that Jesus and his Disciples looked, thought and acted just like us. This leads us to misinterpret what the Bible is really saying. For example, without historical knowledge, 19th century slave owners thought the Bible justified what they were doing.	Historical scholarship has created a parade of revisionist Jesuses, all of whom only reflect their creators' concerns and biases. **Albert Schweitzer** shows that all attempts to create a 'historical Jesus' just project the attitudes of the present onto the past. These Jesuses all contradict each other and none is true to the Jesus Christ of the Bible

The Sociological Approach

By the start of the 20th century, scholars were taking more interest in other forms of religion. Experience of other cultures led thinkers to compare Christianity to the other great world religions (Islam, Hinduism, Buddhism) and to so-called primitive religions encountered in Africa, Asia and Australia. It seemed to these thinkers that Christianity was just one response to a 'religious impulse' in mankind.

The **sociological** (or anthropological) **approach** investigates the structures of religious thought in general, not just in Christianity. It looks for similarities between religious ideas rather than the things that make a religion distinctive. It focuses on myths and symbols that recur in religions and how these are rooted in social pressures common to humans everywhere.

Comparative Religion

There are more than 6000 religions in the world. Theology focuses on a single religion from the perspective of a believer, but comparative religion uses a scientific approach to study all religions equally.

The scientific method involves thinking of ways in which our cherished assumptions about the world may prove to be wrong – **Robert Wuthnow**

*You can see how this scientific approach to studying religion grows out of the **Enlightenment**'s focus on scepticism and rationalism.*

In comparative religion, religion is seen as a part of a larger culture or social system.

What the study of religion and culture is not about, however, is finding 'ultimate' truths or answers – **Malory Nye**

Some scholars focus on world religions that go beyond the boundaries of a single culture. These world religions have sacred texts, clearly articulated beliefs and a sense of distinct identity. An example would be Islam which began in Saudi Arabia but spread throughout Africa and Asia and is rooted in the message of **Muhammad** as preserved in the **Qur'an**.

One approach is to categorize religions as being either **universalizing** or **ethnic**. Universalizing religions actively seek converts and cross cultures. Ethnic religions are closely associated with specific ethnic groups and do not seek converts. People "join" ethnic religions by being born into them.

Catherine Albanese defines **ordinary religion** and **extraordinary religion**.

Ordinary religion shows people how to live well within boundaries... extraordinary religion helps people to transcend, or move beyond, their everyday culture and concerns – **Catherine Albanese**

This introduces the idea that people might get different things from religion: for some it simply helps them "*live well*" but for others it offers life-changing experiences and a new way of looking at the world.

> *You could link this to **the debate between Barth and Bultmann** (p39): Bultmann sees the Bible as something that could help modern people live well if it were to be de-mythologized - but Barth sees the Bible as a witness to something transcendent. Bultmann offers ordinary religion but Barth offers extraordinary religion.*

Implications of Comparative Religion

World religions are not the only religions and focusing on them downplays the influence of culture on religious behaviour. For example, US and Mexican Christianity are different, as are Iranian and Saudi Arabian Islam.

This focus on world religions also leads to an over-reliance on interpreting sacred texts like the Bible. This trend is resisted by **anthropologists** who focused on ethnic religions by living with the communities and studying them 'from the inside'. For example, **Bronislaw Malinowski** studied the tribal religion of the **Trobriand Islanders** and **Sir Edward Evans-Pritchard** studied beliefs in witchcraft among the **Azande** of northern Africa.

Some writers refer to non-mainstream religions as "**CULTS**." This term often indicates that the religion is inferior to other religions – that it's sinister or a hoax.

> *'Cults live on the unpaid bills of the churches,'* which is to say that new religious movements arise to meet demands not being satisfied by existing providers **– Philip Jenkins**

Jenkins means that the religious impulse will lead people to create new religions when the old religions no longer answer their questions or provide for their needs.

Christianity seems to have begun as a 'cult'. The Romans considered it *religio prava* (a depraved superstition) rather than *religio licita* (a respectable religion) and persecuted it, but **Rodney Stark** (1965) argues that Christianity triumphed because it offered people a sense of meaning and community that the official pagan religion of the Roman Empire did not. By the 4th century CE, Christianity had become respectable and paganism declined.

This view links to the idea of **secularisation**: sociologists suggest Christianity no longer answers the needs of people living in industrial societies, which is why belief in it is declining in those countries.

> *There's another link here to **Rudolf Bultmann's** idea that modern people have a scientific outlook that cannot relate to the mythological world-view of the Bible.*

Sir James Frazer and *The Golden Bough*

One of the most famous studies in comparative religion was carried out by **Sir James Frazer**. *The Golden Bough* (1915) is a massive 12-volume study of myths and legends from around the world.

In Roman mythology, the golden bough was the branch of a magical tree with golden leaves that enabled heroes to visit the lands of the dead. Frazer's book is like a 'golden bough' because it guides you through the 'underworld' of ancient religions that existed before Christianity.

Frazer considers how religion grows out of magic. The first magical rituals were created to help the tribe survive times of uncertainty (for example, waiting for the harvest and hoping there wouldn't be a flood or drought).

He begins the book with a description of exactly such a ritual: the priest of Nemi is murdered by his rival who then takes his place as priest. Frazer argues that the early magicians evolved into priests and then kings and the ancient rituals were applied to the gods. This led to beliefs in a **dying-and-rising god** whose death benefits the human race but who then comes back to life. Frazer gives several examples:

- **Osiris**, the Egyptian god of life who is murdered by his brother Set and returns as the god of death
- **Adonis**, the lover of Aphrodite (goddess of love) who is killed by a boar
- **Attis**, the consort of the goddess Cybele who went mad and castrated himself

Frazer has two explanations for these myths. One is that the myths are 'echoes' or faint memories of ancient rituals where the ageing leader of the tribe was killed and replaced by a younger rival. The other is that these myths symbolise the agricultural process, where the harvest is followed by winter but there is new growth again in spring.

What made Frazer's book shocking and exciting to many readers is that he places Christianity as another myth alongside these pagan ones. Christianity also has, in Jesus, a dying-and-rising god who is linked to the harvest (Jesus describes himself as the '**Bread of Life**').

Frazer isn't saying that Jesus never existed (although some of Frazer's followers, such as **Gerald Massey**, made this extreme claim). Frazer's point is that the reason Christianity spread and appealed to people is because it closely resembles the ancient pagan myths of the dying-and-rising god.

Implications of Frazer's theory

Frazer's influence was huge. *The Golden Bough* inspired art, novels and other researchers: Malinowski became an anthropologist after reading it. However, it's important to remember that Frazer is an 'armchair researcher' who wrote the entire thing from the comfort of his study. He synthesized a huge amount of ancient records, reports by missionaries and descriptions by explorers, but he never went to any of the tribal societies he described. Instead, Frazer used a rather grand and exciting writing style to give his theories *panache* (imaginative impact). He accepted his views were purely speculative.

Frazer's point boils down to an insight famously made in the Old Testament:

> *What has been will be again, what has been done will be done again;*
> *there is nothing new under the sun* – **Ecclesiastes 1: 9**

In other words, human beings have evolved to have certain psychological and spiritual needs, so religion is **always** going to take a certain sort of form. Our imaginations are stimulated by myths that have patterns like the dying-and-rising-god and we will be drawn to these myths whether they are true or not. In fact, we will be motivated to twist historical events so that they conform to these myths.

> *This links to **David Strauss**' theory that the Disciples believed Jesus rose from the dead because they had an intense emotional need for this to be true (p183). It also links to **Rudolf Bultmann**'s idea (p33) that we still need myths to help us cope with existence, but our scientific world-view means that we have to reinterpret the Bible's old myths which no longer 'work' for us.*

However, few Christians accept Frazer's ideas. **C.S. Lewis** argues that Christianity is an example of "*a myth which is also a fact*". He claims that in the Bible there is a shift from myth to historical fact:

> *an Osiris, dying nobody knows when or where, to a historical Person* crucified under Pontius Pilate. *By becoming fact it does not cease to be myth: that is the miracle* – **C.S. Lewis**

Lewis argues that the pagan myths were in fact hazy and misunderstood anticipations of Christ, rather than Christ being a garbled and misunderstood version of a pagan myth. Lewis also argues that myths are ways for human beings to understand abstract ideas like 'life' and 'death' in an imaginable form.

The idea of myths as stories with great meaning was developed further by the psychologist **Carl Jung**, who saw myths as expressions of humanity's **COLLECTIVE UNCONSCIOUS** – rather like dreams that all humans share. Jung thought that by reflecting on myths and seeing our own life in them, humans could achieve psychological health.

Jung's ideas have been carried forward by **Joseph Campbell,** who argues that the structures of ancient myths conform to a pattern he calls 'the Hero's Journey'. Campbell thinks this pattern of journeying to a heroic crisis then returning to the world altered is the basis for all human storytelling, not just religion. Fans of Campbell map his ideas onto popular books and films, from *Star Wars* to *Pulp Fiction*.

The 'monomyth' (as it is called) involves a hero leaving the security of home, crossing a threshold into an unfamiliar world (or set of experiences), going through trials and being tempted but making allies along the way until they face a supreme ordeal. They then return to their ordinary life with new knowledge, skill or power.

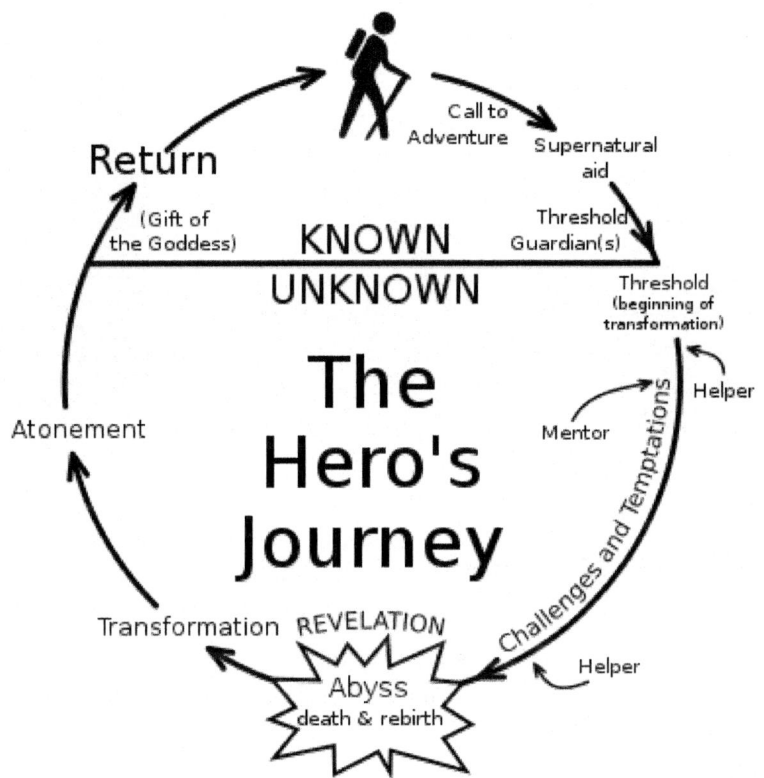

Jesus is called to adventure by the prophecies and visitors like the Magi; he crosses a threshold when baptised by John and immediately has to confront the Devil; his Disciples become helpers but he faces challenges from the Jewish leaders; Jesus dies but is resurrected and transformed into a glorious and divine being; he returns to his heavenly home.

Can you apply Campbell's mythic structure to Lord of the Rings *or* Harry Potter? *How about* Pride & Prejudice *or* An Inspector Calls?

Jordan Peterson & 'Maps of Meaning'

A popular contemporary thinker who writes and talks about religious myths is the Canadian scholar **Jordan Peterson**. Peterson has a huge online following and students can watch his many lectures and interviews on YouTube. Some of his views on gender and political correctness are controversial, but his ideas on myth are helpful for this course.

Peterson's 1999 book *Maps of Meaning: The Architecture of Belief* explains that myths are 'maps' to help guide us through life.

> *myths are centrally and properly concerned with the nature of successful human existence* – **Jordan Peterson**

Peterson argues people can find emotional, moral and political solutions in myths – especially Christian myths, which he particularly values – without having to de-mythologize them first into a set of philosophical propositions the way **Bultmann** does. Peterson argues everyone should imitate Jesus Christ because Jesus is the ideal person/story – the archetypal hero.

> *The Bible is, for better or worse, the foundational document of western civilization … [and] … can reveal things to us about what we believe and how we do and should act that can be discovered in almost no other manner* – **Jordan Peterson**

Peterson's idea of the Bible as a human document with a divine message is close to **Barth**'s view of the 'Story of God'.

Photo: Gage Skagmore

Implications of *Maps of Meaning*

Peterson is wildly popular at the moment and liberal Christians like the way he presents Jesus and the Bible as exciting subjects with meaning for the 21st century. Critics point out that Peterson treats the Bible as a psychological **allegory** and that some of his interpretations are very different from the way traditional Christians have interpreted them.

Peterson is also rather vague on whether he actually believes in God. He argues that religious myths help us to live *as if* God exists (which means living with a sense of purpose, confidence and love for mankind) but this is rather different from the sort of faith that traditional Christians have.

Peterson's views have been attacked as reactionary (old-fashioned and conservative). Basing your life on ancient myths will make you resistant to new developments (like feminism).

Other critics point out that Peterson focuses excessively on Jewish and Christian myths and would draw very different conclusions if he paid more attention to myths from other cultures. However, Peterson regards the Bible as "*the foundational document of Western civilization*" and therefore the most appropriate myth to study and learn from.

You will consider the idea of *Jesus' Resurrection as a myth in more detail in* **Topic 6** *(p180).*

Does the sociological approach help interpret the Bible?

YES	NO
The Bible didn't appear out of nowhere. The first Gentile converts were pagans who brought their myths with them to their new religion. This approach focuses on the essential similarity between the Bible and other religious myths.	This approach ignores the important differences between Christianity and pagan myths. Jesus was a historical person, crucified on a date in history. Christians claim the Resurrection is not a myth but a real event that happened.
This approach helps explain the rapid spread of Christianity and the way it overthrew paganism. Christianity conformed to pagan myths, offering believers a dying-and-returning-god along with a sense of meaning that the disorganised pagan myths could not.	The spread of Christianity is better explained by the heroism and moral goodness of the early Christians who impressed the Romans with their selflessness and willingness to die for their cause. They were willing to do this because they believed Christianity was a fact, not a myth

The Literary Approach

The literary approach to the Bible focuses on Bible texts as literature and how they use literary effects like symbolism and metaphor to express their meaning. It is usually treated as a branch of the **historical approach**: **Form Criticism** looks at the Bible in terms of *pericopae* that are from different genres and **Redaction Criticism** looks at how Biblical authors shape their material to different purposes. However, in the 20th century the **New Criticism** emerged in the 1920s, which focused on reading the Bible as poetry. This led to **narrative theology**, which **Alister McGrath** treats as a separate approach in its own right.

Narrative Theology

Bible scholars since the Enlightenment have wanted to extract **PROPOSITIONS** from the Bible. Propositions are philosophical statements or laws, such as 'love your neighbour' or 'forgive your enemies'. The Bible certainly contains such propositions but they are embedded in **NARRATIVES**, which are lengthy stories with a lot of detail highly specific to a place and time.

> *Enlightenment Biblical interpreters regarded the narrative structure of Scripture as an irritation and aimed to extract propositional truths from it* – **Alister McGrath**

This view is clear in **Hegel**, who regards the Bible as a not-yet-systematized system of thought, inferior to true philosophy. In the **rational approach**, there is a tendency to mock these narrative elements whereas the **historical** and **sociological approaches** tend to chop them up into their key ingredients and assume the real meaning is 'behind' the narrative.

However, **Clark Pinnock** (2000) calls the Bible a *"theodrama"* – the story of God's involvement with mankind. Pinnock argues that the narrative aspect of the Bible (the fact that it is a story with a beginning, middle and end) is not just an unnecessary fairy tale – it's vital for understanding what it means.

'Story' or 'drama' here includes different types of passages in the Bible: not just actual events but prayers, poetry, prophecies, parables, etc. They reveal the character of God through his acts leading up to his self-revelation in Jesus Christ.

Narrative theology focuses on the Bible as a story of God's activity. The Bible does contain **propositions** (philosophical ideas), but narrative theology says that Biblical propositions are intimately wrapped up as part of the *'theodrama'* of God's activity. They can't be separated from the drama.

For example, Jesus told stories (**parables**) and sometimes interpreted these using propositions. A good example would be Jesus telling the **Parable of the Sower** (p81) and then interpreting it for his listeners in **Luke 8: 1-15**.

If the propositions could have made the point better, Jesus would have started with the propositions and then given the story afterwards to "illustrate" what he meant. Since he didn't do this, we should follow his method and respond to the stories first and foremost.

Turning the stories into simple propositions is what **Cleanth Brooks** calls *"the heresy of paraphrase"* – you distort the meaning of a story when you reduce it to a summary or list of bullet-points.

> *You could link this to the **debate between Barth and Bultmann** (p39). Bultmann is stripping the narrative away to expose the propositions behind it, but Barth argues you have to respect the narrative as a witness to Jesus Christ.*

An example of a Biblical proposition would be *"God is love"* (**1 John 4:8**). This needs interpretation. Narrative theology suggests that the way to interpret "God is love" is to look at a Biblical story that reveals God's character through his actions. For example, you could read the story of the **Woman Caught in Adultery (John 8: 1-11)** or reflect on Jesus suffering on the Cross (**Matthew 27: 32-56**).

Implications of Narrative Theology

The task for Christians is to 'finish the story' by living it out in the context of their own lives. For example, **Mark's Gospel** concludes with the women visiting Jesus' tomb, finding it empty and running away:

> *Trembling and bewildered, the women went out and fled from the tomb. They said nothing to anyone, because they were afraid* **– Mark 16: 8**

Once a Christian reader has absorbed this story, they can 'finish the story' by going into the world to do what the women could not: tell other people about Jesus being raised from the dead.

Narrative theology also warns that we cannot interpret the story properly unless we are "living the story" together. This involves being part of a community of faith shaped by the story. Teachings and doctrines are secondary to the story and cannot replace it. This means that doctrines are always revisable when a new and better understanding of the story comes along. This is a more controversial side of narrative theology and it is connected to a movement known as the **Emerging Church**. Emerging Churches regard strict doctrines as less important than living out the story of God in the world today. They support **ECUMENISM** (working alongside people from other churches and religions) and engage in social activism and community work. However, critics argue they are drifting away from the key teachings (propositions) of Christianity.

Narrative theology also rejects the idea of the Bible being **INERRANT** (without error). As **Karl Barth** (p26) says, the Bible is the medium or witness to the story of Jesus Christ and readers can 'meet' Jesus when they read the story. This meeting is what matters, not the propositions you can extract from the text. Of course, conservative Christians reject this because the inerrancy of the Bible is an essential teaching for them.

C.S. Lewis & 'Myth Became Fact'

C.S. Lewis' views on myth appeared in the context of the **sociological approach** to Biblical interpretation (p58). They are worth considering in more detail as part of the literary approach. Lewis was a professor of English Literature who specialised in medieval romances and ancient myths. He wrote an essay called *Myth Became Fact* in 1944. In this essay, Lewis argues that it's impossible to get propositional truths out of the Bible while ignoring the narrative:

> *We are invited to restate our belief in a form free from metaphor and symbol. The reason we don't is that we can't* – **C.S. Lewis**

The reason why we can't is because of the two ways of knowing that humans have: ABSTRACT knowledge and CONCRETE knowledge. Abstract knowledge is purely propositional but concrete knowledge is something we experience in the here-and-now. Lewis gives the example of toothache. When we are in pain, we can't think abstractly about what pain is like. When are not experiencing pain, we can think abstractly but what do we really know about pain? The "dilemma" is that we can only ever experience things as concrete realities (like toothache) or as abstractions (like the idea of pain) but not as both at once.

> *In the enjoyment of a great myth we come nearest to experiencing as a concrete what can otherwise be understood only as an abstraction* – **C.S. Lewis**

Lewis means that stories bring together abstract ideas and concrete situations. He concludes that Christians have to focus on the story of Christ as much as intellectual propositions about him:

> *To be truly Christian we must both assent to the historical fact and also receive the myth (fact though it has become) with the same imaginative embrace which we accord to all myths* – **C.S. Lewis**

Lewis goes even further when he suggests that responding to the story of Christ might even be more important than intellectually agreeing to propositions about Christ (e.g. that he is **the Son of God**):

> *A man who disbelieved the Christian story as fact but continually fed on it as myth would, perhaps, be more spiritually alive than one who assented and did not think much about it*
> – **C.S. Lewis**

Lewis talks about *'feeding'* on a myth, which means allowing yourself to be emotionally, imaginatively and morally inspired by it. He suggests that even scientific theories like Evolution can be seen as myths. Lewis is not saying that the theory of evolution isn't true (he's not a fundamentalist Christian), but he is saying that the story of life evolving on Earth affects the imagination as well as satisfying the curiosity of the intellect. The theory of evolution would not be so popular if it didn't work as a myth *as well as* being a scientific theory. In the same way, the story of the Resurrection is a myth *as well as* a historical event.

Implications of *Myth Became Fact*

Lewis' arguments are an effective criticism of **Rudolf Bultmann**'s programme to **de-mythologize** the Christian story by taking out all the narrative details in favour of a set of propositions from existentialist philosophy. Lewis argues that the narrative, with all its mythological metaphors and symbols, is indispensable.

Lewis' ideas become more controversial (and closer to the view of **Emerging Churches** today) when he suggests that an atheist who 'feeds' on the myth of Christ might be 'more spiritually alive' than a Christian believer who just goes along with it as an intellectual idea. Traditional Christians would disagree, saying that people are saved by confessing that Jesus is their Lord and Saviour, not by being emotionally moved by the Gospel story.

However, the two views might not be so far apart. Traditionalists would admit that confessing Jesus as your Lord and Saviour isn't just intellectual agreement; it involves being transformed or 'Born Again'. A 'Sunday Christian' who agrees intellectually to various propositions about Jesus and God but doesn't really care about them hasn't really been 'Born Again'.

Lewis has a point when he says that the story gives rise to propositions, not the other way around. For example, many Christians believe in the perpetual virginity of Mary, the real presence of Christ in the Eucharist or the idea of God as a Trinity – but none of these propositions are stated in the Bible; instead, they are derived from reflecting on the story.

> *You will study another scholar who adopts the literary approach: **R. Alan Culpepper** (p158) is a key scholar for **Topic 5** and treats John's Gospel as a novel.*

Does the literary approach help us to interpret the Bible?

YES	NO

The Bible is clearly written in narrative form. Stories like **the birth of Jesus**, his Parables and the narrative of his Passion (arrest, trial, torture and death) affect the imagination and the conscience. The teachings of Christianity come from the story, not the other way round.

There are clear propositional truths that are essential to Christianity: that Jesus is the Son of God, that there is judgement after death, that God forgives our sins if we believe in Jesus. Without these, Christianity becomes **SUBJECTIVE** and people can believe whatever they want.

By engaging with the story, Christians can encounter the Word of God more meaningfully than if they just agree to a set of propositions. They can live their lives in a way that 'finishes the story' and the story can be shared by a community of believers. Propositions don't bring people together or inspire their lives.

Groups of Christians like the **Emerging Church** who focus on narrative theology rather than **propositional revelation** end up following false teachings. Christian teachings are supposed to challenge the world, not fit in with it. Propositional truths are needed to keep Christians true to the original *kerygma* (preaching) of Jesus and the Apostles

TOPIC 5: THE KINGDOM OF GOD, CONFLICT, DEATH & RESURRECTION

Texts and interpretations – The Kingdom of God in Luke: parables of the kingdom and eschatology
- The teaching of Jesus concerning the Kingdom of God, differing views on the arrival of the Kingdom, past, present and future.
- The meaning, theological significance and importance for early believers.
- With reference to the ideas of I H Marshall and A Schweitzer.

Why did Jesus have to die?
- Religious and political conflict in the ministry of Jesus as presented in the Fourth Gospel: the religious and political authorities and why they were so concerned about Jesus, the arrest, trials, and charges made against Jesus. References may be made to the Law of Moses, Temple cleansing, Sabbath controversies.
- Other elements to Jesus' challenge to Judaism: Christology, blasphemy, threat to power, political expediency. The context of conflict in Jesus' ministry, its key themes and differing views on who was responsible for the death of Jesus.
- With reference to the ideas of E Rivkin and R A Culpepper.

The crucifixion and resurrection narratives in Luke's Gospel
- Old Testament references, symbolism, fulfilment of scripture, God's saving plan. The religious significance of the crucifixion narratives.
- The meaning and significance of the resurrection narratives for early believers, including terms such as sacrifice, salvation, atonement, power of God, forgiveness of sins, relationship with God, the future of the early Church.
- With reference to the ideas of I H Marshall and F Matera.

KINGDOM OF GOD, CONFLICT, DEATH & RESURRECTION

What's this topic about?

What did Jesus mean when he preached the Kingdom of God? Why did this bring him into conflict with the Jewish leadership of his day? What happened that led to Jesus being sentenced to death and how are we to understand his Resurrection?

KINGDOM OF GOD

This topic looks at the idea of the **Kingdom of God** in Luke's Gospel, the **Parables** that explore this and the different theories of **Eschatology** (past, present or future). Key scholars are **I. Howard Marshall** & **Albert Schweitzer**

WHY DID JESUS HAVE TO DIE?

This topic covers Jesus' **conflict** with the authorities in the Fourth Gospel, his **arrest** and **trial**, with reference to **charges** against him regarding the **Law**, **Temple cleansing** and **Sabbath controversies**, **Christology** & **blasphemy**, **threat to power** & **expediency**. Key scholars are **Ellis Rivkin** and **R. Alan Culpepper**.

DEATH & RESURRECTION

This topic covers the **Crucifixion** and **Resurrection** narratives in Luke, with reference to **the Old Testament** and **fulfillment of Scripture, sacrifice, salvation & atonement, power of God, forgiveness of sins** & **relationship with God**. Key scholars are **I. Howard Marshall** & **Frank Matera**.

Before you go any further...

... there are some things you need to know.

JESUS' EARTHLY MINISTRY

The Gospels don't tell us about Jesus' early life, after his birth but before he begins preaching. We are introduced to Jesus when he is 30 years old, in the company of John the Baptist, where John is baptizing people in the River Jordan. Jesus is baptized too then goes into the Judean desert to fast and prepare himself; it is here that he is tempted by the Devil.

Jesus' 'Ministry' (his career as a preacher) begins back in his homeland of Galilee. His base is the town of Capernaum where he recruits Galilean fishermen to be his first Disciples, notably **Peter** (although **John's Gospel** represents Jesus attracting followers from John the Baptist's group first).

Jesus preaches in the Synagogues and travels around the region performing miracles and healings; in particular, he casts out evil spirits who are possessing people (exorcisms). His miracles attract wonder but also suspicion.

His preaching (*kerygma*) is more controversial. Jesus teaches that the **Kingdom of God** (p75) is arriving or has already arrived and that God is going to upset all the traditional power structures, raising up the weak and the downtrodden and casting down the powerful and the proud. Needless to say, the poor people love this message but the Jewish leadership are troubled by it. Even more troubling for them are Jesus' claims to have a special role in this APOCALYPSE (revelation at the end of time) – Jesus claims to be the judge and redeemer promised in the Old Testament.

Jesus preaches – but what exactly was his *kerygma*?

Jesus' ministry is divisive. On the one hand, he attracts a large following. He appoints an 'inner circle' of Disciples called 'the Twelve' who symbolise the new Israelites (who were originally from twelve tribes). He has other followers too, including the sisters **Mary** and **Martha** and the woman **Mary Magdalene**: Jesus' message is popular with women.

However, Jesus is rejected by his own family and town of Nazareth as well as by the Jewish leadership, the scribes and the Pharisees. For this reason he occasionally ventures out of the Jewish heartland of Galilee, preaching and healing in the Gentile towns of the Decapolis, Samaria and Phoenicia.

At Passover, Jesus travels south to Jerusalem in Judea. He predicts his own death at the hands of the Jewish leaders. Although his followers do not understand his prophecies, they know they are going into danger. On a mountaintop in Judea, the Disciples have a religious experience, seeing Jesus as a divine being in the company of the prophets Moses and Elijah: this is known as the Transfiguration.

These events take place over a year. However, **John's Gospel** tells a slightly different story that seems to take place over 3 years. Readers who HARMONISE these stories recognise that Jesus made several journeys between Jerusalem and Galilee

JESUS' PASSION WEEK

The final week of Jesus' life is covered in great detail in the Gospels and is known as the 'Passion' (from the Latin *Passionem* meaning 'suffering').

Jesus enters Jerusalem to an ecstatic welcome from the crowd. He is greeted as a king: the Messiah and the heir to King David.

Jesus goes directly to the Temple and causes a scene there by driving out the animals for sale and overturning the tables of the money-changers.

The priests at the Temple are alarmed by this and begin plotting to have Jesus killed.

(In **John's Gospel**, the cleansing of the Temple happens right at the start of Jesus' ministry, so he either carried out this demonstration twice or John as reordered events. In John's Gospel, it is the final Sign of **raising Lazarus from the dead** that convinces the High Priest that Jesus must be killed.)

At Passover, the pilgrims celebrate their ancestors' escape from slavery in Egypt by sharing a meal of bread, bitter herbs and wine and eating lamb. Jesus shares a meal with his followers, telling them that a new Passover is taking place, with his own body and blood as the sacrifice.

One of the Twelve Disciples, **Judas Iscariot**, leaves to betray Jesus to the priests.

Jesus takes his remaining Disciples outside Jerusalem to the Mount of Olives where they spend the night in the Garden of Gethsemane. Jesus prays while the Disciples sleep. Then Judas and the guards turn up to arrest Jesus (p121). Most of the Disciples run away in fear when Jesus is taken back to Jerusalem as a prisoner, however Peter (and, according to **John's Gospel**, a mysterious person known as the Beloved Disciple) follow at a distance. As Jesus predicted he would, Peter denies knowing Jesus three times when bystanders accuse him of being one of Jesus' followers.

A trial is arranged by the Sanhedrin (a council of senior priests, led by the High Priest). They find Jesus guilty of blasphemy and send him to the Roman governor, **Pontius Pilate**, to be sentenced. Pilate is unwilling to execute an innocent man simply to appease the priests, but a mob has gathered calling for Jesus' death.

Pilate agrees, sending Jesus to be crucified (p140) at a hill called Golgotha (the 'place of the skull'). Jesus' female followers, including his mother, are present to witness his death.

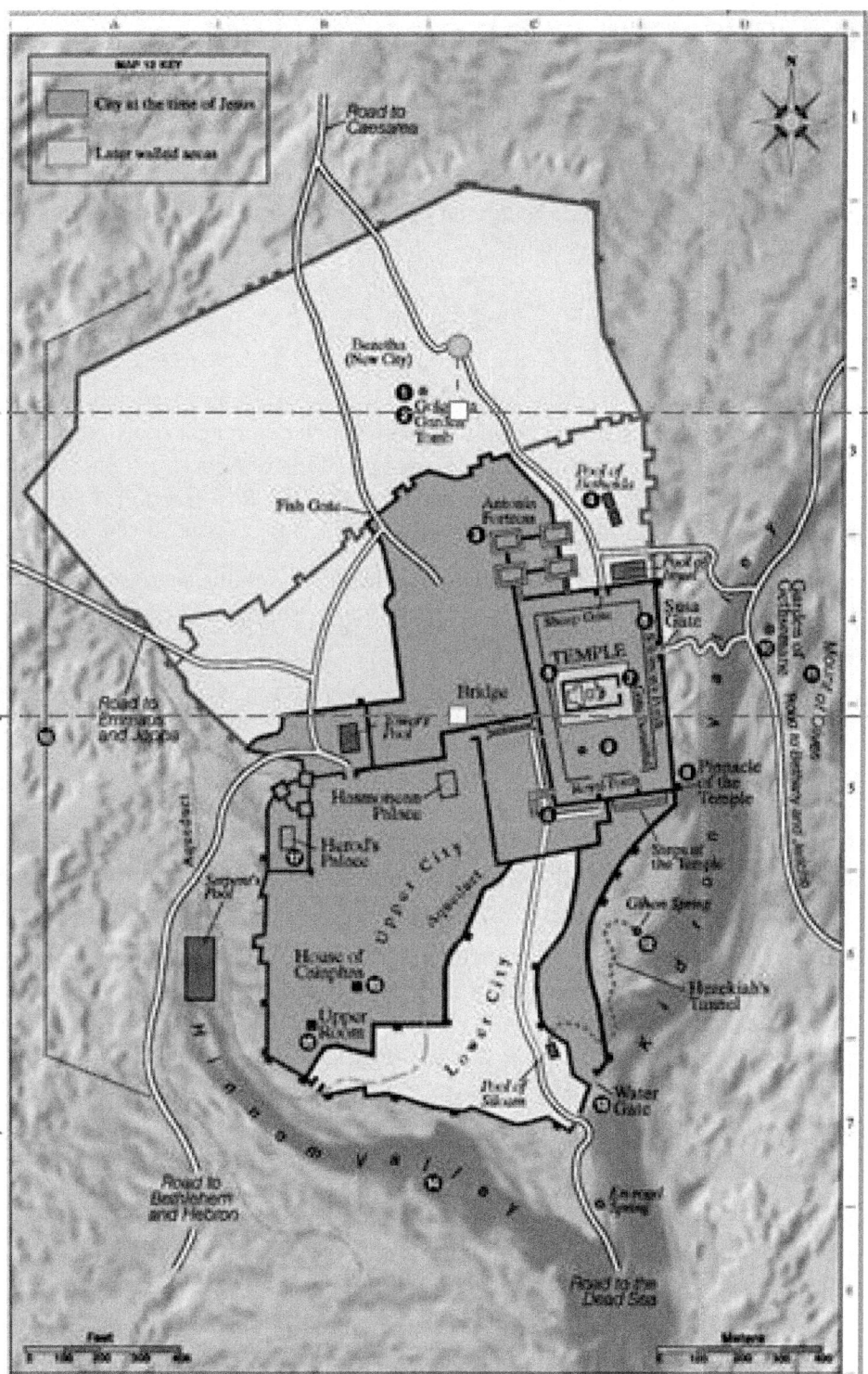

Jerusalem at the time of Jesus (c. 30 CE)

TOPIC 5.1 KINGDOM OF GOD IN LUKE

The idea of the **Kingdom of God** is a core part of Jesus' original *kerygma* (preaching). It features in all four Gospels (although **Matthew** substitutes the term 'Kingdom of Heaven' and **John** prefers to write about **Eternal Life**).

Luke's Gospel explores the idea of the Kingdom of God through Jesus' use of **Parables** – stories or brief narratives with a hidden meaning.

Introducing Luke's Gospel

Luke is the longest Gospel. It is traditionally believed to be written by a travelling companion of Paul who was a doctor; many scholars claim to find evidence of medical knowledge in the details in this Gospel. Whoever wrote the Gospel also wrote the **Book of Acts** which describes the birth of the Early Church and the activities of **Peter** and **Paul** after the Resurrection. Taken together, **Luke-Acts** takes up a quarter of the New Testament.

Luke begins with a Prologue addressed to someone called **Theophilus**, in which the author claims to have gathered the information in this Gospel from earlier sources.

> *since I myself have carefully investigated everything from the beginning, I too decided to write an orderly account* – **Luke 1: 3**

Who is 'Theophilus'? Some scholars think Theophilus is Luke's patron, a wealthy Christian convert who wanted to know more about the background of Christianity; others suggest Theophilus might be a Roman official, since Luke's Gospel seems to go out of its way to present Christianity as a respectable Roman religion that is no threat to the Roman Empire. Since 'Theophilus' means 'loving God' then the name might not be a single person at all: it might refer to everyone in Luke's church.

In Luke's Gospel, Jesus performs 21 miracles (compared to the 7 **Signs** in John) and many involve Jesus casting out evil spirits who recognise him as the **Son of God**. This fits in with Luke's view of Jesus' ministry as a 'cosmic drama' involving Heaven and Hell as well as Earth – in Luke's Gospel there are more mentions of angels than in any of the others, Jesus' birth is attended by angels and angels are present at his empty tomb.

Another distinctive feature in Luke's Gospel is the use of **Parables**. Six of these Parables are present in **Mark** and **Matthew** but Luke adds another 18 from his own sources.

As a **redactor**, Luke alters material from **Mark**: not just correcting Mark's Greek, Luke moves material about to produce a more logical and coherent story and alters the representation of Jesus into something more respectful, removing scenes where Jesus is harsh, angry or emotional. At Jesus' trial, Luke avoids describing Jesus being mocked and whipped by the soldiers.

Luke's main concern is with the poor and the outcast. This Gospel is sometimes termed the 'Gospel of compassion' and it shows Jesus in a very compassionate light. Jesus blesses the poor and condemns the rich. Women and Gentiles feature prominently in this Gospel.

Luke is the only Gospel-writer to use the word 'Saviour' to describe Jesus and his most common title for Jesus is 'Lord' (*Kyrios*) – a title also applied to God. In fact, 'salvation' is the big theme in Luke, who explores the idea of salvation through the Old Testament, through the ministry of Jesus and afterwards, through the subsequent history of the Church.

Eschatology

Eschatology is based on the Greek *eschatos* meaning 'last'. It refers to the end of the world and the afterlife: the famous 'last' things (death, judgment, heaven and hell).

> *the part of theology concerned with death, judgment, and the final destiny of the soul and of humankind* – **Oxford English Dictionary**

Hellenic beliefs were that the world passed through *aeons* or 'ages'. Eschatology for the Greeks referred to the end of one age and the beginning of another.

Jewish beliefs were more dramatic, with the idea of just two ages: this age and the Messianic Age to come. For Jews, the end of the age was going to be an APOCALYPSE (literally, an unveiling or **revelation**) in which God makes his presence known to everyone. The arrival of this new age would be a great crisis brought about by the arrival of the **Messiah**. Different Jewish sects had different hopes about the Messiah and the Messianic Age. Most expected some sort of earthly kingdom, ruled over by the Messiah, with the other empires in the world conquered by the Messiah. In this new world order, the Jews would no longer be persecuted.

The **Pharisees** went further than this, believing that the dead would be returned to life and judged by God or God's representative, the **'Son of Man'**. This was based on Old Testament prophecies such as:

> *Multitudes who sleep in the dust of the earth will awake: some to everlasting life, others to shame and everlasting contempt* – **Daniel 12: 2**

In **Luke 21** there is an extended discourse called the 'Little Apocalypse' where Jesus describes the destruction of Jerusalem and its Temple and the persecution of loyal Christians; these events culminate in a cosmic crisis where the **Son of Man** appears to judge the world.

Christians interpret this in four ways:

- **Preterist:** the Apocalypse refers to the events of Jesus' lifetime and the lifetime of his immediate followers who experienced his Resurrection and founded his Church (in other parts of the Gospels, the destruction of the Temple symbolises the crucifixion of Jesus)
- **Futurist:** referring to the end of time, which is still to come (the destruction of the Temple symbolises the literal end of the world)
- **Literal:** describing factual events that really happen in this word (the Temple was literally destroyed in 70 CE)
- **Symbolic:** describing spiritual events in the soul or after death (the destruction of the Temple symbolises the death that happens to everyone).

Critics like **Johannes Weiss** argue that Jesus preached a **preterist eschatology**. In other words, he thought that the End Times were literally imminent. One famous remark by Jesus backs this up:

> *this generation will certainly not pass away until all these things have happened* **– Luke 21: 32**

C.S. Lewis calls this *"the most embarrassing verse in the Bible"* because, despite what Jesus says, his Disciples **did** all die without the world ending. Because of this, many Christians interpret Jesus' apocalyptic language **symbolically** rather than literally, referring to the punishment for sin and the distress of a life without God.

	Literal	Symbolic
Preterist	The 'Little Apocalypse' in **Luke 21** refers to the persecution of Christians under Nero and the destruction of Jerusalem by the Romans in 70 CE	Apocalyptic statements describe the birth of the Church: the end of the old world of Judaism and the creation of a new world of Christianity
Futurist	Luke's 'Little Apocalypse' describes the end of the world and the return of Christ as the Judge of mankind; this might be far in the future.	Apocalyptic statements describe what the Church will experience in future (persecution, perseverance, hope) and what happens after we die

Albert Schweitzer [*right*, p162] argues that Jesus believed the world would literally end with his own Crucifixion and that the first Christians believed the world would end when Christ returned to Earth (which is called *PAROUSIA*), which was supposed to happen very soon after the Resurrection.

Schweitzer thinks Jesus died disappointed and the first Christians were disappointed too. In response to this disappointment, Christians reinterpreted Jesus' teachings and started claiming that *Parousia* wouldn't take place until a date far in the future.

I. Howard Marshall (p159) sums up the problem for believers of Jesus' having a mistaken belief in an imminent Apocalypse that never happened:

> *how the teaching of Jesus can in any way be valid when it rests on a set of mistaken assumptions ...concerned with the central theme of his message* **– I. Howard Marshall**

C.H. Dodd (*c.f.* **Topic 2: The Person of Jesus**) also thinks Jesus preached that the Apocalypse was taking place ***during*** his ministry (REALISED ESCHATOLOGY). However, Dodd claims the Apocalypse is **symbolic** for Jesus and not literal – it is a dramatic change in how people live and not the literal 'end of the world'.

The Kingdom of God

There are 39 references in Luke's Gospel to the 'Kingdom of God' or just 'the Kingdom'. Luke's Gospel contains 'the Lord's Prayer' (**Luke 11: 2-4**) which asks for the Kingdom of God to appear:

> *Father, hallowed be your name, your kingdom come* **– Luke 11: 2**

The big scholarly debate is about ***when*** this Kingdom is supposed to happen?

- The **Past:** a 'Golden Age' that people hope might come again
- The **Present**, being an opportunity to connect with God in the here-and-now
- The **Future**: as an **eschatological** event, probably at the end of time

KINGDOM IN THE PAST: The Kingdom of God is an eternal kingdom: it has always existed. When God created the world, he extended his kingdom to Earth, but Adam and Eve rebelled against him. The story of the Old Testament is the story of God's Kingdom breaking through into the world. God extended his kingdom by taking the Israelites to be his Chosen People. He appointed kings like David to be his representatives on Earth. This produced a 'Golden Age' when the Kingdom of God was also a political kingdom of Israel, ruled over by David and his son Solomon.

However, David's descendants were unworthy in various ways and the Israelites kept rebelling. **Luke's Gospel** shares this view of the Kingdom extending from the distant past into the present:

> *The Law and the Prophets were proclaimed until John. Since that time, the good news of the kingdom of God is being preached, and everyone is forcing their way into it* **– Luke 16: 16**

Luke sees John the Baptist as the end of the God's Kingdom in the past and the beginning of a new phase introduced by Jesus, with the Kingdom now available to everyone and humans (Gentiles as well as Jews) are crowding to get into it.

KINGDOM IN THE PRESENT: The Kingdom of God is something that happens during the ministry of Jesus and his first Disciples. Jesus refers to the Kingdom of God being *entos hymon estin*: the Greek phrase is translated as 'within you' or 'among you' or 'in your midst':

> *The coming of the kingdom of God is not something that can be observed, nor will people say, 'Here it is,' or 'There it is,' because the kingdom of God is IN YOUR MIDST* **– Luke 17: 20-21**

However, Luke seems to treat many references to the Kingdom in the spiritual sense: it is *"within you"* in the sense of being a special state of mind, being spiritually close to God rather than living in a society that follows religious rules. This is linked to **symbolic** interpretations of eschatology.

KINGDOM IN THE FUTURE: The Kingdom of God is a future reality that will take place at the end of the age. This is linked to the futurist view of **eschatology**. Christians expect the 'Second Coming' of Christ (*Parousia*) and the Judgement of the living and the dead, with some going to Heaven and others to Hell:

But when you enter a town and are not welcomed, go into its streets and say, 'Even the dust of your town we wipe from our feet as a warning to you. Yet be sure of this: The kingdom of God has come near.' – **Luke 10: 10-11**

However, within this futurist view of the Kingdom, there are more distinctions: the Future Kingdom could be IMMINENT (in the future, but soon) or REMOTE (in the far future).

This seems to create a lot of contradictions. Is the Kingdom something that has always existed, something that is going to exist, or a symbolic state that exists in the souls of believers? Many scholars argue that 'Kingdom' refers to a 'reign' rather than a place or a literal kingdom.

'Kingdom of God' should be taken to refer primarily to God's sovereignty rather than to the realm over which he is sovereign – **I. Howard Marshall**

In other words, the Kingdom is not a place on Earth or in Heaven; it is a state of affairs where God is in charge. When God rules over people's lives, there will be no more sin or greed or cruelty. This means that the spiritual Kingdom of God can exist at the same time as an earthly empire. The spiritual Kingdom grows when more people join it but it doesn't have territory or borders.

This idea is summed up in the famous hymn *I Vow to Thee my Country*:

And there's another country, I've heard of long ago,
  Most dear to them that love her, most great to them that know;
We may not count her armies, we may not see her King;
  Her fortress is a faithful heart, her pride is suffering;
And soul by soul and silently her shining bounds increase,
  And her ways are ways of gentleness, and all her paths are peace.

This rather lovely hymn is often sung at Remembrance Day services. It looks forward to an end to war because people abandon fighting over physical kingdoms that exist on maps and choose to serve a spiritual kingdom instead – the Kingdom of God – which exists inside people's souls

This idea is also expressed by the previous Pope like this:

The Kingdom of God comes by way of a listening heart – **Pope Benedict**

This view is dominant in **John's Gospel** where the idea of an Apocalypse is downplayed. Instead, the Kingdom of God is linked to being spiritually born-again:

no one can see the kingdom of God unless they are born again – **John 3: 3**

In this view, the Kingdom of God can be past, present **and** future. The Kingdom grows or shrinks through history according to how many people submit to God's rule over their lives. In the future, there may be a state of affairs where everyone is ruled by God; this is when God's Kingdom will have fully arrived.

Salvation-History in Luke

Hans Conzelmann (1954) proposes a popular theory that Luke was faced with a Christian community confused and disappointed by the failure of Christ to return – this is the PAROUSIA DELAY. To answer their complaints, Luke reinterprets the idea of the **Kingdom of God** in a new historical sense.

- Throughout the Old Testament, the Prophets urge the Jews to live within God's Kingdom, but they are often ignored. This is the 'Age of Israel' which comes to an end with the preaching of John the Baptist.
- Jesus' ministry is a new age in salvation-history when salvation is made available to everyone who believes in him; in this time, Satan is defeated.
- After Jesus' Ascension into Heaven, a third age of salvation-history begins. Jesus' followers have to spread his message and win converts. This age will eventually end with *Parousia* but that is in the future and the Church has to prepare for a 'long haul' through history until Christ returns. During this age, Satan's power returns, so Christians will experience temptation and persecution.

Salvation-history views the Kingdom of God as an ongoing historical project: it was begun in the ancient past by the Prophets of Israel, demonstrated in practice by Jesus and has to be carried on into the future and spread by the Christian church. The eschatological passages in the New Testament describe in **symbolic** terms what happens to humans after they die. Conzelmann distinguishes the 'message of the Kingdom' (repent your sins, love your neighbour) from the Kingdom itself (a future state when there will be no sin).

> *It is the* message *of the Kingdom that is present, which in Luke is distinguished from the Kingdom itself* – **Hans Conzelmann**

For Conzelmann, Luke is different from Mark and Matthew by breaking away from apocalyptic thinking and viewing Christianity as a religion that guides how you live your whole life in a society that isn't going to be destroyed by God any time soon.

In support of Conzelmann's idea, Luke's Gospel **does** have a strong social message: an emphasis on feeding the hungry, caring for the poor and settling disputes peacefully. These are not usually concerns for writers who think the world is going to end soon. Luke introduces the 'Lord's Prayer' (**Luke 11: 2-4**) in which Christians pray for their *"daily bread"* while waiting for the *"Kingdom to come"*. This is not the prayer of someone who thinks the end of the world is imminent.

However, **I. Howard Marshall** (p159) opposes Conzelmann's theory. Marshall points out that there are still moments of urgent apocalyptic discourse in Luke's Gospel, such as the 'Little Apocalypse' and the embarrassing **Luke 21: 32**.

> *They demonstrate that, for Jesus, the kingdom was already present in his ministry* – **I. Howard Marshall**

If Luke is a **redactor** who wants to change Jesus' original apocalyptic *kerygma* to a new less-apocalyptic message, why would he leave these passages in? These passages count against Conzelmann's view.

The views of scholars that you are familiar with could be set out like this:

Jesus taught the Apocalypse is:		
Immediate (now)	Imminent (soon)	Future (far away)
Schweitzer (literal – and Jesus was mistaken) **C.H. Dodd** (symbolic – 'Realised Eschatology')	**Marshall** (symbolic & literal, e.g. his own Crucifixion or the destruction of Jerusalem and the Temple in 70 CE)	**Conzelmann** (symbolic & literal, e.g. the Afterlife or Judgement Day in the far future)

Is the Kingdom of God in Luke to be interpreted as in the future?

YES

NO

Jesus warned his followers that the Kingdom of God was *"near"* and predicted specific things that would happen when the Kingdom arrived – such as the 'Little Apocalypse' in **Luke 21**. Christians expect the *Parousia* when Jesus returns in glory; this was the *kerygma* (preaching) of the early Church.

The *Parousia* the first Christians expected did not occur. They were interpreting Jesus wrongly. The Kingdom he describes is *"in your midst"* or *"within you"* – it is a spiritual state in the present rather than a physical reality in the future. Marshall calls it God's *reign* rather than God's *realm*.

Jesus should be interpreted as preaching a salvation-history, where the Kingdom of God existed in the past in a partial and incomplete way, was demonstrated by Jesus in a full sense and then becomes a project for the Church to spread. However, it will be completed at a future date when Jesus returns, but we cannot know when that will be.

There's no getting around the embarrassing verses like **Luke 21: 32** where Jesus clearly talks about the Kingdom of God arriving in an apocalypse in a few year's time. This doesn't fit in with salvation-history but it does fit in with Schweitzer's theory that Jesus was a *"failed messiah"* who believed in an apocalypse that never happened.

Interpreting the Parables in Luke

Parables are stories with a spiritual meaning. They often work like riddles and Jesus seems to have used Parables as a teaching tool: his followers debate the meaning of a Parable before Jesus explains it more clearly.

> *A list of Luke's Parables describing the **Kingdom of God** are found in Anthology extract #5. Only the first (**Sower**, p81) and two others (**Great Banquet** on p87, **Ten Minas** on p93) are 'Parables' in the strict sense of the word. You will study 3 more of Luke's Parables in **Topic 6** (p225)*

These Parables had a meaning for Jesus' original audience. However, they also had a meaning for the 1st century Christians who preserved them as part of the church's ORAL TRADITION. This later interpretation could be different from what Jesus originally meant.

- **Form Criticism** views these Parables as *PERICOPAE* or textual units that owe more to the beliefs of 1st century Christians than to Jesus' original teachings
- **Redaction Criticism** views these Parables as being edited by Luke to serve his own viewpoint (i.e. **Conzelmann** would say, to promote the idea of salvation-history and explain the '*Parousia* delay').

Each of these Parables can be used as evidence FOR or AGAINST Conzelmann's idea of salvation-history in Luke's Gospel.

- Some back up **Conzelmann**'s idea that Luke's Gospel shows the **Kingdom of God** as happening in the far future or being symbolic for judgement in the Afterlife; Luke seems to have **redacted** (edited) the original preterist meaning to suit his futurist agenda

- Some support **Marshall**'s theory that Luke still believes in a Kingdom that is **imminent** (coming soon) but not **immediate** (happening already); this means Luke faithfully reproduces the earliest traditions about Jesus without editing them.

- **C.H. Dodd**, who was a key scholar in **Topic 2 (Person of Jesus)**, argues that Jesus preached a REALISED ESCHATOLOGY, which is the idea the Apocalypse is happening during his own ministry, in the here-and-now. Dodd thinks this is a **symbolic** Apocalypse: a chance to start your life over, break free from a corrupt society and live life in a new way, free from sin. **Marshall** argues against Dodd's view too, but there are passages supporting Dodd's idea of 'Realised Eschatology' such as *"the kingdom of God is in your midst"* (**Luke 17: 21**).

> *Most Christians today think of the Apocalypse as something that will happen in the far future but there are some Christian groups (usually Fundamentalists) who expect it to happen very soon indeed. These believers aren't put off by the fact that all the Christian groups in previous centuries who expected an imminent Apocalypse turned out to be wrong.*

Do the Parables show that the Kingdom will arrive in the future?

YES	NO
The Parables support the idea of salvation-history, with centuries to pass after Christ's ascension to even until his return to Earth and judgement happening in the Afterlife instead. For example, the Kingdom is said to be *"in the midst of you"* and apocalyptic passages in Matthew have been removed by Luke.	There is still a note of apocalyptic urgency in many of these passages. Although **Matthew** adds more apocalyptic material, Luke mostly follows **Mark**, whose references to the Apocalypse are more toned down and less specific. Jesus still preaches the end of the age as an event in the imminent future.
Luke's Parables offer a lot of advice to Christians in the 1st century living in a world that isn't about to end. They encourage charity and concern for the poor, the urge perseverance and commitment to Christian ideals over 'the long haul' rather than an imminent ending.	Luke uses material from **Mark** or the **Q-Source** without removing apocalyptic material when it would be easy to do so. Luke seems to be less interested in the Crucifixion and Resurrection and more interested in Christ's Ascension to Heaven as the beginning of the Apocalypse but he still writes as if the end is coming.

NB. In **Topic 6** you will examine three more of Luke's Parables from a different perspective: analyzing what they reveal about Jesus' ethical teachings.

The Parable of the Sower (Luke 8: 1-15)

This Parable is introduced with a description of Jesus' followers: the Twelve Disciples, of course, but also a group of women, including Mary Magdalene, Joanna the wife of one of Herod's officials (perhaps it was her son Jesus healed in **John 4: 43-54**), Susanna and others. These women support Jesus' ministry financially and Jesus has cured them of diseases and evil spirits. These women will be loyal to Jesus to the end: they are present for the Crucifixion and Mary Magdalene discovers the empty tomb.

This group of independent women is unusual in both Jewish and **Hellenic** culture in the 1st century – at least one of them seems to have left her husband to follow Jesus. This perhaps illustrates the **Kingdom of God** in action: people cooperating to support each other with no prejudice based on gender or class. Women seemed to be particularly receptive to the Christian message; **Paul**'s epistles (letters) mention several women leading churches (Priscilla, Phoebe and Chloe are named).

But how did this unusual group come together? Jesus' Parable illustrates this:

> [4] While a large crowd was gathering and people were coming to Jesus from town after town, he told this parable: [5] "A farmer went out to sow his seed. As he was scattering the seed, some fell along the path; it was trampled on, and the birds ate it up. [6] Some fell on rocky ground, and when it came up, the plants withered because they had no moisture. [7] Other seed fell among thorns, which grew up with it and choked the plants. [8] Still other seed fell on good soil. It came up and yielded a crop, a hundred times more than was sown."

The Parable of the Sower appears in all the Synoptic Gospels with only minor variations. Jesus explains the meaning of the Parable to his Disciples:

- The seed represents the Word of God – the Christian *kerygma* (preaching) about the Kingdom of God
- The soil represents the personality of the people who listen to this preaching
- The *path* represents people who are not interested in the Word of God; this might be because of their ignorance, selfishness or the Devil tempting them
- The *rocky ground* represents shallow people who are attracted to Christianity because of its novelty value but miss out on the deeper meaning
- The *thorns* represent worldly pressures (your job, your family, etc) that stop people from prioritizing the Christian message
- The *good soil* represents the ideal listeners: people who are attentive and deep, people who prioritise their faith over their other commitments and put it into practice.

This Parable fits in well with the idea of salvation-history. There's no reference to the Apocalypse or *Parousia*. The Kingdom of God exists inside the hearts of believers where it grows and produces a harvest of goodness and happiness.

> When he said this, he called out, "Whoever has ears to hear, let them hear."

> [9] His disciples asked him what this parable meant. [10] He said, "The knowledge of the secrets of the kingdom of God has been given to you, but to others I speak in parables, so that, "'though seeing, they may not see; though hearing, they may not understand.'

Jesus concludes his Parable by echoing **Isaiah 6:9**, predicting that some listeners will hear his words, but never understand what he means. These listeners are like the path or the rocky soil where seed cannot grow. This passage echoes **Mark 4: 11-12** (and Mark is probably Luke's **source** here). This links to Wrede's theory of the **Messianic Secret** in **Topic 1**– that Jesus deliberately speaks in confusing Parables because he doesn't **want** the ordinary people to understand him.

> *You have to make up your own mind whether Jesus is being deliberately mysterious (as Wrede thinks) or if Jesus is being more regretful about the fact that his teachings fall on 'deaf ears' but pointing out that this was predicted by **Isaiah** long ago*

Luke's 1st century readers: These readers would understand that they are the *good soil* and the *crop*. The other types of soil represent former-Christians who *received the word with joy* and were enthusiastic converts at first, but who didn't *persevere* and have drifted away from Christianity – probably a reference to the persecutions Christians experienced in the 1st century and afterwards. This Parable describes the importance of *persevering* for a Christian church that is ready for the 'long haul' until the *Parousia* happens on some future date and this fits in with **Conzelmann**'s idea of salvation-history. However, the fact that this Parable is in all the Synoptic Gospels supports **Marshall**'s view that Luke has **not** altered the earliest traditions about Jesus.

Jesus and Beelzebub (Luke 11: 14-28)

'Beelzebub' (BEE-YELL-ZEE-BUB) is an ancient pagan god, but for 1st century Jews it was a common name for the Devil. The name means 'lord of the flies' or 'lord of dung'.

In this episode, Jesus heals a mute man by driving out the evil spirit inside him. Driving out evil spirits is called EXORCISM. Some in the crowd accuse Jesus himself of being in league with the Devil, since evil spirits obey him.

This episode occurs in all three Synoptic Gospels. In **Mark**, it is Jesus' family from Nazareth who accuse him of being mad; in **Matthew** the accusers are Pharisees. **Luke's Gospel** doesn't specify who the accusers are (but they seem to be Pharisees, as you will see later).

Jesus answers his critics with several short Parables:

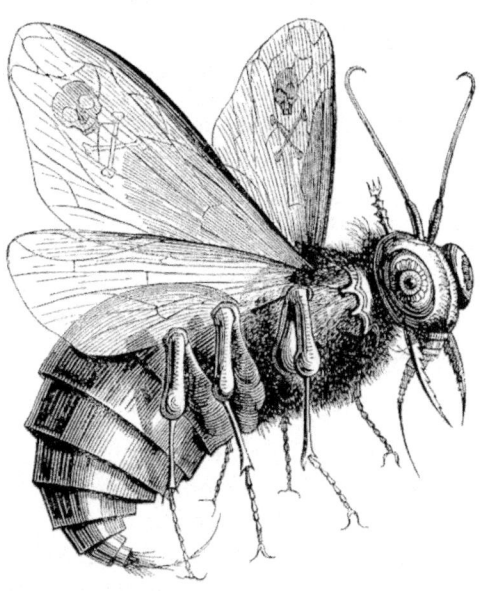

Beelzebub – Lord of the Flies

> [17] Jesus knew their thoughts and said to them: "Any kingdom divided against itself will be ruined, and a house divided against itself will fall. [18] If Satan is divided against himself, how can his kingdom stand? I say this because you claim that I drive out demons by Beelzebul. [19] Now if I drive out demons by Beelzebul, by whom do your followers drive them out? So then, they will be your judges. [20] But if I drive out demons by the finger of God, then the kingdom of God has come upon you.

This Parable creates the image of Satan's Kingdom – a rival kingdom to the **Kingdom of God**. Jesus cannot be in league with Satan, because his exorcisms would mean that Satan's Kingdom is at war with itself.

This imagery is part of the cosmic drama that features heavily in Luke's Gospel: the world is a battleground between the forces of God and the forces of Satan.

> *Although Luke doesn't specify the Pharisees, the reference to "your followers" who also drive out demons suggests that Jesus is talking to Pharisees, who claimed to be able to exorcise demons too.*

Jesus' remark that *"the kingdom of God has come upon you"* suggests the Kingdom of God is here in the present, not still-to-happen in the future: **I. Howard Marshall** uses this passage to argue against **Conzelmann**'s idea of salvation-history.

Jesus goes on to tell a short **Parable of the Strong Man**:

> [21] "When a strong man, fully armed, guards his own house, his possessions are safe. [22] But when someone stronger attacks and overpowers him, he takes away the armor in which the man trusted and divides up his plunder.

The 'house' here is the soul of a person trying to resist Satan. The 'strong man' is a person who trusts in their own willpower or goodness to keep them safe. Instead, the Devil *overpowers him* because willpower and following the Law are not enough to defeat Satan.

Alternatively, the 'house' might be the House of Israel, i.e. the Jewish religion with the Temple as its base. The 'strong man' is the Jewish **Law** which is strong, but not strong enough to defeat sin and evil. The *plunder* being divided up by *someone stronger* is the destruction of Jerusalem by the Romans. This interpretation makes the Parable an **eschatological** warning (preterist and literal).

> [24] "When an impure spirit comes out of a person, it goes through arid places seeking rest and does not find it. Then it says, 'I will return to the house I left.' [25] When it arrives, it finds the house swept clean and put in order. [26] Then it goes and takes seven other spirits more wicked than itself, and they go in and live there. And the final condition of that person is worse than the first."

This extends the Parable, because Satan is relentless. Even if cast out once, he returns to the house and invades it again. The fact that the house is *swept clean and put in order* shows the efforts of people to lead a good life on their own or by following the Law – this lasts only until the next time the Devil attacks them. Only Jesus has the power to drive out Satan once and for all.

This mythological world-view - a universe full of invisible spirits who possess people and have to be exorcised - is part of the reason **Rudolph Bultmann** *(p33) argues that the Gospels have to be DE-MYTHOLOGIZED to make them meaningful to modern people with scientific outlooks. You should ask yourself whether you have to have a literal belief in demons to appreciate this Parable.*

Luke's 1st century readers: These Christians understand that they are the *house* that is under constant attack by Satan. This is part of Luke's salvation-history: now that Jesus has ascended to Heaven, Christians must continue the war against Satan themselves. There will be setbacks when they give in to temptation or experience persecution for their beliefs. They would remember Jesus saying *"whoever does not gather with me, scatters"*. This refers to gathering together as a church to resist the power of Satan.

The Sign of Jonah (Luke 11: 29-32)

This Parable follows directly on from **Jesus & Beelzebub** but is worth looking at separately.

Jonah is an Old Testament prophet. Jonah was sent by God to warn the sinful people of the city of **Nineveh** that they were going to be destroyed. Jonah tries to avoid going but, after being swallowed by a giant fish, he eventually arrives in Nineveh. The Ninevites take the message to heart and change their sinful ways, so God spares them (much to Jonah's disappointment).

The **Queen of the South** is the 'Queen of Sheba' in the Old Testament. This mysterious figure visited King Solomon to test his wisdom.

Jesus uses these two examples to criticize his audience. The 'Sign of Jonah' is an APOCALYPTIC warning of God's Kingdom arriving soon. In the ancient past, people listened to these warnings and changed their ways:

- the *men of Nineveh* listened to Jonah
- the *Queen of the South* listened to Solomon

Jesus accuses his audience of not listening to him, even though he is greater than any prophet. The listeners are like the *path* or the *rocky ground* in the **Parable of the Sower** (p81): they hear Jesus preach but they don't take the message seriously.

This passage is also in **Matthew 12: 38-45**. However, in Matthew's version, the 'Sign of Jonah' refers to the Crucifixion and Resurrection. Jonah spent three days in the belly of the fish and Jesus will spend 3 days in the tomb. Luke removes this explanation, making his 'Sign of Jonah' passage seem rather incomplete.

> *This is one of those passages that is in Matthew and Luke but not in Mark - it could therefore be from the **Q-Source** (from **Topic 3**).*

Luke's 1st century readers: There is a tone of urgency here: this links with the idea that some 1st century Christians still expected the *Parousia* to happen any day, as **Marshall** argues. However, **Conzelmann** argues that Luke seems to have **redacted** this passage, removing the reference to the Crucifixion and Resurrection found in **Matthew**. This downplays the idea that the Apocalypse has already begun. Luke's rather vague 'Sign of Jonah' is just a general warning that the Apocalypse will happen 'one day' but not necessarily 'soon'. In the Old Testament, the people of Nineveh were *not* destroyed because they turned to God. This could be Luke's solution: the Apocalypse has been postponed because of the faith of the Christian church and people repenting their sins.

The Narrow Door (Luke 13: 22-30)

This Parable is unique to Luke, although **Matthew 7: 13-14** contains a warning about the broad gate to Hell and the narrow gate to Heaven and, in **John 10: 7-9**, Jesus refers to himself as the Door or Gate that leads to salvation.

> He said to them, [24] "Make every effort to enter through the narrow door, because many, I tell you, will try to enter and will not be able to. [25] Once the owner of the house gets up and closes the door, you will stand outside knocking and pleading, 'Sir, open the door for us.'

This is an apocalyptic discourse, because the *owner of the house* is God and those who *stand outside knocking* are souls being judged and wanting to enter the Kingdom.

> "But he will answer, 'I don't know you or where you come from.'
>
> [26] "Then you will say, 'We ate and drank with you, and you taught in our streets.'
>
> [27] "But he will reply, 'I don't know you or where you come from. Away from me, all you evildoers!'

Once again, these souls are like the inferior soil in the **Parable of the Sower**: they are people who attended Jesus' preaching and *received the word with joy* but the Word of God didn't take root in them. The owner sending them away represents God sending souls to Hell.

> *Do you think this Parable stands for what will happen when the Kingdom of God arrives on Earth in a literal sense – or what happens after we die, with some people wanting to get into Heaven but being sent to Hell instead?*

Luke's 1st century audience: As with the **Sign of Jonah**, there is a tone of urgency here, but it's very non-specific about timing. Is the door to salvation about to close imminently? or in the future? or does it close when you die? This could support either **Conzelmann** or **Marshall**. The sinners who try to get into the house are similar to the demons that return to the strong man's house.

This leads to a different interpretation: the house represents the church which must *close the door* to people who converted to Christianity but lapsed back into their pagan ways and now want to return to Christianity again. The early Church had a particular problem with believers who gave up on Christianity when persecutions started but then wanted to re-join when it was safe. The Parable's message is, don't let them in. Therefore, the Parable perhaps reflects the debates going on in the early churches and not the original *kerygma* of Jesus.

The Parable of the Great Banquet (Luke 14: 15-24)

This Parable also occurs in **Matthew 22: 1-14**, but Luke's version is very different from Matthew's.

> [16] Jesus replied: "A certain man was preparing a great banquet and invited many guests. [17] At the time of the banquet he sent his servant to tell those who had been invited, 'Come, for everything is now ready.'
>
> [18] "But they all alike began to make excuses. The first said, 'I have just bought a field, and I must go and see it. Please excuse me.'
>
> [19] "Another said, 'I have just bought five yoke of oxen, and I'm on my way to try them out. Please excuse me.'
>
> [20] "Still another said, 'I just got married, so I can't come.'

The man organizing the banquet is God, the banquet is the **Kingdom of God** and the guests are humans whom God wants to save.

In Matthew's version, the organizer of the feast is a king and the banquet is his son's marriage feast. The ungrateful guests assault and kill several servants, so the king sends his army to destroy their homes.

Matthew's version has an apocalyptic tone. The servants are the prophets and the ungrateful guests are the Jews who persecuted them. The son, of course, is Jesus. The army represents the Apocalypse, with God destroying the world.

Luke removes all of this apocalyptic material and focuses on the worldly reasons the guests have for declining the invitation: they resemble the different types of soil in the **Parable of the Sower** (p81). Luke also includes just one servant – the Servant here represents Jesus who is inviting his listeners to enter the Kingdom of God.

> [21] "The servant came back and reported this to his master. Then the owner of the house became angry and ordered his servant, 'Go out quickly into the streets and alleys of the town and bring in the poor, the crippled, the blind and the lame.'
>
> [22] "'Sir,' the servant said, 'what you ordered has been done, but there is still room.'
>
> [23] "Then the master told his servant, 'Go out to the roads and country lanes and compel them to come in, so that my house will be full. [24] I tell you, not one of those who were invited will get a taste of my banquet.'"

Since the guests who were invited don't attend, the banquet is thrown open to anybody at all. This represents the Kingdom of God being available to the **Gentiles** since the Jews (the guests who were originally invited) have refused the offer of salvation.

The phrase *"compel them to come"* in has had unfortunate consequences. **Augustine of Hippo** uses it to justify putting pressure on people to convert to Christianity and it was used in the Middle Ages to justify the forced conversion of pagans, Jews and Muslims to Christianity.

The Banquet also represents the Last Supper and the Eucharist inspired by it

Luke's 1ˢᵗ century audience: This text fits in well with **Conzelmann**'s concept of salvation-history. The apocalyptic symbolism that was present in Matthew's version of the Parable has been removed by Luke so the banquet could represent a Heavenly reward in the Afterlife rather than the Apocalypse happening on Earth. 1ˢᵗ century Christians who no longer believed in an imminent Apocalypse would feel the pressure to maintain Christian commitment their whole life. They too could be like the invited guests who miss out on the banquet if they let their Christianity lapse like the *thorny soil* in the **Parable of the Sower** (p81).

The invitation to *the poor, the crippled, the blind and the lame* reinforces Luke's social concerns: the Parable encourages Christians to share their own wealth with the less fortunate in society. This morality becomes important when *Parousia* is postponed.

The Coming of the Kingdom (Luke 17: 20-37)

This passage is similar to one in **Matthew 24** that is an extended apocalyptic discourse. Luke includes part of the discourse here and the rest appears in the 'Little Apocalypse' in **Luke 21**.

Luke starts with Jesus saying that *"the Kingdom of God is in your midst"*. This could be interpreted in two ways:

- **Symbolically:** The Kingdom of God is a spiritual state in hearts and minds, not a physical reality
- **Immediate:** The Kingdom of God is happening in the present moment. (Specifically, it might represent Jesus who is literally standing in the midst of the crowd).

> ²² Then he said to his disciples, "The time is coming when you will long to see one of the days of the Son of Man, but you will not see it. ²³ People will tell you, 'There he is!' or 'Here he is!' Do not go running off after them. ²⁴ For the Son of Man in his day will be like the lightning, which flashes and lights up the sky from one end to the other. ²⁵ But first he must suffer many things and be rejected by this generation.

This is a warning against interpreting eschatological statements as imminent events: Jesus warns that people will claim that the Apocalypse is happening, but his Disciples should not believe the rumours. When the Apocalypse does happen, it will be *like the lightning*, which is very sudden and also very obvious. Jesus adds *"but first…"* because his own Passion must occur, which reinforces the point that the Kingdom of God isn't appearing right away.

Jesus goes on to make two links to the Old Testament: the stories of **Noah** and of **Lot**.

- **Noah (Genesis 7):** Noah was warned by God that a flood would wipe out all life on Earth. Right up until the moment of the Flood, ordinary life was going on, then the disaster hit.
- **Lot (Genesis 19: 1-26):** Lot was the only good man living in the evil city of Sodom. He was warned by God that the city would be destroyed and fled along with his family. Again, the citizens were getting on with ordinary life when God destroyed them. Lot's wife looked back and was turned into a 'pillar of salt'.

The point of these stories is that they were both 'mini-apocalypses' that took humans completely by surprise. Jesus warns that the arrival of the Kingdom of God will be just as surprising. Jesus concludes with a series of startling images where people will find their neighbours, work-mates and spouses snatched away to Heaven or Hell by God, with no time to react.

> *Some fundamentalist Christians believe the Apocalypse will take a form known as "the Rapture". They think true Christians will be RAPTURED (taken or seized) up into Heaven, leaving sinful humans back on Earth to suffer the dreadful disasters at the end of the world.*

God destroys Sodom but Lot and his daughters escape

Although this discourse contains a lot of apocalyptic imagery, it's actually warning ***against*** believing people who say that the Apocalypse is happening or about to happen. The REAL Apocalypse will happen so quickly there will be no time to speculate about it.

Luke's 1st century audience: Many 1st century Christians still believed in the *Parousia* but thought it had been delayed. There was a danger they would become complacent and their commitment would slip. This passage encourages readers to carry on living ***as if*** the Apocalypse could happen at any moment.

This means it fits both **Conzelmann**'s idea of salvation-history (with the Apocalypse indefinitely postponed and Christians living through the 'long haul' of history) and **Marshall**'s idea that Luke and his church still believed in an imminent Apocalypse.

The Rich and the Kingdom of God (Luke 18: 18-30)

This passage also occurs in **Mark 10: 17-31** and **Matthew 19: 16-30**. Matthew's version is more strongly apocalyptic, ending with Jesus describing *"the renewal of all things"* by God.

> *This passage is a good example of the **Synoptic Problem**, with close word-for-word similarities between the three Gospels but also differences. For example, Luke agrees with Mark in calling the character a "ruler" but for Matthew he is just "a rich young man"*

Jesus is questioned by a wealthy ruler who wants to know how to enter the Kingdom. Jesus gives a very conventional answer: keep the Ten Commandments. The ruler replies that he keeps all the Commandments.

> [22] When Jesus heard this, he said to him, "You still lack one thing. Sell everything you have and give to the poor, and you will have treasure in heaven. Then come, follow me."
>
> [23] When he heard this, he became very sad, because he was very wealthy. [24] Jesus looked at him and said, "How hard it is for the rich to enter the kingdom of God! [25] Indeed, it is easier for a camel to go through the eye of a needle than for someone who is rich to enter the kingdom of God."

Many readers detect a sort of dry humour in the way Jesus treats this man. Since Jesus regards just thinking about sinning as the same as actually sinning (e.g. **Matthew 5: 28**), the man's claim that he has kept ***all*** the Commandments is an empty boast. He is like the *rocky soil* in the **Parable of the Sower** (p81): he's just not deep enough to appreciate what it means to live in the way God expects. Therefore Jesus gives him a new Commandment guaranteed to upset him: give away all your wealth. The man isn't prepared to do this; his wealth is like the *thorns* in the **Parable of the Sower**.

Jesus adds the famous and baffling metaphor of the camel going through the eye of a needle. Given the humourous way Jesus has treated the rich man, this might be just a wild piece of imagery for something impossible to do. However, two interpretations are popular:

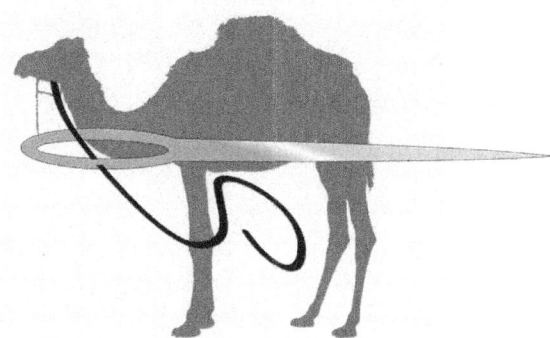

- *Kamêlos* ("camel") is a mistranslation of *kamilos* ("rope"). Jesus is referring to trying to thread a thick rope through a needle.
- There was a narrow gate in Jerusalem called 'the Needle's Eye' and camels could only pass through it if their baggage was unloaded first. Therefore, wealth has to be taken away before any camel can pass through the Needle's Eye gate.

Jesus' Disciples are upset by the tough standard Jesus is proposing. He reassures them that, *"What is impossible with man is possible with God."* This means that, even though the standard is high, God will help Christians live up to it.

> [29] "Truly I tell you," Jesus said to them, "no one who has left home or wife or brothers or sisters or parents or children for the sake of the kingdom of God [30] will fail to receive many times as much in this age, and in the age to come eternal life."

It's interesting that Jesus moves from talking about giving up money to giving up family. The two are connected. Many early Christians really did lose their families when they converted – either because they were ostracized by the Jewish community or because they had to cut themselves off from their pagan past. It's ironic that Christianity is often linked to "family values" today – but Jesus rarely says positive things about family ties.

Jesus praises people who make great sacrifices for the sake of the Kingdom; they will be rewarded both in *this age* (the here-and-now) and in *the age to come* (which could mean either the Apocalypse or the Afterlife). This is similar to the *good soil* in **The Parable of the Sower** that produces a *crop*.

In Matthew's Gospel, this passage is more strongly apocalyptic: Matthew refers to the Disciples on thrones, judging the Twelve Tribes of Israel in the *age-to-come*. Luke is less specific about the reward except that it will involve **Eternal Life**. Notice that Luke still uses the apocalyptic theme of two ages: this current *age* (or *aeon*) and the eschatological *age to come* but Luke is much more vague than Matthew about when and where the *age to come* is happening.

Luke's 1st century audience: The earliest Christians gave up their personal wealth when they converted and it was shared communally. This passage might refer to that practice. Later Christians interpreted the passage in a weaker way: that you should be ***prepared*** to give up all your wealth if it was required of you, but not that you should automatically have to do so. The idea of the *age to come* started to mean the Afterlife for many Christians, rather than the Apocalypse.

This fits in with **Conzelmann**'s idea of salvation-history, although **Marshall** points out that the distinction between this age and the age to come is also in Mark, so Luke didn't alter the original passage to fit with a new anti-apocalyptic way of thinking.

The Parable of the Ten *Minas* (Luke 19: 11-27)

This Parable is also in **Matthew 25: 14-30**. However, the two Parables are written differently and seem to come from different sources. In Matthew's version, there is no framing story of the king going on a journey and the servants are entrusted with *talents* (bags of gold weighing 30 kg each!) rather than *minas*.

> *This Parable relates to the **4-Source Solution** to the **Synoptic Problem** (in **Topic 3**), because it does not seem to come from Matthew and Luke both using the **Q-Source**. Instead, their own special sources (M and L) both contain different versions of this Parable*

Jesus describes a nobleman going away to be crowned king and leaving his 10 servants with money to handle on his behalf. Each servant gets one *mina*. A *mina* is a unit of currency that divides into 50 shekels. It's about a quarter of the annual wage for an agricultural worker in the 1st century, so a *mina* is a lot of money by the standards of Jesus' audiences.

When the nobleman (now a king) returns, the servants have invested the money and made a profit for their boss and they are rewarded. However, one servant has not done this.

> [20] "Then another servant came and said, 'Sir, here is your mina; I have kept it laid away in a piece of cloth. [21] I was afraid of you, because you are a hard man. You take out what you did not put in and reap what you did not sow.'
>
> [22] "His master replied, 'I will judge you by your own words, you wicked servant! You knew, did you, that I am a hard man, taking out what I did not put in, and reaping what I did not sow? [23] Why then didn't you put my money on deposit, so that when I came back, I could have collected it with interest?'

The king is furious that the servant has wasted the opportunity that was given to him – and is angry at the implied criticism that he is *a hard man* who treats people unfairly.

The king handles the matter in an odd way. The money is taken from the 'wicked servant' and given to the one who has already been rewarded the most.

> [26] "He replied, 'I tell you that to everyone who has, more will be given, but as for the one who has nothing, even what they have will be taken away. [27] But those enemies of mine who did not want me to be king over them – bring them here and kill them in front of me.'"

The king represents God and the servants are his worshipers. Previous Parables (like the **Great Banquet**, p25) suggest that God rewards those who have **least**, but here God seems to reward those who have **most**.

However, the Parable isn't really about money. The *minas* are like the *seeds* in the **Parable of the Sower** (p81): the good servant is like the *good soil* that produces a *crop* and the 'wicked servant' is like the *path* or the *rocky soil* where the seed is wasted.

> If the *minas* represent Jesus' teachings, that makes the king's anger a bit more understandable (after all, he's got loads of money – why should he be so furious about a paltry *mina*?). God is angry with people who receive Jesus' teachings but don't put them into action in their lives – but he doubly rewards those who do!

The story of the nobleman going away to be crowned is hard to interpret. Some scholars think there is a reference here to **Herod Archelaus** who went to Rome in 4 BCE to be crowned King of Judea after his father, Herod the Great, died. However, his Jewish subjects rebelled against him and were brutally put down. According to Josephus, Archelaus had 3000 of his enemies brought to the Temple and executed.

A coin showing Herod Archelaus as 'king of the Jews'

Archelaus is an odd comparison for God. However, the Parable seems to have an apocalyptic meaning: the return of the king stands for God's arrival at the end of the age, to punish the wicked and reward the faithful. The wicked servant might represent the Jews who treat God as a *hard man* to be appeased through animal sacrifices rather than loved as a Father in Heaven. Ironically, they are then treated by God the same way they treated him: without love.

Luke's 1st century audience: On the face of it, the apocalyptic tone of this Parable doesn't fit well with **Conzelmann**'s idea of salvation-history. However, 1st century Christians would view the king as Christ. He is currently absent, because he has ascended to Heaven to be crowned there. He will return at *Parousia*, but no one knows when that will be. In the meantime, Christians must do Christ's work on Earth.

Interpreted this way, the Parable **does** fit in with salvation-history, because Christ's return hasn't happened yet and Christians are living through the time of his absence. When he does return (or perhaps, in the Afterlife), there will be a reckoning. People who converted to Christianity but then had nothing more to do with the church – or who behaved fearfully and hid when persecution came along – are like the wicked servant and will be punished. Those who commit to the Christian life will be rewarded.

TOPIC 5.2 WHY DID JESUS HAVE TO DIE?

All four Gospels describe Jesus' final days, but **John's Gospel** is particularly rich in detail. Although this Gospel is usually thought of as being late in composition (90s CE, long after the death of people who were eyewitnesses to these events), it does contain some details about Jerusalem in the 30s CE that seem to be more accurate than the Synoptic Gospels.

Other than the Gospels, our main source of knowledge about the background to Jesus' death is the Jewish historian **Flavius Josephus** (37-100 CE).

The Religious & Political Authorities

Several groups held power in **1st century Palestine** and all might have had reasons to want to see someone like Jesus executed.

The High Priest & the Sanhedrin

The High Priest was **Joseph Caiaphas**, a man who had held office for a decade and served under two Roman governors. The High Priest was appointed by the Romans for his willingness to collaborate with them, not for his religious faith. Nevertheless, Caiaphas seems to have been particularly successful at keeping **Pontius Pilate** happy while presenting himself to the Jewish people as the leader of their religion.

Caiaphas' mission was to please the Romans by preventing outbursts of religiously-inspired violence and, in return, to persuade the Romans to be as reasonable as possible in their dealings with Jews. Arresting a religious troublemaker with a dangerous following would not have been a problem for a man like Caiaphas. He would not have wanted the Romans to think he had 'lost his grip'.

Caiaphas knew that he stood or fell with Roman power. The anti-Roman **Zealots** tried to assassinate High Priests (and in 60 CE they eventually succeeded in murdering one of Caiaphas' successors). As a Sadducee, Caiaphas couldn't expect much help from the Pharisees. He needed the protection of the Romans.

Caiaphas also needed backing for his actions and achieved this by convening a 'parliament' of Jewish leaders called the SANHEDRIN. **Ellis Rivkin** (p161) argues that the Sanhedrin was essentially a political council rather than a religious body, but senior priests hand-picked by Caiaphas would have been members.

The Sadducees

The Sadducees were a sect of wealthy and conservative Jews who rejected the newfangled beliefs of the Pharisees (such as life after death and religious laws other than those in the Torah). They were particularly associated with the Temple-cult and maintaining the strict sacrifices as laid down in the Torah, dictated by God to Moses.

Not all priests in the Temple were Sadducees, but perhaps most were. They would have dominated the membership of the Sanhedrin (indeed, Caiaphas the High Priest was a Sadducee). This group would have disapproved of a religious innovator like Jesus who seemed to be developing new teachings and who challenged the authority of Moses and the Torah.

Even more than religious innovation, the Sadducees would have wished to protect the Temple from threats. Various Jewish groups opposed the Temple: they saw it as corrupt since it had been built by Herod the Great and the Temple's High Priest was appointed by the Romans. The idea of the Temple being destroyed would have frightened the Sadducees since it was the source of their status and wealth as well as their religion.

The Pharisees

The Pharisees were the most numerous of the Jewish religious leaders. They taught a belief in life after death for Jews who followed the strict Law – not just the laws in the Torah but the traditional 'Oral Law' that covered every aspect of life. They were highly respected by ordinary people. Breakaway Pharisees had created the **Zealot** movement that wanted to overthrow the **Roman occupation**.

The Pharisees would certainly have been threatened by the sudden growth of a religious movement that told people they didn't need to follow the Pharisees' laws. Most Pharisees preferred to argue with Jesus and his followers rather than use force, but some Pharisees were priests in the Temple and members of the Sanhedrin and had some political power.

John's Gospel reports that a senior Pharisee named **Nicodemus** supported Jesus and argued against his execution.

The Herodians

Two of Herod the Great's sons ruled in Palestine: **Herod Antipas** was the *tetrarch* of Galilee and **Herod Philip** was *tetrarch* of territories further east. These rulers are often (wrongly) termed 'kings' by the Gospels, although ordinary people perhaps saw them as kings. In fact, they were more like governors, appointed (and sometimes removed from office) by the Romans.

The Herodians depended on the goodwill of the Romans to stay in power. Their older brother **Archelaus** had been banished by the Romans after too many revolts by his subjects. The younger brothers learned a lesson from this. Herod Antipas had **John the Baptist** arrested and executed. The Gospels say this is because John the Baptist criticised Antipas' sex life, but **Flavius Josephus** claims that John the Baptist's following had grown so large that Antipas feared there would be a rebellion against him.

Herod Antipas got away with executing John the Baptist without serious repercussions, but several of the Baptist's followers joined Jesus' movement (in fact, Jesus himself had been baptised by John) so Antipas probably saw Jesus' followers as a threat too.

The Romans

The Roman Empire wanted two things from provinces like Judea: the payment of taxes and peaceful law and order. Unfortunately, it only got the taxes.

Although **Herod the Great** had kept the peace well enough, after he died in 4 BCE the province erupted in revolt. Herod's son **Archelaus** only made matters worse with his reprisals and he was banished by the Romans in 6 CE and a Roman governor was sent to rule Judea directly. The **Zealot** movement formed to resist Roman rule, especially the payment of taxes which the Zealots saw as no different from worshiping the Roman Emperor as a god.

The Roman governor at the time of Jesus' execution was **Pontius Pilate**, who had been in charge of Judea since 26 CE. Pilate was a harsh, stubborn man with no love for the Jewish religion nor any sensitivity to religious feelings. Pilate's first act as governor was a blunder. He brought flags and images of Roman gods into Jerusalem during the night and when the Jewish citizens discovered them in the morning there were protests. These turned into conflict when Pilate refused to remove the pagan symbols. Eventually Pilate had to back down and the Emperor himself wrote a letter criticising Pilate's handling of things. On other occasions, Pilate sent in his soldiers to beat and kill Jewish protesters.

Besides the Romans themselves, there were the Jewish PUBLICANS who worked for the Romans by collecting taxes. These collaborators were despised by the common people and threatened and attacked by the **Zealots**. Pilate clearly had no problem with executing Jewish troublemakers who threatened his authority or the safety of his publicans. However, he had also learned to be careful about provoking the Jewish crowds. He probably let himself by guided by **Caiaphas the High Priest** on matters like this but he had a reputation for ignoring good advice.

Jesus' Arrest & Trials

John's Gospel differs from the Synoptics on one crucial point. For John's Gospel, Jesus is arrested on the night *before* the Passover feast and executed on the day of the feast itself, but in the Synoptics he is executed the day *after* the feast.

The Passover Feast

The Passover (*Pesach*) is perhaps the central act of Jewish celebration, commemorating the ancient escape of the Israelites from slavery in Egypt, as recorded in the **Book of Exodus**. It is a Spring festival, which culminates in a ritual meal (*Seder*). During this meal, four cups of wine are drunk and unleavened (flat) bread is shared while the story of the salvation of the Jewish people is re-told.

In the 1st century, thousands of pilgrims crowded into Jerusalem for Passover, many sleeping rough because the city was full. The Roman governor would stay in the city with his soldiers during the festival, because the theme of freedom from oppression inspired revolutionaries. In the Temple, the High Priest sacrificed an unblemished (spotless) lamb known as the Paschal Lamb. This sacrifice commemorated the blood of the lamb that marked the homes of the Israelites, so that the spirit of death passed over them when God cursed the Egyptian families (read the story in **Exodus 12**).

> *Modern Jews still celebrate Passover but they no longer sacrifice lambs – that ritual ended when the Temple was destroyed in 70 CE.*

The Last Supper

In the Synoptic Gospels, Jesus and his Disciples gather for a *Seder* meal on Passover. Jesus shares the bread and wine and declares that these are his body and his blood. This is the creation of the **Eucharist**, the central act of Christian worship. Jesus is arrested that night and executed the next day, which is the Sabbath.

Leonardo Da Vinci's famous painting of *The Last Supper*

However, in **John's Gospel**, Jesus shares a meal with his followers and is arrested a day earlier. He is executed on the eve of Passover at the same time as the sacrifice of the Pascal Lamb. This reinforces John's point that Jesus is the *Lamb of God*, sacrificed on our behalf.

> *Who got the date right, John or the Synoptics? Both have a reason to fudge the dates: the Synoptics want Jesus' Last Supper to be a Passover Meal because of its symbolism of Christianity being a continuation of Judaism; John wants Jesus to die at the same time as the Paschal Lamb to reinforce his ideas. Objectively speaking, John is more likely to be correct, because Jews wouldn't usually execute criminals on the Sabbath.*

Gethsemane

After the meal, Jesus and his Disciples leave the city to spend the night in a garden called **Gethsemane** on the nearby Mount of Olives. With Jerusalem full of pilgrims celebrating Passover, many would have to camp outside the city itself, under trees. However, this seems to be a favourite spot for Jesus. Amongst the olive trees, Jesus prays but his exhausted Disciples fall asleep.

Jesus experiences the 'agony in the garden' because he knows what lies ahead for him but needs to submit to the will of God. **Luke's Gospel** emphasises this agony until Jesus is comforted by angels. **John's Gospel** misses out the agony completely.

> *The Garden of Gethsemane still exists in Jerusalem and the olive trees there have been scientifically tested and found to be some of the oldest in the world: they are at least 1000 years old and could have grown from the roots of the trees Jesus stood among.*

Olive trees in Gethsemane today

A group of soldiers arrives to arrest Jesus (p121), guided there by the traitor **Judas Iscariot**. In the Synoptic Gospels, Judas indicates which man the soldiers are to arrest by kissing Jesus on the cheek (although **John** misses out this detail). All the Gospels describe a fight when one Disciple (John names him as **Peter**) cuts off the ear of a servant of the High Priest. Jesus orders them to put away their weapons. In **Luke's Gospel**, Jesus miraculously heals the wounded man.

The Trials

Jesus is led away and interrogated by the High Priest **Caiaphas**. In the Synoptic Gospels, a full meeting of the Sanhedrin has gathered to judge Jesus. Witnesses testify that Jesus boasted he was going to destroy the Temple. However, the final straw is when the High Priest asks Jesus if he is the **Son of God**: Jesus says that he is and this is regarded as **blasphemy** and worthy of death.

John's Gospel includes a different scene with Jesus being interrogated by a former High Priest named **Annas** (p123). John mentions Jesus being taken to the High Priest but misses out the whole Sanhedrin trial.

Meanwhile, all the Gospels describe Jesus' Disciple **Peter**, waiting nearby for news, denying three times that he knows Jesus, exactly as Jesus had predicted (p125).

First thing in the morning, Jesus is taken to the palace of the governor, **Pontius Pilate**. In the Synoptic Gospels, this is the first day of Passover and the Sabbath; in **John's Gospel** it is the Passover Eve. All the Gospels describe Jesus' trial before Pilate. **Luke** adds an extra detail that Pilate sends Jesus to the nearby palace of **Herod Antipas**, who is also in Jerusalem for the Passover. However, Jesus refuses to answer Antipas' questions and is returned to Pilate.

All the Gospels include a tradition where Pilate would release a condemned man every Passover. He offers the crowd a choice between Jesus or a notorious outlaw called **Barabbas**. Mark and Luke add that Barabbas' crime was starting a riot and John's Gospel calls him *"lestes"*, a word that usually means 'rebel'. The crowd outside demands that Barabbas is released instead of Jesus. Reluctantly, Pilate sentences Jesus to death by crucifixion.

*The idea that someone like Pilate would release prisoners as a publicity stunt sounds fishy, but it is attested in all four Gospels. **Ellis Rivkin** suggests that Pilate was mocking the Jewish crowd by doing this, which makes more sense than it being a 'tradition'.*

The trial scene is regarded by most scholars as historical since it passes the CRITERION OF MULTIPLE ATTESTATION (it is in all four Gospels with only minor differences) and the CRITERION OF EMBARRASSMENT. This last point is worth expanding.

It was deeply embarrassing for the 1st century Christians that Jesus was condemned as a criminal by the Roman Empire. This made their religion look like a dangerous cult that encouraged rebellion.

Christians would never have invented a story like this about Jesus. If Jesus were truly a **myth**, Christians would surely have told a story about him being stoned to death by the Jews (as happened to the martyr **Stephen** or Jesus' brother **James**) and not crucified by the Romans.

Christians would have wanted to 'play down' the involvement of the Romans in Jesus' death and the nature of his crime. However, it was clearly too well known that Jesus had been crucified for rebellion for anyone to change the story.

Instead, the Gospels go out of their way to show Jesus as being innocent of the charges against him and the Roman governor as recognizing this. Jesus' crime is represented as a religious one (**blasphemy**), not a political one (**insurrection** – or rebellion against Rome), and Pilate is described as condemning Jesus with extreme reluctance.

- **Hermann Reimarus** (p44) argues that Jesus REALLY WAS a political rebel and that the Romans were quite right to execute him – but that 1st century Christians tried to hide this when they wrote the Gospels.
- **Albert Schweitzer** (p162) argues that Jesus was innocent of rebellion but *wanted* the Romans to execute him because, according to Schweitzer, Jesus (mistakenly) believed that the death of God's innocent servant would bring on the Apocalypse. This explains why Jesus didn't deny the charges brought against him.

Conflict with the Authorities in John

All the Gospels show Jesus in conflict with the authorities, especially *"the scribes and the Pharisees"* or the *"teachers of the Law"* (which **Ellis Rivkin** regards as the same group, whom he terms the 'Scribe-Pharisees'). However, in **John's Gospel** the conflict is especially intense, perhaps echoing disputes in the former-Synagogues of the **Johannine Community**.

> *A selection of conflicts in John's Gospel is found in Anthology extract #6*

These disputes had a meaning for Jesus' original followers. However, they also had a meaning for the 1st century Christians who preserved them as part of the church's ORAL TRADITION. As with the Parables, this later interpretation could be different from what Jesus originally meant. They represent later Christian beliefs about why Jesus had to die.

Scholars like **Ellis Rivkin** argue that the later Christians misunderstood the relationship between the different Jewish sects and their philosophy of 'live and let live'. He maintains that 1st century Pharisees would not want to have someone executed for breaking their rules or blasphemy.

The Examiner may expect you to interpret these passages in the light of four themes:

- **Christology:** This refers to beliefs about Jesus' relationship with God, especially those that go against standard Jewish beliefs. In Judaism, God is one and is not multiple Persons, so God cannot be both a Father and a Son. God is utterly transcendent: it's wrong to picture him as a human or attribute human features to him. This means that a human being cannot be God and the phrase 'Son of God' can only be **symbolic**. In Judaism, Jesus could be a prophet but he could not be a human EXALTED to God-like status or God INCARNATED in human form. These Christological beliefs would be offensive to many 1st century Jews, possibly even **blasphemous**.

- **Blasphemy:** Blasphemy is a crime against God. Some Christological ideas (above) could be seen as blasphemous by 1st century Jews. So could attacks on the Temple (where God dwells) or the Torah (the Old Testament Scriptures that are the Word of God). Breaking the **Pharisee** rules on Sabbath-keeping could also be seen as blasphemy. Since the **Sadducees** did not believe in life after death, they might regard **Eternal Life** as blasphemy too. Some 1st century Jews would regard death as an appropriate punishment for blasphemy but others would see it as up to God, rather than humans, to punish blasphemers either in this life or the Afterlife.

- **Threat to Power:** Several groups in 1st century Palestine enjoyed power and influence (and with this, safety from mistreatment by the Romans or attacks by the **Zealot** rebels). The **Sadducees** enjoyed great wealth and respect from managing the Temple in Jerusalem. Although not as wealthy, the **Pharisees** enjoyed respect as the recognised interpreters of the **Law of Moses**. Such groups would react with hostility to anyone threatening their livelihood and the source of their status: the Temple and the Law respectively. In addition, the **Romans** saw any large crowds as potential rioters and rebels.

- **Political Expedience:** 'Expedience' means doing the practical thing even if you don't believe in it. The **Romans** had demonstrated in the past that they would put down any rebellion with great brutality and were easily provoked by riots or large crowds gathering around popular leaders. The Jewish leaders (**Sadducees** and **Pharisees**) wanted to protect their own people from these reprisals. This meant that they would be willing to arrest and execute Jewish rabble-rousers to keep the peace, even if (religiously speaking) they had no objection to what these troublemakers were teaching. **Ellis Rivkin** argues that this is the real reason Jesus was executed.

The conflicts involve three different disagreements:

- **Law of Moses:** The **Law** was contained in the Torah, a set of scrolls believed to be written by **Moses** around 1300 BCE and containing the 'Written Law' dictated by God (the Torah is the same as the first 5 Books of the Old Testament). The Sadducees based their version of Judaism on the 613 rules in the Torah. The Pharisees added the 'Oral Law' (the later books of the Old Testament and further traditions). These laws gave rules on how a Jew should live, right down to food, clothing, work and sex. The Pharisees' laws were particularly detailed and required their expertise to interpret how they applied to particular situations. When the Law was broken, a religious court called a *BET DIN* decided how the law-breaker should be punished.

- **Sabbath Controversies:** The Sabbath is part of the **Law of Moses** that is worth considering by itself. The Sabbath is the 'day of rest', established by God, when he rested on the 7th Day of Creation (**Genesis 2: 2**). Jews would do no work (Hebrew *MELAKHA*) on the Sabbath. The **Sadducees** interpreted this in a fairly simple way, but the **Pharisees** developed detailed rules about what counted as 'work' and what didn't. There were 39 types of forbidden work (*MELAKHOT*) and many more rules covering special cases. Sabbath rules prevented lighting a candle or looking in a mirror fixed on a wall – but hiring a Gentile to light a candle for you was acceptable. Christians criticised Sabbath-keeping as LEGALISTIC – putting laws before loving God or your neighbours.

- **Temple Cleansing:** The Jerusalem Temple stood on the site of the original Temple of Solomon. It had been rebuilt by **King Herod the Great** with magnificent luxury. The construction started in 19 BCE and building was still going on in Jesus' time; the Temple was finally finished only a few years before its destruction by the Romans in 70 CE. The Temple was a massive complex with golden roofs and marble pillars. The huge outer courtyard was a market and tourist trap. The inner courtyards were reserved for Jews. The whole complex was managed by the **Sadducees**. Nevertheless, many Jews opposed the Temple and the animal sacrifices that went on there. The **Essenes** regarded the Temple priesthood as corrupt and the rituals there as unnecessary. The **Zealots** regarded the Temple priests as collaborators with the Roman occupiers. The idea of 'cleansing' the Temple of everything that was wrong with it and replacing it with a purer form of worship was popular with many people, but this was seen as **blasphemy** and a **threat to the power** of the priests who ran it.

Jesus Clears the Temple Courts (John 2: 12-25)

This dramatic event is recorded in all the Gospels, but **John** positions it at the start of Jesus' ministry (soon after the **Sign of Turning Water into Wine** – *c.f.* **Topic 2**) whereas the Synoptic Gospels position it at the end, right after Jesus enters Jerusalem during his Passion Week. **Culpepper** (p158) suggests a thematic reason for John's Gospel to place this at the start of the story:

> *Jerusalem is established as the locus of Jesus' sharpest conflict with unbelief which has been hardened by misunderstanding of the scriptures, institutions and festivals of Judaism* – **R. Alan Culpepper**

For **John**, the Jewish religion has entirely mistaken the Old Testament (which is supposed to predict Christ), so Jesus is angry at the grand scale of the Temple which misses the point of the Scriptures. That's why this is the only example of Jesus using violence.

> [13] When it was almost time for the Jewish Passover, Jesus went up to Jerusalem. [14] In the temple courts he found people selling cattle, sheep and doves, and others sitting at tables exchanging money. [15] So he made a whip out of cords, and drove all from the temple courts, both sheep and cattle; he scattered the coins of the money changers and overturned their tables. [16] To those who sold doves he said, "Get these out of here! Stop turning my Father's house into a market!" [17] His disciples remembered that it is written: "Zeal for your house will consume me."

The *cattle, sheep and doves* are being sold as sacrificial animals. The people *sitting at tables exchanging money* are exchanging the hated Roman coins (with the Emperor on them) for the silver shekels that can be used to pay the Temple Tax.

What with buying an animal to sacrifice and paying the Temple Tax – with the sellers and money-changers taking their cut – worshiping at the Temple could be an expensive business for ordinary Jews and at Passover the authorities could expect to make a lot of money.

This is why Jesus condemns them for turning the Temple into a *market.* The Synoptic Gospels are actually more explicit about this, calling the Temple authorities *thieves* for robbing worshipers in this way.

Jesus proclaims his authority by saying: *"Destroy this temple and I will raise it again in three days."* This is a **symbolic** reference to himself as the true Temple and his Resurrection after 3 days. However, this claim will be used against Jesus. In the Synoptic Gospels, at Jesus' trial, witnesses claim he ***threatened*** to destroy the Temple himself.

In the Synoptic Gospel, this disturbance is what persuades the authorities that Jesus is politically dangerous and they decide to have him killed. In John's Gospel, this is just the opening salvo in Jesus' campaign against the Jewish establishment and it is the **Sign of Raising Lazarus from the Dead** (*c.f.* **Topic 2**) that persuades them that Jesus must die.

What did Jesus really say? As historians, we can't decide between the priests (who think Jesus threatened to destroy the Temple) and the Gospel-writers (who insist he merely predicted it would be destroyed and predicted his own Resurrection).

This scale model shows the Temple and the huge outer courtyard which was filled with market stalls. Did Jesus really drive *everyone* out of this big place?

The Cleansing of the Temple is likely to be a historical event. It passes the CRITERION OF MULTIPLE ATTESTATION (it's in all four Gospels with few differences other than the dating) and it contains details about the layout and organization of the Temple that seem to be historically accurate too.

The priests' complaint mentions that it has taken *"forty six years to build this Temple"*. Since we know Herod the Great started the Temple in 19 BCE, we can date Jesus' protest to 27 CE, possibly 30 CE if the priests are referring specifically to the Outer Court where the market was. That also fits well with the dating of Jesus' crucifixion in 30 or 33 CE.

Christology: Jesus calls the Temple *"My Father's House"* which refers to being the **Son of God**. Of course, Jesus encouraged his followers to call God *Father* (e.g. in the Lord's Prayer) but here he seems to be referring to God as his *Father* specifically. He claims the authority of a son to driver intruders out of his father's home.

Blasphemy: By attacking the Temple as a *market* (or worse, a *den of thieves* in **Matthew 21: 13**), Jesus is insulting a holy place. By putting a (temporary) stop to the selling of animals, he is preventing the sacrifices to worship God. Finally, by suggesting he can rebuild the Temple in three days he is claiming to be greater than the Temple – in fact, to be the TRUE Temple where the TRUE Word of God is found.

Threat to Power: This attack is a threat to the Sadducees' power, as custodians of the Temple. It is also a threat to the Pharisees' power, as the ones who interpret the calendar of feasts and sacrifices by which the Temple runs. If Jesus' followers were to imitate Jesus and start attacking the Temple, they might be joined by other anti-Temple groups (like the **Essenes**) and the priests would all suffer.

Political Expediency: During Passover, the city of Jerusalem was crammed with pilgrims, so news of this disturbance would spread and encourage others who hated the Temple or just wanted to provoke conflict with the Romans. With more pilgrims flooding into the city daily, the authorities would want to prevent any further disturbances by arresting the ringleader – Jesus.

The Authority of the Son & Testimonies about Jesus (John 5: 16-47)

> *This passage follows directly on from the **Sign of Healing at the Pool** which you studied in Topic 2 (The Person of Jesus).*

Jesus has healed a man on the Sabbath and made clay out of soil – breaking the regulations for the Sabbath which forbid any kind of work on the day of rest. Jesus defends himself saying that, since God never rests, neither does he.

> **5** [16] So, because Jesus was doing these things on the Sabbath, the Jewish leaders began to persecute him. [17] In his defence Jesus said to them, "My Father is always at his work to this very day, and I too am working." [18] For this reason they tried all the more to kill him; not only was he breaking the Sabbath, but he was even calling God his own Father, making himself equal with God.

Jesus says some surprising things: that God never rests and that, therefore, as God's Son, the Sabbath Laws don't apply to him.

Ellis Rivkin objects to the way John's Gospel interprets this debate. He argues that the Jewish sects in the 1st century all followed a code of 'Live and Let Live'. He believes the **Pharisees** and **Sadducees** did not try to persecute each other over religious differences and left other sects (like the **Essenes**) alone too. Therefore they would not have wanted to kill Jesus just for saying this.

Jesus goes on to claim that, as God's Son, he knows all the things his Father knows and can do all the things his Father does – including granting **Life** and judging sinners. Criticisms of him are the same as criticising God. Jesus goes into an apocalyptic discourse, predicting the future arrival of the **Son of Man** (himself) and the return to life of all the dead to be judged (by him).

Jesus compares himself to **John the Baptist**:

> [36] "I have testimony weightier than that of John. For the works that the Father has given me to finish – the very works that I am doing – testify that the Father has sent me. [37] And the Father who sent me has himself testified concerning me. You have never heard his voice nor seen his form, [38] nor does his word dwell in you, for you do not believe the one he sent. [39] You study the Scriptures diligently because you think that in them you have eternal life. These are the very Scriptures that testify about me, [40] yet you refuse to come to me to have life.

The Jews regard John the Baptist as a good man, perhaps as a prophet, but Jesus claims to be something greater than John. He claims the Jews have missed the point of their own Scriptures, because the Scriptures predict Jesus, but the Jews don't recognise him. Jesus drives his point home by saying that the Jews have set their hearts on **Moses** (the Prophet who received the Law from God), but they *"do not believe what he wrote"* because they do not recognise Jesus is the *Logos* who spoke to Moses.

Culpepper (p158) argues that, in passages like this, the Jews don't necessarily stand for the Jewish religion, but for all the people who don't believe in Jesus and *set their heart* on something else:

> *The real conflict is not between Jesus and the Jews... but between Jesus and those who refuse to accept the revelation he brings. Unbelief is the real opponent* – **R. Alan Culpepper**

Christology: As the passage says, Jesus claims to be God's Son and, going further, part of God himself. Jesus is part of God's creative process described in the **Book of Genesis** when the world was made in 6 days; he knows God's secrets and has God's powers. This links to Jesus being the *Logos* as described in **John's Prologue**.

Blasphemy: Not only does Jesus break the Sabbath but he denies the Scriptures, which claim that God rested on the 7th Day of Creation: Jesus claims God never rests. He claims the Jewish leaders have misread the Scriptures and that he himself is greater than the Scriptures.

Threat to Power: The Pharisees preached that people could have **Eternal Life** by following the **Law** in their Scripture and the Oral Law passed down in Jewish tradition. Jesus claims that *he* alone offers Eternal Life and that the Pharisees' laws do not.

Political Expedience: John the Baptist was arrested and executed by Herod Antipas. One of the reasons for this was that the large crowds John attracted made Antipas nervous. If Jesus was viewed as similar to John the Baptist, it would have made him a target for the authorities, either Roman or Herodian, who would want to remove him.

Division over Who Jesus Is & Unbelief of the Jewish Leaders (John 7: 25-52)

Jesus starts off in John's Gospel with a large and loyal following (some of whom were previously followers of John the Baptist). These Disciples recognise him as **Messiah, King of Israel** and **Son of God**. However, in **John 6** there is a crisis when Jesus preaches his controversial **"I Am" sayings**, presents himself as superior to **Moses** and introduces the idea eating his flesh and blood in the **Eucharist**. **Culpepper** (p158) argues that many followers then *"defect"* because they cannot accept these *hard teachings* (**John 6: 66**), leaving Jesus with just his core Twelve Disciples (and one of them is **Judas**, the ultimate defector).

---

*This perhaps reflects the history of the **Johannine Community**, who might have been a large group of Jewish Christians originally, but as their beliefs about Jesus grew more extreme (high Christology), the ordinary Jews defected, until they were left as a small and unpopular minority in the Synagogue.*

Jesus goes to Jerusalem for the Feast of Tabernacles. He speaks about going back to the one who sent him, saying, *"Where I am, you cannot come"*. There is a classic Johannine misinterpretation here. Christian readers know Jesus refers to going back to God, when he ascends to Heaven after his Resurrection. The Jews wonder if he just means he is going to the **Diaspora** (the Jewish communities living in the Roman Empire) to *"teach the Greeks"*. They are right, but not in the way they think: Christ's message will go out into the Greek world, becoming a new religion and leaving the Jews behind:

Jesus will go to the Diaspora but not as the Jews think – **R. Alan Culpepper**

By this point, no one can work out who or what Jesus is supposed to be:

[40] On hearing his words, some of the people said, "Surely this man is the Prophet."

[41] Others said, "He is the Messiah."

Still others asked, "How can the Messiah come from Galilee? [42] Does not Scripture say that the Messiah will come from David's descendants and from Bethlehem, the town where David lived?"[43] Thus the people were divided because of Jesus. [44] Some wanted to seize him, but no one laid a hand on him.

Viewing Jesus as a 'Prophet' would be perfectly normal for Jews to do. However, the Age of Prophecy was supposed to have ended with the last prophet, **Malachi** (c.420 BCE). Many Jews would have been suspicious of Jesus as a 'False Prophet'.

Viewing Jesus as the **Messiah** would not be unusual, but Jesus doesn't meet the standard definition of the Messiah since he comes from Galilee and does not appear to be descended from the **line of David** (*c.f.* **Topic 1**).

> *John's Gospel never mentions the **birth-narratives** that describe Jesus being born in Bethlehem and of the **line of David**. For John, this sort of legalistic approach to the Old Testament prophecies is completely mistaken and only leads to confusion. When you believe in Jesus, **then** you understand the Scriptures – not the other way round.*

These confusions perhaps echo debates later in the 1st century within the Synagogues of the **Johannine Community**, where some members could accept Jesus as a prophet or even the **Messiah**, but could not accept him as God incarnate. **Raymond E. Brown** argues that John's Gospel was specifically written to convert these *crypto-Christians* (*c.f.* **Topic 3**).

The Pharisees interpret the letter of the Old Testament prophecies and conclude that none of the prophecies refers to a Messiah (or anyone else of any importance) coming from Galilee. Yet their grip on the people (whom they despise) and even their own soldiers is slipping. **Nicodemus** is a Pharisee who urges his allies to listen to what Jesus has to say, but he is shouted down.

Christology: Jesus claims to know God because he is from God and will return to God. This is similar to **John's Prologue** which describes the *Logos* coming from God, dwelling among men (and the Feast of Tabernacles means the feast of *dwellings*) but not being recognised by his own people; exactly what happens in this passage (*c.f.* **Topic 2** for details on the *Logos*).

Threat to Power: The Pharisees know that their influence over the population has been challenged. When they send soldiers to arrest Jesus, the soldiers come back inspired by Jesus' words. Even some of their own members (like Nicodemus) seem to be on Jesus' side.

Political Expediency: This takes place during the Feast of Tabernacles, a harvest festival that brought pilgrims to Jerusalem. It is another opportunity to arrest Jesus before he can incite the crowd to riot. Furthermore, the divisions in the crowd also encourage the authorities to put a stop to things, because Jesus is creating disagreement and tension.

Disputes & Jesus' Claims about Himself (John 8: 12-59)

This is a lengthy passage, but it builds to a dramatic conclusion and one of Jesus' most explosive **"I Am" statements** (*c.f.* **Topic 2**).

At the start of this debate, Jesus delivers his **"I am the Light of the World"** statement (it is still the Feast of Tabernacles and the Temple is lit up by giant torches – but Jesus is the true Temple of God); *c.f.* **Topic 2** for a fuller analysis of this statement.

Jewish **Law** demands two witnesses to prove a statement. Jesus declares that he is one witness and God the Father is his other witness. As before, Jesus refers to how he has come from somewhere and is going somewhere: the unbelieving Jews do not know his origin or destination but **John's Prologue** explains that he is the *Logos* who has come from God and will return to God. Jesus similarly says he is *"from above"* (i.e. from the spiritual world, rather than being of the **Flesh**).

Jesus cannot be arrested yet because *"his hour had not yet come"*. This *hour* is his hour on the Cross, when he is raised up and glorified. The Jewish leaders are mystified but finally seem curious and awe-struck. They wonder about Jesus' identity.

> 25 "Who are you?" they asked.
>
> "Just what I have been telling you from the beginning," Jesus replied. 26 "I have much to say in judgment of you. But he who sent me is trustworthy, and what I have heard from him I tell the world." 27 They did not understand that he was telling them about his Father. 28 So Jesus said, "When you have lifted up the Son of Man, then you will know that I am he and that I do nothing on my own but speak just what the Father has taught me. 29 The one who sent me is with me; he has not left me alone, for I always do what pleases him." 30 Even as he spoke, many believed in him.

"From the beginning" here is a reference to **Genesis**, the first Book of the Old Testament, called *BERESHIT* ('In the Beginning') in Hebrew. Who Jesus is has been made clear right from the start of the Scriptures. **John's Prologue** also makes this clear: the *Logos* was with God *"in the beginning"*.

The debate turns into an argument about ancestry. The Jews believe they are descended from **Abraham** and, spiritually, from God. Jesus replies that, though they may be biologically descended from Abraham, they do not have Abraham's faith and their spiritual father is the Devil.

> 39 "Abraham is our father," they answered.
>
> "If you were Abraham's children," said Jesus, "then you would do what Abraham did. 40 As it is, you are looking for a way to kill me, a man who has told you the truth that I heard from God. Abraham did not do such things. 41 You are doing the works of your own father."

Jesus' argument is that 'actions speak louder than words' – the Jews may *claim* to act in God's name, but since they reject Jesus and plot to kill him, they *really* act in the Devil's name.

> "We are not illegitimate children," they protested. "The only Father we have is God himself."
>
> 42 Jesus said to them, "If God were your Father, you would love me, for I have come here from God. I have not come on my own; God sent me. 43 Why is my language not clear to you? Because you are unable to hear what I say. 44 You belong to your father, the devil, and you want to carry out your father's desires. He was a murderer from the beginning, not holding to the truth, for there is no truth in him. When he lies, he speaks his native language, for he is a liar and the father of lies. 45 Yet because I tell the truth, you do not believe me! 46 Can any of you prove me guilty of sin? If I am telling the truth, why don't you believe me? 47 Whoever belongs to God hears what God says. The reason you do not hear is that you do not belong to God."

When Jesus claims to have God's power to grant **Life**, they mock him, saying he is possessed by a demon. When Jesus claims to have met **Abraham** (who lived 2000 years before), they think he is mad.

> 57 "You are not yet fifty years old," they said to him, "and you have seen Abraham!"
>
> 58 "Very truly I tell you," Jesus answered, "before Abraham was born, I am!" 59 At this, they picked up stones to stone him, but Jesus hid himself, slipping away from the temple grounds.

Jesus' final remark is a bombshell: he claims to be older than Abraham (i.e. older than the Jewish religion itself), a being from outside of time and history itself: he identifies himself by the holy name "I AM" in an unmistakable way. This is too much for the Jewish leaders, who resort to violence, but Jesus escapes.

Christology: With his two **"I Am" statements** (especially the one at the end), Jesus identifies himself as God incarnate – the same God who made a covenant with Abraham in **Genesis** and who spoke to Moses out of the Burning Bush in **Exodus**.

Blasphemy: Jesus claims to be the true Temple, the true meaning of the Torah and the true God of Israel. This is why the Jewish leaders try to stone him to death.

Threat to Power: Jesus' speeches are a total rejection of the power of the Jewish priests and Pharisees: he claims they cannot understand their Scriptures, they cannot understand God, they are children of the Devil doing the Devil's work and, ultimately, that they are not the legitimate descendants of Abraham.

The Pharisees Investigate the Healing (John 9: 13-34)

*You should be familiar with this passage from **Topic 2 (The Person of Jesus)**, where it is part of the **Sign of Healing the Blind Man***

This passage doesn't feature Jesus in person, but it continues the theme of division. The confusions in the crowds about who or what Jesus is have spread to the Pharisees, who are now falling out among themselves over Jesus' identity.

Jesus has broken the Sabbath regulations by healing a blind man (tradition names him as **Celidonius** though he is unnamed in the Bible), making clay to do it and telling him to carry a burden home (violating the 39th Sabbath rule).

> [16] Some of the Pharisees said, "This man is not from God, for he does not keep the Sabbath."
>
> But others asked, "How can a sinner perform such signs?" So they were divided.

For John's Gospel, the fact that God himself *does not keep the Sabbath* is evidence that it is only a man-made rule.

The Pharisees summon Celidonius' parents to help them understand whether Jesus really healed their son:

> [20] "We know he is our son," the parents answered, "and we know he was born blind. [21] But how he can see now, or who opened his eyes, we don't know. Ask him. He is of age; he will speak for himself." [22] His parents said this because they were afraid of the Jewish leaders, who already had decided that anyone who acknowledged that Jesus was the Messiah would be put out of the synagogue. [23] That was why his parents said, "He is of age; ask him."

The parents' cautious answer is because Jews who accept Jesus as the **Messiah** are being banished from the Synagogues, separating them from their families and neighbours.

Ellis Rivkin rejects passages like this in John's Gospel, arguing that the Pharisees debated with their opponents but did not persecute them over religious differences.

Nevertheless, after the destruction of the Temple, the **Council of Jamnia** (90 CE) did rule that Christians be thrown out of the Synagogues of the Roman Empire.

- **Form Criticism** would see this passage as a *pericope* from later in the 1st century, reflecting the fears of the **Johannine Community** in the 80s and 90s CE, not something that happened during Jesus' lifetime
- Alternatively, maybe the persecution of Christian believers by Pharisees started much earlier and the Council of Jamnia only made it official policy to do this

The Pharisees summon Celidonius back, but the formerly-blind man has grown in confidence and answers their questions sarcastically, saying: *"Do you want to become his disciples too?"*

> **28** Then they hurled insults at him and said, "You are this fellow's disciple! We are disciples of Moses! **29** We know that God spoke to Moses, but as for this fellow, we don't even know where he comes from."

The Pharisees make a distinction between Disciples of Jesus and Disciples of Moses. This is ironic because, for John's Gospel, Moses **was** a Disciple of Christ: it was the *Logos* who spoke to Moses and Jesus is the *Logos*. When the Pharisees admit they don't know where Jesus comes from, they are admitting their spiritual ignorance.

Celidonius offers more sarcastic remarks but the Pharisees lose their temper:

> **34** To this they replied, "You were steeped in sin at birth; how dare you lecture us!" And they threw him out.

The Pharisees teach that disabilities like blindness are a punishment for sin (either your own or your parents' sin, passed onto you). Jesus rejects this teaching (**John 9: 3**). The Pharisees cannot recognise the **Sign of Healing the Blind Man**, so they are the ones who are truly blind.

When Celidonius is *thrown out*, this might refer to the final expulsion of the Johannine Community from their Synagogues.

Blasphemy: This shows that, at a certain point, confessing Jesus to be the Messiah came to be seen as blasphemy by the Jewish leadership. John's Gospel claims this began right back during Jesus' ministry, but **Form Critics** argue it developed later on, outside of Judea.

Threat to Power: This passage shows the authority of the Pharisees slipping. They no longer command the respect of the people, but they still lead through fear. They are aware of this loss of status and it makes them angry.

Political Expediency: People who were thrown out of the Synagogues in the Roman Empire were no longer considered Jews and therefore not protected as a *religio licita* (official religion). This meant they could no longer refuse to worship the pagan gods or the Roman Emperor. If they continued to refuse, this was political rebellion and they could be arrested, tortured or executed.

Further Conflict over Jesus' Claims (John 10: 22-42)

This is the final scene in the Johannine ministry of Jesus that perhaps originally brought the Book of Signs to a close (although in the Gospel of John as it exists today, the **Sign of Raising Lazarus from the Dead** acts as a link to the Book of Glory which comes next). Three months have passed and it is the Festival of Hanukkah (around Christmas time). This Jewish festival celebrates the dedication of the Temple and the miraculous relighting of its lamps. John makes it clear that Jesus is the true Temple – another case of the Jews misunderstanding their own rituals.

> *The Jews legalistically maintain their observance of the festivals but do not recognise the reality they celebrate* – **R. Alan Culpepper**

A *hanukkiah* – the candles are lit to celebrate the re-dedication of the Temple in 165 BCE after the Maccabean Rebellion against the Persians

The Jews want to know if Jesus is the **Messiah**, but Jesus still won't give a direct answer. However, he ends up declaring: *"I and the Father are one."* The Jews regard this as blasphemy and try to stone him to death. Jesus sarcastically asks which of his *good works* they are punishing him for:

33 "We are not stoning you for any good work," they replied, "but for blasphemy, because you, a mere man, claim to be God."

Jesus replies with a technical argument, that in the Old Testament the prophets and judges are called *gods* because they listened to the Word of God – but Jesus claims to *be* the **Word of God made flesh**. Since they were called *gods* for listening to *him*, then he can call himself God without blaspheming.

Jesus' riddling answers to his critics are very clever – and very frustrating.

> *Jesus' non-answers allow him to retain control while moving conversations to higher planes, but it is not hard to understand why he provokes hostility* – **R. Alan Culpepper**

Jesus escapes when they try to kill him and this time he leaves Judea.

> [40] Then Jesus went back across the Jordan to the place where John had been baptizing in the early days. There he stayed, [41] and many people came to him. They said, "Though John never performed a sign, all that John said about this man was true." [42] And in that place many believed in Jesus.

By crossing the River Jordan, Jesus leaves Judea and enters the territory of Perea. He returns to the place where **John the Baptist** attracted his followers – the story of Jesus' ministry has come full circle. Jesus has left a place of unbelieving for a place of believing.

> *Tradition states that the Christians in Judea fled to Perea before Jerusalem was destroyed in 70 CE so, according to* **Form Criticism**, *the geography of this passage may be a* pericope *that really refers to later events in the 60s CE.*

This passage also refers to the opening prediction in **John's Prologue** that the Word of God is welcomed outside Judea by Gentiles, but rejected in Judea by Jews.

> *He came to that which was his own, but his own did not receive him* – **John 1: 1**

Christology: In a statement of very high Christology, Jesus claims to be one with God.

Blasphemy: The Jewish leaders regard Jesus' claim to be God as blasphemy. It goes against the central beliefs in Judaism that God is One and that God is not human and cannot be represented by a human.

Political Expediency: Outside Judea, on the other side of the River Jordan, Jesus is beyond the political authority of the High Priest **Caiaphas** and the Roman governor **Pontius Pilate**. He is not in danger unless he returns to Judea.

> *However, Jesus* **will** *return to Judea. In the next chapter he gets the news that his friend* **Lazarus** *is dying and re-enters Judea to heal him. This is described in the* **Sign of Raising Lazarus from the Dead** *(c.f.* **Topic 2***)*

The Plot to Kill Jesus (John 11: 45-57)

> *You should be familiar with this passage from **Topic 2 (The Person of Jesus)**, where it is part of the **Sign of Raising Lazarus from the Dead***

Jesus returns to Judea to raise his friend **Lazarus** from the dead. By crossing the River Jordan into Judea, he is replicating the arrival of the original Israelites into the Promised Land over a thousand years earlier. News travels to **Caiaphas** and his priests in Jerusalem that Jesus has returned and has raised the dead in Bethany, a village just two miles outside Jerusalem.

High Priest **Caiaphas** calls *a meeting of the Sanhedrin*. This term means 'assembly' or 'council'. The 'Greater Sanhedrin' was a group of 71 scholars and priests who met in Jerusalem every day in the Hall of Hewn Stones. They acted as a sort of parliament governing Jewish life in Palestine.

PRIEST.   HIGH PRIEST.   LEVITE.

The Jewish priesthood in the 1st century.

This image of a respectable governing body dominates most interpretations of the Gospels, who all refer to the Sanhedrin meeting to condemn Jesus. However, **Ellis Rivkin** (p161) draws a distinction between two different sorts of council:

1. **The Bet Din:** a religious council that settled religious disputes and punished people for breaking religious laws; Rivkin argues that the Bet Din only had power over people who followed the Pharisees' code. The BET DIN HA-GADOL is the grand council of 71 priests and scholars, but Rivkin doesn't think *that* is the meeting being described here.
2. **The Sanhedrin:** a non-religious 'privy council' or 'star chamber' that met to decide matters of political importance, such as threats to the safety of the country

If Rivkin is right, then the 'Sanhedrin' that Caiaphas assembled was not the impressive parliament of 71 religious experts, but a gang of politicians handling a threat to peace in Judea.

> "What are we accomplishing?" they asked. "Here is this man performing many signs. [48] If we let him go on like this, everyone will believe in him, and then the Romans will come and take away both our temple and our nation."

The fear that the Romans will *take away both our temple and our nation* sounds like a political fear: that Jesus will cause such a commotion that the Romans, suspecting that he is about to lead a revolt, will take a pre-emptive strike and destroy the Jewish community in Judea. This fits in with Ellis' view that the Sanhedrin is a small, political council, not a big religious one.

However, the priests also seem to be concerned that *everyone will believe in him* because he is *performing many signs*. That sounds more like something a big religious council would care about, rather than a political meeting.

> [49] Then one of them, named Caiaphas, who was high priest that year, spoke up, "You know nothing at all! [50] You do not realize that it is better for you that one man die for the people than that the whole nation perish."

Caiaphas' argument sounds like a classic political calculation: it's better to execute one troublemaker rather than risk a full-blown war with the Romans that could destroy the country. It's certainly not a religious argument about the importance of stopping Jesus' teachings or signs. In fact, Caiaphas says that the priests who are fretting about the religious implications of Jesus *know nothing at all* – they are fools. The political problem, not the religious problem, is what they have to deal with. This supports Rivkin's argument that the 'Sanhedrin' is a political meeting.

(It's also a classic piece of Johannine irony. Jesus is going to die an ATONING DEATH so *one man* really **will** *die for the people*.)

The Synoptic Gospels all feature a scene where, right before his Crucifixion, Jesus is put on trial before the Sanhedrin, but John's Gospel does not include a full trial-scene. Instead, this scene seems to serve the same function, establishing the mixed motives of the Jewish leaders and the tragic irony of their eventual decision.

The passage ends with Jesus going into hiding in the desert town of Ephraim while the whole of Jerusalem is a-buzz with gossip about whether Jesus will make an appearance during the Passover festival that Spring. The High Priest has his spies everywhere, ready to report as soon as Jesus makes an appearance. The stage is set for the events of the Book of Glory in John's Gospel.

Blasphemy: The priests seem to be concerned about more and more people believe in Jesus; this is presumably bad because they think Jesus' blasphemous teachings are leading people astray.

Threat to Power: The priests seem to be threatened by Jesus attracting followers with his 'signs'.

Political Expediency: Caiaphas persuades the priests that political expediency is what matters most: there will be a massive crackdown by the Romans if Jesus is allowed to carry on, so Jesus must be stopped before his followers get out of control.

Evaluating Jesus' Conflict with the Authorities

All the Gospels show Jesus in conflict with the *"Scribes and the Pharisees"* (whom **Ellis Rivkin** argues were really one group that he terms the *Scribes-Pharisees*). However, John's Gospel depicts Jesus' conflict with the Jewish authorities as being particularly intense.

The idea that Jesus had to die because he offended the Jewish religion has had tragic consequences. It led to antisemitism, the persecution of Jews throughout history and, in the 20th century, the Holocaust. Jews were collectively blamed for DEICIDE (the crime of murdering God) and the Jewish religion was viewed by many Christians as legalistic, soulless and depraved.

> *However, even John's Gospel falls short of the monstrous 'blood curse" in **Matthew 27: 24-25** where the Jewish crowd at Jesus' trial chant 'His blood upon is us and our children!" – essentially, Matthew represents the Jewish people as taking the blame for killing Jesus.*

But how true to history is this idea of a ***religious*** conflict?

a. The conflict is HISTORICALLY ACCURATE. The *Scribes-Pharisees* were offended by Jesus' claim to be the **Son of God** and had him executed for **blasphemy**. This is a traditional/conservative view of why Jesus had to die.

b. The conflict is HISTORICALLY EXAGGERATED. While Jesus may well have been in conflict with the authorities, the really hostile conflict was between Christians and the Pharisees in the Synagogues of the 1st century and came about because of the high **Christology** that emerged after Jesus' death and Resurrection appearances. This is **Raymond E. Brown**'s view that the conflict in John's Gospel represents the experiences of the **Johannine Community** (c.f. **Topic 3.2 Purpose & Authorship of the Fourth Gospel**).

c. The conflict is HISTORICALLY DISTORTED. The *Scribe-Pharisees* argued against Jesus but did not try to silence him by executing him. Instead, Jesus was executed as a matter of **political expediency**. This is **Ellis Rivkin**'s view (p161).

d. The conflict is SYMBOLIC. The Jewish authorities symbolise *"the world's unbelief"*. This is **R. Alan Culpepper**'s view (p158).

There are problems with viewing the conflict as historically accurate. John's Gospel represents Jesus as presenting Eucharistic themes (eating his flesh and drinking his blood) and a high Christology (being God incarnate) whereas most scholars think these ideas developed later among the 1st century churches. Moreover, **Rivkin** argues that

> the Scribes-Pharisees *steered clear of political involvement and ... confined their outrage at religious dissidents to verbal onslaughts* – **Ellis Rivkin**

In other words, the religious authorities of Jesus' time had no power or interest in executing people like Jesus for making outrageous theological claims. The Gospels might preserve memories of Jesus arguing with the Jewish leaders, but these arguments would have been more like friendly debates.

The idea that these conflicts are exaggerated or distorted is based on **Form Criticism**, because the conflicts are textual units (*pericopae*) created by the 1st century Christians, influenced by their own bitter confrontations with the Jewish leadership. They are 'putting words into Jesus' mouth'.

Redaction Criticism suggests that the Gospel passages where Jesus is in conflict with the authorities have been reinterpreted in the light of later beliefs. This means that Jesus did not really claim to be God– but later Christians offended the Pharisees by making those claims *about* Jesus. The Gospels represent Jesus as having the sort of arguments with the Pharisees (and receiving the same threats) that the later Christians experienced.

There are criticisms of this view. The Jewish **Law** does sentence blasphemers to be executed:

> *One who blasphemes the name of the Lord shall be put to death* – **Leviticus 24: 16**

1st century Christians certainly were threatened and attacked by the Jewish authorities for their beliefs. **Acts 7: 58-60** describes **Stephen** (the first Christian martyr, *see right*) being stoned to death by Jewish priests, witnessed by **Paul** back when he was still called Saul.

Later, Paul (now converted to Christianity) writes about being beaten and stoned for his own beliefs by his Jewish enemies.

> *Three times I was beaten with rods, once I was pelted with stones* – **2 Corinthians 11: 25**

Ellis Rivkin's idea that the *Scribes-Pharisees* only ever dealt peacefully with their opponents is contradicted by these passages from writers who lived alongside 1st century Jewish opponents.

(Of course, Paul and Luke might be exaggerating too, but they would hardly invent assaults that everyone knew to be preposterous and unrealistic so there is surely *some* truth to them).

There clearly was a risk of religiously-inspired violence when Paul was writing (in the 50s CE) and when Luke was writing (in the 70s or 80s CE), so why not during Jesus' ministry (around 30 CE) as well?

> *How accurate you think these passages are will depend on how persuasive you find **Form** and **Redaction Criticism**. If you think it is likely that 1st century Christians could have created stories about Jesus to express their own anger and fear towards the Jewish leadership of their day, then it's probable that the accounts of Jesus in conflict with the Jewish authorities of his day are at least exaggerated and possibly invented.*

Culpepper views 'the Jews' in John's Gospel as **symbolic**. They do not represent the historical Jews of Jesus' time, but stand for unbelievers everywhere, at every time. Culpepper calls the Jews in John the *"representatives of the world's unbelief"* and says:

> *Through the Jews, John explores the heart and soul of unbelief. As the representatives of unbelief, their misunderstandings touch on all the vital issues* – **R. Alan Culpepper**

If we take Culpepper's view, then Jesus may well have argued with the *Scribes-Pharisees* about **Temple cleansing** and **Sabbath regulations** and may have made high **Christological** claims about himself, but the vicious conflict in John's Gospel is not meant to be a historical account of what Jesus' enemies did: it's an **allegory** for how all humans respond to Christ's claims (rather like the different types of soil in Luke's **Parable of the Sower**, p81).

Did Jesus have to die because he offended the Jewish authorities?

YES	NO
Jesus is accused of **blasphemy** in all four Gospels, so this is well-attested. The first Christians were martyred by Jewish opponents and **Paul** describes being beaten and stoned. Jesus' claims to be God and later Christian claims about him would have been very offensive to devout Jews in the 1st century.	The conflicts in the Gospels, especially John's Gospel, reflect conflicts experienced by 1st century Christians and are not things that happened to Jesus. Jesus might have opposed **Sabbath regulations** and called for **Temple cleansing** but he didn't call himself God and wasn't executed for **blasphemy**.
Since the 1st century Christians experienced violence at the hands of Jewish leaders, why shouldn't this have happened to Jesus too? **Leviticus 24: 16** gives a religious justification for executing blasphemers in Judaism so there's no reason to treat the execution of Jesus for blasphemy as unhistorical.	**Ellis Rivkin** argues that, in **1st century Palestine**, different **Jewish sects** had arrived at a compromise of 'Live & Let Live' and did not persecute each other. The *Scribes-Pharisees* would have debated Jesus and even insulted him but what not have killed him for his blasphemous ideas.

Jesus' Arrest, Trial & Sentence To Be Crucified (John 18:1 – 19:16)

This lengthy extract can be divided into 3 sections.

Jesus Arrested

Jesus arrives in Jerusalem for the week of his Passion. He avoids attempts to arrest him and finally meets with his Disciples for an evening meal. In the Synoptic Gospels, this is the Passover *seder* meal, which Jesus reinterprets as a celebration of his own approaching death: the **Eucharist**. In John's Gospel, the final meal is the day before Passover so there is no sharing of bread and wine. Instead, Jesus washes his Disciples' feet, urges his Disciples to love one another and predicts that Peter will deny him 3 times.

Jesus and his Disciples leave the city to spend the night in an olive garden. The Synoptic Gospels name the garden as Gethsemane, although John (oddly) leaves it unnamed. The Synoptic Gospels describe Jesus praying in anguish that God will spare him from having to go through with the torment ahead, using a metaphor that the *"cup"* God wishes him to drink may pass from him untasted. John removes all this: the Johannine Jesus (being the **Word of God made Flesh**) has no doubts or fears.

The traitor **Judas** arrives with *"a detachment of soldiers and some officials from the chief priests and the Pharisees"*. In the Synoptic Gospels, Judas identifies who Jesus is to the soldiers by kissing him. John's Gospel presents the scene differently:

⁴ Jesus, knowing all that was going to happen to him, went out and asked them, "Who is it you want?"

⁵ "Jesus of Nazareth," they replied.

"I am he," Jesus said. (And Judas the traitor was standing there with them.) ⁶ When Jesus said, "I am he," they drew back and fell to the ground.

⁷ Again he asked them, "Who is it you want?"

"Jesus of Nazareth," they said.

⁸ Jesus answered, "I told you that I am he. If you are looking for me, then let these men go." ⁹ This happened so that the words he had spoken would be fulfilled: "I have not lost one of those you gave me."

Jesus is completely in control of the situation. He goes to his enemies, rather than them coming to him; Judas has no power to betray him, instead Jesus interrogates them: *"Who is it you want?"* has symbolic meaning because, of course, Christ is what every soul searches for. Jesus' reply of *"I am he"* echoes his earlier **"I Am" statements** and the soldiers are knocked to the ground with religious awe. They are powerless to arrest Jesus unless he allows them to. Jesus refers back to his **I Am the Bread of Life** discourse **(John 6: 39)** when he does not lose any of his followers.

All the Gospels describe a scuffle in which a 'servant of the High Priest' has his ear cut off. **Luke 22: 51** adds the detail that Jesus miraculously heals the man's wound, but the other Gospels do not mention this. John's Gospel identifies **Peter** as the Disciple with the sword:

> [10] Then Simon Peter, who had a sword, drew it and struck the high priest's servant, cutting off his right ear. (The servant's name was Malchus.)

> [11] Jesus commanded Peter, "Put your sword away! Shall I not drink the cup the Father has given me?"

Jesus heals Malchus

Jesus takes control of the situation. He tells Peter to put his sword away and references the symbolism of *"the cup the Father has given me"* which shows that the author of John's Gospel knew about the prayer in Gethsemane but chose not to include it (because he doesn't include details that make Jesus look weak).

The CRITERION OF EMBARRASSMENT suggests that this event is historical because Jesus' followers would not have invented an episode which showed them being violent. However, there is also **symbolism** here: the loss of hearing, like blindness, represents the inability of the High Priest's followers to hear the Word of God.

John's Gospel names the man as '**Malchus**', which is a name meaning 'King' in Hebrew. This is probably symbolic. Later, Jesus will claim that he is a king, but his kingdom is *"not of this world"*. The Kingdom of God cannot be brought about by violence, so the episode where Peter tries to use violence against a 'king' but is stopped by Jesus emphasizes this.

This is one of many passages in John's Gospel where Peter fails to understand Jesus properly – as opposed to the 'Beloved Disciple' who does understand. This probably represents some friction between the Johannine church and the other Christian churches which looked back to Peter as their founder.

__A.N. Wilson__ offers an even more imaginative theory, that "Malchus" is a code name for someone the early Christians knew well but who was controversial. Now __Paul__, who preached to the Gentiles, was named Saul in his earlier life as a servant of the High Priest – and Saul is the name of the first 'King' of Israel. In his epistles (letters), Paul mentions the "thorn in his flesh" and the "mark of Jesus" on his body. Tradition says Paul suffered pain in his head or ear. Was Paul the mysterious 'servant of the High Priest' and code-named 'Malchus' by the Johannine Community?

Christology: Jesus' *"I am he"* statement echoes his **"I Am" statements** that identify Jesus as God as does the awe-struck reaction of the soldiers.

Political Expediency: Arresting Jesus in the night fits with John's Gospel's symbolism of **Light & Dark**, but it also makes political sense. The authorities want to make Jesus 'disappear' and then execute him before Jesus' supporters can mobilize. All the Gospels attest to the struggle with the High Priest's servant and the fact that some of Jesus' followers carried swords. Presumably Jesus has even more armed followers who are not with him this night (they are perhaps in Bethany where Mary and Martha live, only two miles away). This is why **Judas** helps the authorities capture Jesus in a remote place, away from the public eye.

The High Priest Questions Jesus & Peter's Denials

Jesus is taken to by interrogated by **Annas**, a senior priest. The other Gospels describe the Disciples running away in fear (at least one of them naked, according to **Mark 14: 52!**). John does not include undignified details like this. The Disciples simply fade from the story except for two:

> [15] Simon Peter and another disciple were following Jesus. Because this disciple was known to the high priest, he went with Jesus into the high priest's courtyard, [16] but Peter had to wait outside at the door. The other disciple, who was known to the high priest, came back, spoke to the servant girl on duty there and brought Peter in.
>
> [17] "You aren't one of this man's disciples too, are you?" she asked Peter.
>
> He replied, "I am not."

The story of Peter's denial of Christ is attested in all the Gospels. It too passes the CRITERION OF EMBARRASSMENT (why would Christians invent a story that makes their main leader look bad?).

John adds further details. Peter denies Jesus by saying *"I am not"* – a reversal of Jesus' distinctive **"I Am" sayings**.

The 'other disciple' accompanying Jesus into the High Priest's house isn't named, but most scholars believe this to be the 'Beloved Disciple' who is perhaps the author (or at least, the inspiration) of John's Gospel.

> *John seems to get confused about who is questioning Jesus here: is it Annas or Caiaphas? Annas is a **former** High Priest, but Caiaphas is the **current** High Priest.*

Inside Jesus is questioned by Annas (or maybe Caiaphas, it's hard to tell). Jesus responds by asserting his innocence and drawing attention to the illegality of this whole proceeding.

> [20] "I have spoken openly to the world," Jesus replied. "I always taught in synagogues or at the temple, where all the Jews come together. I said nothing in secret. [21] Why question me? Ask those who heard me. Surely they know what I said."
>
> [22] When Jesus said this, one of the officials nearby slapped him in the face. "Is this the way you answer the high priest?" he demanded.

The instruction, *"Ask those who heard me,"* refers to the later followers of Jesus too: the **Johannine Community** who *know what Jesus said*. There is also a reference back to the High Priest's servant with no ear who cannot hear, just as the High Priest cannot hear Jesus either.

The slap is an unusual detail in John's Gospel. The Synoptic Gospels describe Jesus being beaten, spat on and mocked, but John always shows Jesus as dignified and in control. This detail might be a concession by John's Gospel to the widely-known stories of Jesus' sufferings or it might refer to the experiences the Johannine Community later at the hands of the leaders of their Synagogues before they were expelled.

The Synoptic Gospels describe a full trial before the Sanhedrin with witnesses, but John describes only this brief and violent interrogation, very unofficial and 'off-the-record'. Which is correct?

The Gospels can be HARMONISED if this interrogation took place **before** the trial before the Sanhedrin. However, **Ellis Rivkin** (p161) argues that Jesus' trial really was a small, political affair involving just a few influential people, not a formal religious meeting. If Rivkin is right, then John's version is closer to the truth.

> 25 Meanwhile, Simon Peter was still standing there warming himself. So they asked him, "You aren't one of his disciples too, are you?"
>
> He denied it, saying, "I am not."
>
> 26 One of the high priest's servants, a relative of the man whose ear Peter had cut off, challenged him, "Didn't I see you with him in the garden?" 27 Again Peter denied it, and at that moment a rooster began to crow.

This concludes Peter's denial of Christ. John links the final denial to *the man whose ear Peter had cut off*, as if Peter's lack of faith and his resort to violence are connected.

The Synoptic Gospels describe Peter remembering that his denials were predicted by Jesus and breaking down and weeping. **Luke 22: 61** adds the detail that Jesus, being brought out of the High Priest's house, turns and looks at Peter at this moment, driving home Peter's realization that he has betrayed Jesus too.

John's Gospel adds none of these touching details. This Gospel is more interested in the Beloved Disciple than Peter – but in **John 21: 15-17** Peter meets the Resurrected Christ who asks Peter three times if he loves him. This is seen as a rehabilitation of Peter: the Risen Jesus forgives him (and perhaps represents the Johannine Church forming a more positive view of the other Christian churches founded by Peter).

> 28 Then the Jewish leaders took Jesus from Caiaphas to the palace of the Roman governor. By now it was early morning, and to avoid ceremonial uncleanness they did not enter the palace, because they wanted to be able to eat the Passover. 29 So Pilate came out to them and asked, "What charges are you bringing against this man?"
>
> 30 "If he were not a criminal," they replied, "we would not have handed him over to you."

Christology: Jesus' prediction about Peter comes true, showing that Jesus is at the very least a prophet.

Blasphemy: Jesus talks back to the High Priest, showing no respect for the man's religious status.

Threat to Power: Jesus undermines the power of the High Priest by questioning the legality of his trial. As usual, this provokes violence from (or in the case, on behalf of) the people in power who are accustomed to instant and unquestioning obedience.

Political Expediency: The 'trial' before the High Priest is not strictly trial at all: Jesus has not been 'arrested' so much as abducted by the authorities. In the 21st century, when political enemies are kidnapped and taken away to be secretly tortured or killed it is called 'rendition'. It's illegal today and it was illegal back in the 1st century too, though people then didn't have the protection of human rights.

Jesus Before Pilate

John's Gospel enters its most dramatic phase. The Romans have been a sinister force in the background so far, but now we meet their representative: **Pontius Pilate**.

The Jews believe they will become spiritually unclean if they enter a Gentile's house. Since this is this eve of Passover (or the Sabbath, in the Synoptic Gospels), they stay outside Pilate's palace since they don't with to pollute themselves on a holy day. The irony is that they are worrying about *ceremonial uncleanness* while they are trying to kill the Son of God.

The conversation between Christ and Pilate is very different from that involving the High Priest. It reads like a fencing match, with each person attacking and blocking. Jesus talks to Pilate like an equal. As usual with John's Gospel, everything drips with irony.

> 33 Pilate then went back inside the palace, summoned Jesus and asked him, "Are you the king of the Jews?"
>
> 34 "Is that your own idea," Jesus asked, "or did others talk to you about me?"
>
> 35 "Am I a Jew?" Pilate replied. "Your own people and chief priests handed you over to me. What is it you have done?"

Pilate's question goes to the heart of things: is Jesus the true King of the Jews (i.e. the **Messiah**)? Of course, Pilate is thinking only of an earthly king, but his question is deeper than he knows.

Jesus starts interrogating Pilate in return. Pilate's reply sums up his disdain for religious ideas: *"Am I a Jew?"* means 'Why would someone like me care about things like this?'

But of course, in John's Gospel *'Jew'* symbolises 'unbelief', so Pilate's question means: 'Am I an unbeliever?' This is the question the trial is going to answer, for it is Pilate, not Christ, who is really on trial here.

> *It is [Pilate] who is on trial and his judgment will be a verdict on himself as much as it is on Jesus* – **R. Alan Culpepper**

> 36 Jesus said, "My kingdom is not of this world. If it were, my servants would fight to prevent my arrest by the Jewish leaders. But now my kingdom is from another place."
>
> 37 "You are a king, then!" said Pilate.

Jesus declares his identity to Pilate: the king of a spiritual realm of which unbelievers know nothing. Pilate's reply is meant to be sarcastic, but, without meaning to, Pilate has answered his own question: Jesus is indeed a king.

Jesus tells Pilate about the truth of God, but Pilate replies, *"What is truth?"* Pilate represents agnostics and atheists who don't recognise the Truth even when it takes human form and stands in front of them.

Pilate is unwilling to execute Jesus. He seems to find Jesus fascinating. He goes over the heads of the Jewish leaders and appeals to the crowd: they can ask to have Jesus released as part of the 'Passover amnesty' when a prisoner is released. The crowd instead calls for the release of a criminal called **Barabbas**.

Barabbas is mentioned in all the Gospels as the prisoner released instead of Jesus. **Matthew** refers to Barabbas as "*a well-known prisoner*" but **Mark** and **Luke** add the detail that Barabbas had committed murder during an "*uprising*". John's Gospel uses the word *lestes* to describe Barabbas: a rebel. The irony is that, instead of Jesus, Pilate is forced to release a **real** revolutionary who *is* a threat to Roman power.

After that, things acquire a momentum of their own:

19 Then Pilate took Jesus and had him flogged. ²The soldiers twisted together a crown of thorns and put it on his head. They clothed him in a purple robe ³ and went up to him again and again, saying, "Hail, king of the Jews!" And they slapped him in the face.

The Synoptic Gospels go into more detail on Jesus' humiliation and torture but John's Gospel, as usual, preserves Jesus' dignity. The soldiers imagine they are mocking Jesus but really they are dressing him as what he truly is: the King.

Pilate is still trying to wriggle out of executing Jesus. **Matthew 27: 19** claims that Pilate's wife had a dream about Jesus and she begs him to have nothing to do with the trial; John's Gospel suggests that Pilate himself is becoming aware that Jesus is somebody special. Pilate hopes the crowd will be satisfied with seeing Jesus whipped but it only makes them more determined to see Jesus crucified.

Pilate insists Jesus is innocent: "*I find no basis for a charge against him.*"

The issue becomes, is Pilate strong enough to do what is right, in spite of the demands of the mob, or will he cave in to the demand to crucify Jesus, despite knowing him to be innocent?

> *From this point on, the issue is not Jesus' guilt or innocence but whether Pilate will defend Jesus against the Jews* – **R. Alan Culpepper**

> [7] The Jewish leaders insisted, "We have a law, and according to that law he must die, because he claimed to be the Son of God."

The Jewish leaders state their motives outright: Jesus must die because he is a **blasphemer** who claims to be the **Son of God**. This is news to Pilate, who seems to have assumed up till now that Jesus merely broke one of the many senseless (to Roman ways of thinking) Jewish rules. Pilate sees Jesus in a new light: someone who *may be God*. Pilate is now *afraid* of what is taking place.

> [8] When Pilate heard this, he was even more afraid, [9] and he went back inside the palace. "Where do you come from?" he asked Jesus, but Jesus gave him no answer. [10] "Do you refuse to speak to me?" Pilate said. "Don't you realize I have power either to free you or to crucify you?"

> [11] Jesus answered, "You would have no power over me if it were not given to you from above. Therefore the one who handed me over to you is guilty of a greater sin."

Pilate asks "*Where do you come from?*" but Jesus has been answering this question all through John's Gospel – it was answered in **John's Prologue**, which explained that the *Logos* comes from God. Jesus *gave no answer* – because Pilate knows enough to arrive at the answer for himself now. It is cowardice, not lack of explanation, that is holding Pilate back,

Pilate tries to assert his power: as the representative of the Roman Emperor, he has the power of life and death.

Jesus' reply is devastating: Pilate has no power except that which is given to him *from above* – from the Emperor but ultimately from God. Pilate is a puppet, playing his part. Jesus is the true lord of life and death and Jesus, not Pilate, will choose whether to live or die.

Pilate makes a last appeal to the Jewish leaders, but they threaten him that he is *no friend of Caesar* if he doesn't do as they demand. They are right: Caesar (the Emperor) insists that governors like Pilate keep the peace and execute troublemakers. Pilate has no choice.

"Here is your king," Pilate said to the Jews.

15 But they shouted, "Take him away! Take him away! Crucify him!"

"Shall I crucify your king?" Pilate asked.

"We have no king but Caesar," the chief priests answered.

The Jewish priests condemn themselves in their own words. *"We have no king but Caesar"* is a denial of God.

Pilate has run out of options and *hands Jesus over* to be crucified. Roman justice and Pilate's personal integrity have been put to the test and found to be weak.

Christology: Jesus claims to be a spiritual rather than a physical king. This fits in with the Christological views of the other Synoptic Gospels, especially **Luke**'s view of **salvation-history**. However, the higher Johannine Christology is revealed when Jesus reveals himself as *"I am he!"* and knocks the soldiers down with his mere presence.

Blasphemy: The Jewish leaders explicitly state that blasphemy is the reason they want Jesus to be executed: *"he claimed to be the Son of God"*.

Threat to Power: If Jesus claims to be a king, then he is a threat to Roman power (because the Emperor appoints puppet-kings like Herod and doesn't allow anyone else to set themselves up as kings); however, Pilate realises that Jesus is only claiming to be a spiritual king, which he doesn't view as a threat

Political Expediency: Pilate fears two things: that a Jewish mob will riot, possibly leading to a full-scale revolt; and that the Jewish leaders will report him to the Emperor for not dealing firmly with troublemakers, which will lead to him losing his job. Therefore, he is forced to sentence Jesus to death.

Evaluating Jesus' Arrest & Trial

All the Gospels describe Jesus' arrest by the soldiers of the High Priest and the Synoptic Gospels describe a trial before the Sanhedrin on charges of **blasphemy**; all the Gospels then describe the trial before Pilate.

> *John doesn't feature a trial scene in front of the Sanhedrin, but it is implied to have taken place in **John 18: 24** and, in any event, John's Gospel describes a lot of behind-the-scenes plotting by the priests, such as the **Plot to Kill Jesus (John 11: 45-57**, p54).*

John's Gospel emphasizes the illegality of the arrest and interrogation by the High Priest, with Jesus being slapped when he tries to defend himself. This is perhaps why John's Gospel omits the Sanhedrin trial scene: the Gospel-writer wants to present Jesus' arrest as a complete corruption of the legal process.

The **Trial before Pilate** shows Jesus being judged for a *political* crime of INSURRECTION (rebelling against Roman rule). The CRITERION OF EMBARASSMENT applies here: Christians would never have invented the story that their Messiah was executed by the Roman Empire as a rebel. The fact that Jesus had been crucified as a criminal was very well-known. It is reported by the Roman historian **Tacitus** (116 CE), who doesn't know much about 'Christianity' except that:

> *Christus, from whom the name had its origin, suffered the extreme penalty during the reign of Tiberius at the hands of one of our procurators, Pontius Pilatus* – **Tacitus**, *The Annals 15: 44*

The Gospels all face the same task: representing Jesus as being sentenced to death as a political criminal (which was undeniable) but suggesting he was really innocent, that the Roman official *knew* he was innocent and that the whole thing was a miscarriage of justice.

But how accurate is this description of Jesus' trial before Pilate?

a. The trial is HISTORICALLY ACCURATE. The priests wanted Jesus to be executed for **blasphemy** but, since blasphemy against the Jewish God wasn't a crime under Roman law, they had to bully and manipulate the governor into finding Jesus guilty of insurrection instead.

b. The trial is HISTORICALLY DISTORTED. The High Priest and Pontius Pilate were allies who executed Jesus for reasons of **political expediency** but the 1st century Christians misunderstood this. This is **Ellis Rivkin**'s view (p161).

c. The trial is SYMBOLIC. Pontius Pilate symbolises *"the impossibility of compromise"* when it comes to judging the claims of Jesus Christ. This is **R. Alan Culpepper**'s view (p158).

There are problems with viewing the trial as historically accurate. All the Gospels depict Pilate as indecisive and weak and John's Gospel describes him as *"afraid"* when he realises he may be sentencing the **Son of God**. This does not fit the description of Pontius Pilate known from history.

Philo of Alexandria (25 BCE-45 CE) describes Pilate as *"a man of inflexible, stubborn and cruel disposition"* and lists *his violence, his thefts, his assaults, his abusive behavior, his frequent executions of untried prisoners, and his endless savage ferocity* – **Philo of Alexandria**

Philo may be exaggerating, but it's clear that Pilate cared nothing for the Jewish religion or giving offence to Jews. His first act in office was to bring pagan images into Jerusalem, supposedly to show respect to the Emperor, but *"not so much to honour Tiberius as to annoy the crowds"* according to Philo.

This does not seem like a man who would have second thoughts about executing a Jewish prophet accused of causing trouble at Passover. It also doesn't sound like someone who was easily bullied or manipulated.

The idea that the trial scene is distorted is based on **Form Criticism**, because the scenes between Pilate and Jesus are textual units (*pericopae*) created by the 1st century Christians. These episodes are influenced by their own disputes with the Jewish leadership and also their need to present themselves as a respectable religion (*religio licita*) in the Roman Empire.

Redaction Criticism suggests that Jesus was convicted of insurrection by Pilate in a very straightforward way, but that the Gospel-writers have changed the story to make Pilate seem unwilling and the Jewish leaders to be the true instigators of the crucifixion.

*How accurate you think the trial scene is will depend on how persuasive you find **Form** and **Redaction Criticism**. If you think it is likely that 1st century Christians created stories about Jesus to present their religion in a good light to the Roman authorities, then it's probable that the accounts of Jesus' trial are distorted to absolve Pilate of the blame.*

Ellis Rivkin (p161) argues that Pilate and Caiaphas the High Priest had been political allies for years and worked together to keep the peace in Judea. If Caiaphas claimed that someone was a political problem, Pilate would need no further argument to execute him.

For Pontius Pilate, the judgment of his trusted high priest, Caiaphas, would have been enough – **Ellis Rivkin**

Rivkin suggests that Pilate *"was given to provoking Jews with wily strategems"* and that he offered the crowd the choice between freeing Jesus the 'King of the Jews' or the robber Barabbas as a political trap. If the crowd chose Jesus, Pilate would order his soldiers to attack them as rebels who were defying Caesar: the crowd ***had no choice*** but to choose Barabbas. Pilate went through this pantomime for no better reason than to enjoy watching the Jews squirm.

This explanation does fit Pilate's nasty temperament rather better than the Gospels. It also explains the rather baffling 'tradition' of freeing prisoners, which no Roman governor would do unless there was a good reason for it.

Rivkin proposes that Jesus' followers were politically naïve and didn't understand the political reasons for what was happening.

> *Jesus' disciples, who believed him to be the Christ, would attribute religious motives to the high priest and his Sanhedrin, since for the disciples, Jesus was exclusively a religious instrument of God, not a political figure* – **Ellis Rivkin**

This would explain why the Gospels present Jesus as the victim of the Jews' religious hostility rather than Pilate's political brutality.

However, there are arguments against Rivkin's view. Jewish leaders certainly **could** complain to the Emperor about Pilate – and they did. At the start of his term of office, the Emperor responded to complaints by ordering Pilate to be more diplomatic with the Jews. The Jewish historian **Josephus** explains how Pilate lost his job in 37 CE: he massacred a group of Samaritan followers of a holy man, the authorities complained to the Emperor and Pilate was recalled to Rome.

> *Pilate's successor seems to have had a very "hands off" policy towards the Jewish leaders, which might explain why they felt bold enough to execute Christian martyrs like Stephen and James without involving the Romans at all.*

It's possible that Pilate didn't understand the religious situation with Jesus: would executing Jesus trigger an uprising among his loyal followers? or would refusing to crucify Jesus cause the Jewish leaders to complain to the Emperor again? If Pilate was torn between these unpleasant alternatives, then perhaps the Gospels preserve a more accurate account of the trial.

Culpepper (p158) views the character of 'Pilate' in John's Gospel as **symbolic**. He does not represent the historical Prefect of Judea, but stands for people who try to avoid making a commitment regarding Jesus.

> *Although he seems to glimpse the truth, a decision in Jesus' favour proves too costly for him* – **R. Alan Culpepper**

For Christians in the late 1st century, there were definite 'costs' for recognising Jesus as **Son of God**: being expelled from the Synagogues by the Jews, being persecuted by the Romans for refusing to worship the Emperor. **Raymond E. Brown** argues that John's Gospel was written for an audience of *"crypto-Christians"* (Jews who believed in Christ but didn't dare state this openly), in which case Pilate represents **them**: if they don't 'come out' and acknowledge Christ, they are siding with the people who condemned Jesus in the first place:

> *In this manoeuvre to force the reader to a decision regarding Jesus, the evangelist exposes the consequences of attempting to avoid a decision* – **R. Alan Culpepper**

Whatever happened to Pontius Pilate?

Pilate was recalled to Rome a few years after Jesus' trial but, by the time he got there, the Emperor Tiberius had died. Pilate disappears from history after that, but there are a lot of traditions about him.

One early Christian tradition was that Pilate became haunted by guilt over what he did to Jesus and converted to Christianity. Pontius Pilate is considered to be a saint in the Coptic Church in Africa.

There might have been political reasons for this story. The early Church wanted to persuade the Roman Empire that Christianity was not a threat, so it avoided accusing a Roman official of murdering God. Pilate is presented as an unwilling accomplice in Jesus' execution.

This meant that the blame had to be shifted onto the Jews instead. In the 3rd century, **Origen** writes: "*it was not so much Pilate that condemned [Christ] as the Jewish nation*". This strengthened the basis for Christian antisemitism in later history.

Pilate continues to fascinate readers. Is he a hero or a villain or a victim himself?

> *His dilemma – to do the right thing or the popular thing – is every ruler's quandary. Perhaps that is why people can sympathise with him: we too must sometimes face a difficult choice* – **Kevin Butcher**

Did Jesus have to die because of political expediency?

YES	NO
Historical records from Philo and Josephus tell us Pilate was a man who had no hesitation about executing prisoners, whether they were innocent or not. High Priest Caiaphas was Pilate's loyal lieutenant and they worked together to remove suspected troublemakers like Jesus.	The historical records also show that Pilate was afraid of getting into trouble with the Emperor for provoking riots. The Jews had complained about him before and a few years later another complaint cost him his job. The Gospels accurately portray Pilate torn between conflicting duties.
Jesus' naïve followers wouldn't have understood the political calculations Pilate had to make. That's why they distorted the trial story into a religious debate about blasphemy. They also wanted to exonerate the Romans by suggesting Pilate executed Jesus against his better judgment. This enabled them to present Christianity as a religion friendly to Rome.	After Pilate left office, the Jewish leaders used the opportunity to execute a number of Christian martyrs like Stephen and James. This shows that their motivation was religious and only Pilate's strong influence held them back. Josephus and Philo agree on how stubborn Pilate was. He would not have executed a holy man purely to please the Jewish priests.

TOPIC 5.3 CRUCIFIXION & RESURRECTION IN LUKE

All four Gospels describe Jesus' crucifixion and the discovery of his empty tomb. **Mark's Gospel** originally ended there, but chapters were added describing appearances of the Risen Christ to his followers; the other Gospels all describe the Risen Christ's appearances, words and actions.

In **Luke's Gospel**, the description of Jesus' death and Resurrection reinforce the themes in the rest of Luke's Gospel:

- Jesus as supremely patient, compassionate and forgiving
- Jesus offers no violent resistance and extends love to his enemies
- The idea of salvation for all people
- The concept of a delayed Second Coming (*Parousia*), with the Church being formed to spread the Good News about Jesus before the End Times arrive

> *The Crucifixion and Resurrection in Luke's Gospel is found in Anthology extract #7*

What is Crucifixion?

Crucifixion is a method of execution invented in Persia but enthusiastically adopted by the Romans. It was considered a shocking and shameful way to die. The victim was usually nailed (but sometimes tied) to a post – not always in the classic T-shape, sometimes with arms above the head – and left to hang there, completely naked. Death followed within 24 hours and the body would be left exposed to be pecked at by birds and infested by flies.

Since the arms bore most of the victim's weight, it would eventually become too exhausting to breathe – or too painful, because the shoulders became dislocated. Death followed by asphyxiation, but could be speeded up by breaking the victim's legs with a cudgel so that they had to use the strength in their arms to raise themselves enough to breath. Most victims were whipped beforehand and made to carry their crossbeam to the post, further exhausting them.

> *Despite what you see in films, most victims were not nailed through their palms but through their wrists. The palms would not be strong enough to support the weight of the body. However, sometimes the victim was tied by the wrists and nailed through the palms.*

Crucifixion was a striking display of the punishment for resisting Roman rule. **Cicero** calls it *the most cruel and disgusting penalty.* Another Roman writer explains:

> *the most crowded roads are chosen, where most people can see and be moved by this fear* – **Quintillion**

To add to the horror and shame, victims were hung up along busy roads and passing crowds were encouraged to mock and ridicule them as they died.

Roman citizens were not executed this way: crucifixion was reserved for foreigners and outlaws; it was used especially on slaves to so terrify them they wouldn't try to escape or rebel.

Jews (as a foreign race) could be crucified, but the punishment was just as shameful for them. The Old Testament teaches that criminals hanged on trees or posts are cursed by God:

> *you must not leave the body hanging on the pole overnight. Be sure to bury it that same day, because anyone who is hung on a pole is under God's curse* – **Deuteronomy 21: 23**

Jesus' Crucifixion

Jesus was made to carry his own cross-beam to the scene of his execution, a hill outside Jerusalem called *Golgotha* (the 'place of the skull'). In the Synoptic Gospels, a man called **Simon of Cyrene** is pulled from the crowd and forced to carry Jesus' cross the rest of the way. Jesus is stripped and nailed to the cross *at the third hour* (9am), according to **Mark's Gospel**.

All the Gospels describe the guards dividing Jesus' clothes out as loot and Mark, Matthew and John add the detail that Jesus is offered a sponge soaked in vinegar-wine to drink. Another detail shared by all the Gospels is that Jesus is crucified between two other convicts. The Romans always put a sign (*titulum*) on top of the cross identifying a criminal's crime. The sign on Jesus' cross reads: 'King of the Jews'.

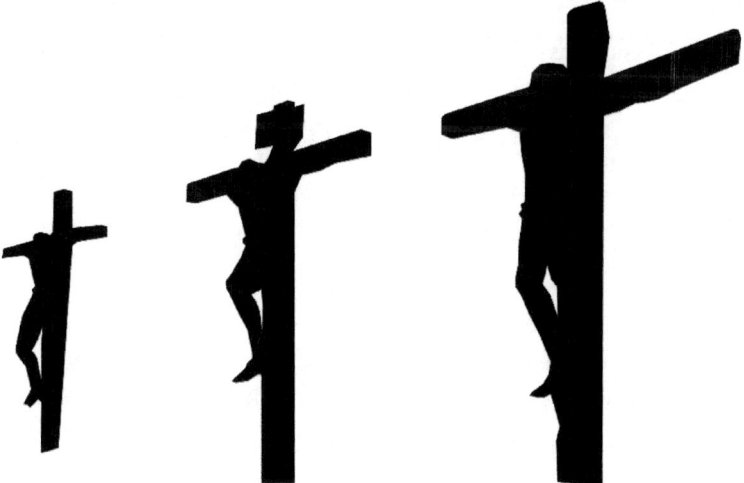

All the Gospels describe a group of Jesus' female followers watching the crucifixion. Luke does not name these women but the others identify **Mary Magdalene** and John's Gospel adds that Jesus' mother and the 'Beloved Disciple' (naturally!) are present.

Jesus suffers on the cross for 6 hours and dies *at the ninth hour* (3pm).

> *Six hours is not a long time to survive on the cross – but remember Jesus had been multiply beaten and whipped beforehand.*

Between them, the Gospels report 7 statements Jesus makes from the cross (the 'Last Words'):

1	Father, forgive them, for they do not know what they are doing.	Luke 23:34
2	[*To the thief*] Truly, I say to you, today you will be with me in paradise.	Luke 23:43
3	[*To his mother*] Woman, here is your son. [*To the Beloved Disciple*] Here is your mother.	John 19:26–27
4	My God, My God, why have you forsaken me?	Matthew 27:46 & Mark 15:34
5	I am thirsty.	John 19:28
6	It is finished.	John 19:30
7	Father, into your hands I commend my spirit.	Luke 23:46

The Synoptic Gospels describe a supernatural darkness covering the world in the last hours of Jesus' life. Matthew mentions an earthquake too but John (for whom **Darkness** is symbolic right back as far as the **Prologue**) leaves out these details. All the Gospels describe one of the soldiers present being struck by Jesus' holiness.

Jesus is taken down from the cross in order to obey the instruction in **Deuteronomy** not to leave a body hanging overnight. A member of the Sanhedrin called **Joseph of Arimathea** appears; he is sympathetic and offers a family tomb to lay Jesus' body in. This is a cave cut into the rock with a big stone that can be rolled over the entrance, sealing it.

The Empty Tomb

After the Sabbath has ended, the women who watched Jesus die travel to the tomb in order to prepare Jesus' body for burial. They arrive first thing in the morning, around sunrise. The Gospels disagree slightly on the identities of the women, but all include **Mary Magdalene** first and foremost.

The women find the tomb empty and the body of Jesus gone. Mark and Luke describe strange men at the empty tomb with shining clothes; Matthew explicitly describes an angel. The women are told that Jesus has risen, just as he predicted.

Mark's Gospel (in its original form) ends with the terrified women running away. Matthew and Luke describe the women returning to the Eleven Disciples (no longer Twelve, now that Judas has gone) but not being believed.

John's Gospel has Mary Magdalene going alone to the tomb and finding it open and empty. There are no angels or strange men there. She runs to the Disciples and says, *"They have taken the Lord out of the tomb, and we don't know where they have put him!"* (**John 20: 2**).

> *John's Gospel is certainly the most realistic of the accounts of the empty tomb, but it contradicts the Synoptics because they claim the women reported Jesus had risen from the dead but John has Mary merely claim that someone has stolen Jesus' body.*

Resurrection Appearances

The Gospels end with a series of Resurrection-appearances by Jesus to different Disciples in different places. Matthew, Mark and John all agree that the women (notably, **Mary Magdalene**) were the first people to meet the Risen Christ, followed by the Eleven Disciples, then other followers in other places. There is considerable disagreement about whether these meetings take place around Jerusalem or back in Galilee, so that HARMONISING these events into a single narrative is difficult.

The Synoptic Gospels describe these meetings coming to an end with an event known as the ASCENSION. Jesus leaves this world and goes to Heaven instead. Matthew locates this on a mountain in Galilee; Luke in Bethany outside Jerusalem; Mark is not specific. According to Luke (in **Acts 1: 3**), the Ascension takes place 40 days after the Resurrection.

> *The Gospels describe Jesus being taken "up" into Heaven, but most Christians don't think of Jesus 'flying away' like Superman. The idea of the Ascension is that Jesus has moved from an earthly type of existence to a heavenly type of existence. However, it must be said that, when Luke describes the Ascension in the **Book of Acts**, Jesus literally does fly into the sky and go through the clouds, leaving the Disciples looking up after him. That is exactly like Superman.*
>
> *This is an example of the 'triple-decker universe' with heaven on top and hell underneath that **Rudolf Bultmann** (p33) argues has to be DE-MYTHOLOGIZED for modern people.*

The Religious Significance of the Crucifixion & Resurrection

For Christians, the Crucifixion and the Resurrection are the heart of Jesus' mission and message: he predicts them throughout his preaching (though the Disciples do not understand him until later) and his death in some way reconciles sinful humans with God.

The Resurrection is not just a matter of Jesus coming back to life the way Lazarus did in the **Sign of Raising Lazarus from the Dead** (*c.f.* **Topic 2**). The Resurrected Christ enjoys a new type of life and a new type of body. He is not a ghost or a spirit being, but the laws of nature no longer seem to apply to him. This is not just intriguing: it is also a promise, because Jesus followers are promised the same sort of resurrected life as well. Jesus' death and Resurrection have changed the nature of life and death for the entire human race.

Liberal Christians focus more on the **symbolism** of Jesus' death and Resurrection: it shows the triumph of love and goodness over evil. For Conservative Christians, the Resurrection is a physical event and the promise of resurrected life for all Christians is to be taken **literally** rather than symbolically.

Atonement: Atonement means making amends for something you did wrong. In a religious sense, it means making up for sin and restoring your relationship with God that was ruined by sin. Judaism had many rituals for removing the effects of sin, such as ceremonial washing and sacrificing animals at the Temple.

Jesus dies an ATONING DEATH because his death on the cross removes the power of sin to separate human beings from God. There are several theories about how this works:

- **Moral Influence theory:** Jesus' perfect life and forgiving death are a powerful inspiration, leading people to live changed lives that are closer to God
- **Ransom theory:** Because of sin, humans are the rightful property of the Devil and Death; Jesus' **sacrifice** pays the 'ransom', freeing humans from the control of evil
- **Satisfaction theory:** Similar to ransom theory, but the debt humans owe is to God, because our sins offend his goodness; only Jesus' perfect suffering and death can satisfy God's demand for reparation
- **Penal Substitution theory:** Similar to satisfaction theory, but humans are under a sentence of death for their sins (the *"wages of sin is death"* in **Romans 6: 23**) and Christ suffers the punishment that ought to be ours (he is our 'substitute')

Forgiveness of Sins: Human beings are sinners in two senses. First and foremost, they think and do evil and selfish things. From God's morally perfect perspective, even faults that don't strike humans as particularly important are still unacceptable and God judges thoughts and motives as well as actions.

However, there is also a sense that human beings are sinners because they are descended from Adam and Eve and would inherit sin even if they did nothing wrong as individuals (this is called ORIGINAL SIN).

Therefore, human beings need to have their sins forgiven and to be forgiven you first have to repent and ***want*** to be forgiven. Repenting every thing you ever did wrong (never mind the stuff you only thought about doing) is psychologically impossible, but Jesus' ATONING DEATH brings about forgiveness of sins on our behalf.

Future of the Church: The first Christians seem to have expected Christ's return (*Parousia*) to be IMMINENT, but **Luke's Gospel** is written for a Christian community that is adapting to a delay before *Parousia* occurs; in fact, Christians might die of old age before *Parousia*. Therefore, Luke interprets Jesus' death and Resurrection in this new context and includes passages specifically aimed at advising Christians how to live and keep their faith strong. The solution is the institution of the 'Church' – a Christian community that extends through time and preserves Jesus' key teachings. This involves Christianity transforming from a fairly loose collection of individuals inspired by their experiences of Christ and the Holy Spirit, into an organisation with a mission and a structure.

Power of God: The Greek word for 'power' is *dynamis*, the word also used in the Synoptic Gospels for 'miracle'. This word is used in **Luke 1: 35** when the Angel tells Mary she will conceive by the Holy Spirit, saying that *"the power of the Most High will overshadow you"*; it is used in **Luke 22: 69** when Jesus tells the Sanhedrin *"the Son of Man will be seated at the right hand of mighty God"* (or *"right hand of the power of God"* in some translations). God's power is explored in Jesus' crucifixion and Resurrection.

- **God's Secret Power:** Luke presents God's power as acting in a *"veiled and secret"* way, according to **I. Howard Marshall** (p159).
- **The Return of Prophecy:** Jews believed the 'Age of Prophecy' ended with the destruction of the original Temple. Luke presents Jesus as a Prophet who introduces a new 'Age of Prophecy' according to **Frank Matera** (p160).
- **Power over Death:** Ever since Adam and Eve, the power of death has ruled over humanity, but in the Resurrection the power of God shows itself to be greater than death itself

Sacrifice: A sacrifice is a gift offered to God as an expression of love and loyalty. Sacrifices involve destroying something you treasure because you value God more. Sacrifices feature prominently in the Old Testament: Cain and Abel make sacrifices to God as does Noah; the laws for making sacrifices to God are revealed to Moses and set out in the Torah; the Temple in Jerusalem is the site for these ongoing sacrifices right up to the 1st century.

However, many reflective Jews wondered about the value of these sacrifices. Why would a perfect God wish to be worshiped through the death of animals? The **Essenes** abandoned animal sacrifices and the **Pharisees** emphasised the personal sacrifice of living in accordance with the Laws of Moses. Christians believe that Jesus' death represents a single perfect sacrifice, rendering all other sacrifices unnecessary.

Salvation: Salvation means being saved from death and/or suffering. It is a key term in Luke's Gospel, featuring more prominently than in the other Gospels. Luke presents God as a Saviour and Jesus is introduced as the Saviour who brings forgiveness of sins in **Luke 1: 77**. Salvation comes about when people repent their sins and believe in Jesus. It is an opportunity open to everyone – Jews and Gentiles – but if the opportunity is missed or rejected, there will be terrible punishment instead (**Luke 19: 44**).

The Crucifixion & Death of Jesus (Luke 23: 26-49)

The soldiers lead Jesus to the place of execution, which is the hill called *Golgotha* ('place of the skull') outside Jerusalem. The place is often called 'Calvary' (from the Latin name for it).

> *This location would now be inside the modern city of Jerusalem. It has not been identified conclusively but a very ancient church, the Holy Sepulchre, is built on the traditional site of the Crucifixion and the empty tomb. However, archaeologists suggest other locations. **Ian Wilson** (p198) considers the location of the Crucifixion in more detail.*

All the Synoptic Gospels describe **Simon of Cyrene** being made to carry the cross for Jesus. Cyrene is in Africa (modern Libya), so Simon was a pilgrim from a long way away. Mark's Gospel identifies him as *the father of Alexander and Rufus* – presumably these were two well-known Christians in Mark's church and their father had been present at the Crucifixion. Luke removes the reference to Rufus and Alexander since, presumably, they weren't known in his church.

The idea of someone carrying Jesus' cross for him is a model for discipleship: good Christians can ease Christ's burden by giving up their own comfort for the sake of others. Jesus explains this earlier in Luke's Gospel:

> *Whoever wants to be my disciple must deny themselves and take up their cross daily and follow me –* **Luke 9: 23**

Simon carries the cross *behind* Jesus – so he is literally following Jesus, like a good disciple should.

Luke includes Jesus prophesying to the 'daughters of Jerusalem', a group of mourning women. His prophecy is APOCALYPTIC, referring to the coming destruction of Jerusalem (or perhaps, the end of the world). The reference to wishing the hills could fall on you to protect you from the impended disaster is a reference to the Old Testament prophecy in **Hosea 10: 8** (*"they will say to the mountains, "Cover us!" and to the hills, "Fall on us!""*):

> *Upon entering the city, [Jesus] wept over it and prophesied its destruction (19: 41-44). Now, as he leaves ... he pronounces his last prophetic word –* **Frank J. Matera**

32 Two other men, both criminals, were also led out with him to be executed. 33 When they came to the place called the Skull, they crucified him there, along with the criminals – one on his right, the other on his left. 34 Jesus said, "Father, forgive them, for they do not know what they are doing." And they divided up his clothes by casting lots.

The two thieves and the dividing up of Jesus' clothes feature in all the Gospels. These details fulfill prophecies in the Old Testament:

> *A pack of villains encircles me; they pierce my hands and my feet -* **Psalm 22: 16**

and

> *They divide my clothes among them and cast lots for my garment –* **Psalm 22: 18**

Mark's Gospel calls the convicts *lestes* (the same word John's Gospel uses for **Barabbas** and implying that they are guilty of insurrection), but Luke changes it to *kakourgos* which just means 'criminal' or 'evil-doer'. Luke is removing the association of Jesus with political revolution against the Roman Empire, so Jesus doesn't die in the company of rebels, just ordinary thieves.

Luke features the first of the 'words from the Cross' when Jesus calls on God to forgive his enemies. Forgiveness of enemies is a theme in all the Gospels but is particularly prominent in Luke's Gospel.

> *Despite being so famous and fitting in so well with Luke's presentation of Jesus as compassionate and forgiving, this saying is missing from some early versions of Luke's Gospel. It's thought Christian scribes might have taken it out because of the leniency it shows towards the Jews! Can you imagine Jesus in **John's Gospel** forgiving the Jews for what they have done?*

Jesus is mocked on the cross by three levels of society: the *rulers* (i.e. the Jewish authorities), the soldiers and then the criminals. They sneer at Jesus because he cannot *save himself*. **Frank Matera** calls this *"the paradox of the cross"* which Jesus has already explained:

> Whoever wants to save their life will lose it, but whoever loses their life for me will save it – **Luke 9: 24**

In their mocking, the crowd uses specific titles: *Christ of God, Chosen One, King of the Jews* and *Christ*.

> Jesus is everything that the rulers, soldiers and criminal mockingly call him. But they do not understand the truth of their own speech since they cannot comprehend the paradox of the cross – **Frank J. Matera**

The sign above the cross is also ironic: *"this is the King of the Jews"* is meant to be a joke but is true on a spiritual level because Jesus shows true kingship by suffering for his people.

> **John's Gospel** makes it clear that Pilate placed the sign there. It reads in full "Jesus of Nazareth, King of the Jews" and is often shortened to its initial letters in Latin: I.N.R.I. for Iesus Nazarenus, Rex Iudaeorum.

The other Synoptic Gospels describe the two criminals mocking Jesus along with the crowd; however, Luke includes a further exchange.

> [39] One of the criminals who hung there hurled insults at him: "Aren't you the Messiah? Save yourself and us!"
>
> [40] But the other criminal rebuked him. "Don't you fear God," he said, "since you are under the same sentence? [41] We are punished justly, for we are getting what our deeds deserve. But this man has done nothing wrong."
>
> [42] Then he said, "Jesus, remember me when you come into your kingdom."
>
> [43] Jesus answered him, "Truly I tell you, today you will be with me in paradise."

The first thief misunderstands the idea of the **Messiah** and **Salvation**: he wants to be rescued from the cross but not from sin. The second thief does understand: he repents his sins and accepts Jesus as Messiah and King. In response, Jesus promises him **Eternal Life**.

> *The second thief is known as the 'Penitent Thief' because he repents. Tradition names him as* ***Dismas*** *and he is considered a saint in the Catholic and Orthodox Churches.*

> [44] It was now about noon, and darkness came over the whole land until three in the afternoon, [45] for the sun stopped shining. And the curtain of the temple was torn in two. [46] Jesus called out with a loud voice, "Father, into your hands I commit my spirit." When he had said this, he breathed his last.

The 'Crucifixion darkness' is mentioned in **Mark's Gospel** but Luke adds a naturalistic detail, suggesting that the *sun stopped shining*. Luke uses the Greek word *eklipontos* (eclipse), which suggests a solar eclipse. However, there's no evidence for a solar eclipse at this date and an eclipse would only last minutes, not hours.

It's possible that Luke is trying to add a rationale to Mark's supernatural account of darkness at noon. Mark may have intended the darkness to be **symbolic** (the universe mourning the death of Jesus), a **fulfillment of Scripture** (darkness was one of the Plagues that God inflicted on Egypt in the story of Moses) or simply a **literary device** (it was common in ancient literature to describe storms, eclipses or earthquakes accompanying the deaths of great men).

> *John's Gospel does not mention this darkness, despite loving the symbolism of light and darkness all the way through. Perhaps John thought literal darkness during the Crucifixion was a bit over-the-top? Or maybe it's because* ***John's Prologue (John 1: 5)*** *says the Darkness never overcomes the Light.*

All of the Synoptic Gospels describe the tearing of the *veil* or *curtain* in the Temple. This was the barrier that concealed the innermost room of the Temple – the Holy of Holies – where the Ark of the Covenant used to be kept and God was supposed to be present. Only the High Priest could enter this room and only once a year, on the Jewish Day of Atonement (*Yom Kippur*), to sprinkle the blood of sacrificed animals to atone for the sins of the Jewish people.

- The torn veil represents the breaking of the barrier between God and mankind because Jesus' death has reconciled humanity with God
- It also represents Gentiles now having access to God
- It represents the destruction of the Jewish Temple (which is demolished by the Romans in 70 CE) and, more generally, the end of the Jewish religion and its replacement by Christianity
- It represents Jesus as the true 'Holy of Holies' where God is present in the world: Jesus is both the High Priest and the sacrifice and this is the true 'Day of Atonement'

The Roman centurion is the first person to acknowledge Jesus after his death – and he is a Gentile! He calls Jesus *"a righteous man"* but the word Luke uses is *dikaios* which means 'innocent' or 'blameless' and refers to the entire character of Jesus' life, not just to his unjust death. The crowd is also deeply affected by this. Formerly they *stood watching* while Jesus was mocked but now they *beat their breasts* as they walk away. This gesture was used by people repenting their sins. It shows that Jesus' death has already started to bring salvation to people.

Atonement: Luke's Gospel proposes the Moral Influence theory of atonement. Jesus dies a moral death, forgiving his enemies and offering **Eternal Life** to his fellow-sufferers. He is a role model for later Christians to follow when they face persecution for their beliefs. His death powerfully influences the Centurion and the crowd, moving them to admire Jesus and repent. However, he is also a willing sacrificial victim (as indicated by the tearing of the Temple veil and offering up his spirit to God), so there is a link to the ransom, satisfaction and penal substitution theories too.

Forgiveness of Sins: Jesus prays to God to forgive his enemies and this symbolises a wider forgiveness of all human sins. The link to the Temple veil connects Jesus to the sacrifice in the Temple that is supposed to remove sins.

Future of the Church: Simon of Cyrene seems to have become a convert to Christianity (his sons are mentioned in **Mark's Gospel**), so his involvement symbolises the way Christianity spreads through compassion for Jesus' suffering. This idea of Christianity spreading is also shown in the behaviour of the Penitent Thief, the Centurion and the crowd who are also moved by admiration for Jesus' innocent suffering and moral goodness.

Power of God: God's power is shown in what **Marshall** calls a *"veiled and secret"* manifestation. Even on the cross, Jesus transforms lives, triggers repentance and expands God's Kingdom by drawing more and more people into relationships of compassion and love. In the crucified Jesus, God's power is most clearly shown (though the mockers do not recognise it, but the Centurion and the Penitent Thief and later the crowd see the truth). God's power is also revealed through prophecy. Jesus has predicted everything that happens (e.g. **Luke 9: 22**) so, although he *seems* powerless, everything that occurs is going according to God's plan. However, in his apocalyptic prophecy to the 'daughters of Jerusalem', Jesus describes God acting in strength (unveiled, no longer secret) on the future Day of Judgment.

Sacrifice: Jesus is a perfect sacrifice on the cross (which is important for the ransom and satisfaction theories of **atonement**). His death renders the Temple sacrifices redundant, which is why the Temple veil is torn. The idea of disciples imitating Jesus' sacrifice is shown in Simon of Cyrene carrying Jesus' cross.

Salvation: The main character being saved in this passage is the Penitent Thief and he represents all humans in need of salvation. His salvation is triggered by compassion for Jesus' suffering; he feels guilt for his own sins, leading to confession and repentance. The final step is faith in Christ. Despite the emphasis on baptism in Christianity, the Thief is promised **Eternal Life** purely because he has repented and trusted in Jesus. Other characters are shown at different stages along this journey to salvation: the Centurion has compassion for Christ but does not repent, the crowd has begun to repent but does not yet have faith in Christ.

Evaluating the Crucifixion in Luke

All the Gospels describe Jesus' crucifixion in broadly similar ways. **Source Criticism** claims that Luke has taken the basic text from **Mark's Gospel** but altered it in several ways:

- Luke has **removed** material from Mark; e.g. before Jesus dies he cries out in despair: "*My God, why have you forsaken me?*" (**Mark 15: 34**); but Luke omits this
- Luke **changed the order** of material in Mark; e.g. in **Mark 15: 38** the veil of the Temple is torn *after* Jesus dies but in Luke this happens *before* Jesus dies
- Luke has **added** new material that wasn't in Mark; e.g. the 'daughters of Jerusalem', the prayer for God to forgive Jesus' enemies, the Penitent Thief, the darkness being an eclipse, the crowds repenting and beating their breasts

Redaction Criticism argues that these alterations reveal Luke's theological agenda and social setting.

- Luke removes the cry of despair, because he wants to present Jesus as a perfect martyr who suffers without complaining. Some scholars think Luke wants to present Jesus as an ideal Greco-Roman philosopher who practices *apatheia* (a tranquil mind without passion – similar to the calm way that Stoic and Cynic philosophers faced suffering).
- Luke moves the tearing of the Temple veil to before Jesus' death, because he thinks it is Jesus' perfect moral LIFE that leads people to God rather than his DEATH (moral influence theory of **atonement**).
- Luke adds material to emphasise how Jesus inspires people to repent and also tones down some of the supernatural material by adding naturalistic explanations.

But how accurate is Luke's description of the Crucifixion?

a. Luke's Crucifixion is HISTORICALLY ACCURATE. Luke's material can be HARMONISED with material from Mark (such as Jesus crying out in despair *and then* calmly commending his spirit to God his Father). The other changes could come from Luke's own research (as explained to Theophilus in Luke's Prologue, **Luke 1: 1-4**), which might improve on Mark's accuracy. This is **I. Howard Marshall**'s view.

According to his own testimony, Luke wished to be taken seriously as a historian – **I. Howard Marshall**

b. Luke's Crucifixion is HISTORICALLY DISTORTED. Luke is a creative writer who freely adds to or alters his material to convey his theological beliefs about Jesus but is not really a 'historian' and isn't interested in preserving a record of what actually happened. There is a historical core but it may be hard to identify it. This is **Frank J. Matera**'s view.

By calling Luke creative, I mean that he edits and arranges his traditions in a manner which expresses his theological convictions – **Frank J. Matera**

There are problems with viewing the Crucifixion as historically accurate. Luke has clearly idealized Jesus' sufferings on the cross. **Albert Schweitzer** (p162), who argues that Jesus was an apocalyptic preacher who died a disappointed man, thinks that the cry of despair recorded in Mark and Matthew is authentic. By removing it, Luke is substituting the **myth** of Christ who died an atoning death for the historical Jesus who was a *"failed messiah."* In support of this, there are other instances where Luke removes or downplays the apocalyptic content of Jesus' teachings. For example, Jesus' words to the Penitent Thief suggest that the **Kingdom of God** (p75) takes place in the afterlife, not on Earth.

On the other hand, Luke still preserves apocalyptic material and even adds new material (such as the prophecy to the 'daughters of Jerusalem'). Luke alters the Centurion's words from *"Surely this man was the son of God"* in Mark and Matthew to *"Surely this was a righteous man"*, which is a much more plausible comment from a pagan onlooker. Luke presents a more NATURALISTIC scene, ignoring **Matthew 27: 51-53** where there is an earthquake and dead people all over Jerusalem come back to life and suggesting that the darkness at noon is an eclipse. This helps us *take Luke seriously as a historian.*

Does Luke's Gospel describe the Crucifixion accurately?

YES	NO
Luke starts his Gospel by *investigating everything from the beginning* to write *an orderly account.* He writes like a historian, removing implausible supernatural details and offering psychologically believable responses for characters like the Centurion.	Luke is a theologian not a historian. He strips away the historical details of Jesus' apocalyptic beliefs and replaces them with a philosophical Jesus who believes in a Heaven in the afterlife instead of on Earth. He shows Jesus dying an atoning death not a despairing one.
Luke preserves Jesus' apocalyptic teachings and even presents new ones that weren't in Mark. His eschatological beliefs are complex (the Kingdom is on Earth **and** fulfilled in the afterlife). These complex beliefs are present in Mark too. There is a shift in emphasis in Luke but not a complete rewrite of Jesus' teachings.	Matthew and Mark have Jesus asking God *"why have you forsaken me?"* Schweitzer has a good argument that these are the authentic words of a man dying in despair. As the Christian faith developed in the 1st century, these words became an embarrassment and Luke removes them from his narrative.

Burial of Jesus & Jesus Has Risen (Luke 23: 50 – 24: 12)

Joseph of Arimathea is introduced as a good man (*dikaios* – the same word the Centurion used for Jesus). Despite being a member of the Sanhedrin, he *had not consented* to the judgment against Jesus. Luke acknowledges that not **all** the Jewish leaders plotted against Jesus.

> *Can you imagine John's Gospel acknowledging something like this? In John, Joseph of Arimathea is described as "a disciple of Jesus, but secretly for fear of the Jews"*

As well as encouraging tolerance towards Jews, Joseph of Arimathea is here to be a credible witness to Jesus' burial: he is not one of Jesus' loyal followers or a Gentile but a respectable Jew who keeps the **Law** and is a member of the Sanhedrin.

Jesus is taken down from the cross to avoid the shame of being left "*hanging on the pole overnight*" (**Deuteronomy 21: 23**). This has to be done quickly because it is Friday and the Sabbath starts at sunset and no work can be done on the Sabbath. Joseph provides a rock tomb in a garden nearby. **Matthew's Gospel** claims Joseph had built the tomb to be his own resting place. It is a new tomb and unused. This means Jesus is receiving a royal burial (royalty were buried in fresh tombs, but common people would share a family tomb when they died).

There are rituals that must be performed on a dead body, traditionally by women. Jesus' female followers are introduced and named: **Mary Magdalene**, another Mary, Joanna and others. These women intend to anoint Jesus' body with spices and ointments, but first they have to rest on the Sabbath. Luke makes it clear that Jesus' death, just like his life, is entirely in keeping with the **Law**.

> *Again, you can't imagine John's Gospel being so delicate about sticking to the Sabbath regulations. In John's Gospel, Joseph of Arimathea and Nicodemus anoint the body there and then "in accordance with Jewish burial customs". There's no reference to keeping to the Jewish Law.*

The Sabbath lasts from Friday evening to Saturday evening, so the women have no opportunity to visit the tomb again until Sunday morning (Sunday was the *first day of the week* in Jewish culture).

24 On the first day of the week, very early in the morning, the women took the spices they had prepared and went to the tomb.[2] They found the stone rolled away from the tomb, [3] but when they entered, they did not find the body of the Lord Jesus. [4] While they were wondering about this, suddenly two men in clothes that gleamed like lightning stood beside them. [5] In their fright the women bowed down with their faces to the ground, but the men said to them, "Why do you look for the living among the dead? [6] He is not here; he has risen! Remember how he told you, while he was still with you in Galilee: [7] 'The Son of Man must be delivered over to the hands of sinners, be crucified and on the third day be raised again.' " [8] Then they remembered his words.

The women find the heavy stone rolled away and the tomb empty. Mark's Gospel describes just one young man waiting in the tomb *dressed in a white robe*. Luke describes two men and makes their appearance more obviously supernatural. Matthew goes all the way, describing an angel that rolls the stone away and knocks a squad of Roman guards unconscious.

> *John has a simpler version. Mary Magdalene goes alone to the tomb (no reason is given why, since Jesus' body has already been anointed), finds the tomb open and empty and concludes someone has stolen Jesus' body. There are no mysterious men or angels,*

Later on, in the **Road to Emmaus** (p87), this story will be re-told and the appearance of the two men will be described as *"a vision of angels"*.

Luke makes another important change to the version in Mark's Gospel. In **Mark 16: 7**, the mysterious man (or angel) tells the women that the Risen Jesus will meet them back in Galilee. Luke edits this to say that Jesus had predicted his resurrection **while he was back in Galilee**. The rest of Luke's story, with its Resurrection appearances, takes place in and around Jerusalem, whereas Matthew's story takes place back in Galilee.

> *Christians usually HARMONISE these accounts, saying the Risen Jesus appeared in Jerusalem, then later in Galilee.*

The women visit the Eleven Disciples and tell their story, but are not believed. Peter runs to the tomb and investigates the discarded grave wrappings, then leaves *wondering to himself what had happened*.

> *John's Gospel has Peter and the 'Beloved Disciple' race to the tomb. Needless to say, the Beloved Disciple gets there first. Peter is baffled by the empty linen but the Beloved Disciple instantly understands what has happened and "believes". This seems to be simple one-upmanship, with the Johannine Community presenting **their** founder as better than Peter.*

It's important that the mere appearance of the empty tomb doesn't trigger belief in the Resurrection. What is needed is the combination of this evidence with the correct interpretation of Scripture:

> *Of itself, the empty tomb does not bring the women or Peter to faith. But when the two men (angels) remind the women of Jesus' words, the remembrance of his words brings the women to faith* – **Frank J. Matera**

The fact that women are the first witnesses to the empty tomb passes the CRITERION OF EMBARRASSMENT, because women were not considered reliable witnesses in 1st century society.

If the Gospel-writers had wanted to invent a story, they would describe Peter (or the Beloved Disciple) visiting the tomb and finding it empty. But it seems that the testimony of the women was too well known in the early church to be altered.

In **Matthew 28: 9-10**, the women meet the Risen Jesus while on their way to tell the news to the Disciples. **John 20: 11-18** (a very touching scene!) also describes Mary Magdalene as the first person to meet the Risen Jesus and **Mark 16: 9-11** confirms Mary Magdalene as the first witness to the Resurrection (but she was not believed by the men).

> *It is interesting to speculate that women were the original Christians: the first believers in the Resurrection.* **Paul** *names a lot of women church leaders in his epistles (letters) written in the 50s CE.*

By the end of the 1st century CE, churches were largely run by men. Were the women erased from the story, to give more credit to the male disciples in starting the Christian religion? If so, this process begins with Luke's Gospel.

> *In Luke, you can detect the women being "photoshopped" out of the story, because there are no references to the women meeting the Risen Jesus.*

However, in other ways women feature strongly in Luke's Gospel, with Jesus' mother Mary, her sister Elizabeth, a prophetess called Anna and the sisters Mary and Martha (who also feature in John's Gospel) all having prominent roles. In the **Book of Acts** (also by Luke), female Christian converts like Lydia also have major roles. Perhaps Luke only removes the women encountering the Risen Jesus because their testimony would be less convincing to a 1st century audience.

Future of the Church: Whatever the original role of the women in starting Christianity, Luke focuses on the male Disciples, notably Peter, who visits the tomb himself like a detective at a crime scene. Later, there will be a reference to Peter meeting the Risen Jesus and Paul mentions this tradition in **1 Corinthians 15: 3-8**. Luke also wrote the **Book of Acts**, which describes the efforts made by Peter and later Paul to spread the Christian faith and create Christian churches.

Power of God: The Resurrection is the most dramatic proof of God's power to defeat death. However, at this point, God's power is still *"veiled and secret"* because no one yet understands what is happening. This is a metaphor for the **Kingdom of God** generally. Jesus describes the Kingdom of God being *in your midst* but most people do not see it. Only at the final stage, when God acts in strength on Judgement Day, will the Kingdom be obvious to everyone. Until then it is a secret known only to as few. The Resurrection works in the same way: it is a secret that small numbers of people are let in on and share.

Salvation: The Resurrection of Jesus is the promise of salvation for everyone, because those who are saved by their faith in Jesus will be resurrected like him. **Frank J. Matera** (p160) calls the Resurrection of Jesus *"a new creation animated and empowered by God's Spirit"* – not just one person being raised from the dead but the first stage in God's project to create the entire universe all over again, one person at a time. Salvation is more than just rescuing people from sin and suffering: it is the beginning of a new world that can only be entered by first dying.

On the Road to Emmaus (Luke 24: 13-35)

This episode occurs only in Luke's Gospel and takes place on the same day (Sunday). Two of Jesus' disciples are walking the road from Jerusalem to a town called Emmaus.

In the other Gospels, 'disciple' tends to mean one of the Twelve. However, Luke uses the word 'disciple' much more broadly to include *any* follower of Jesus, including the reader. These disciples are not members of the Twelve (or Eleven, as they are now since Judas betrayed them). One of them is named Cleopas and the other is unnamed.

- **John 19: 25** names one of the women at the Cross as *"Mary the wife of Clopas"*. Is Clopas the same person as Cleopas? In which case, is the unnamed disciple his wife, Mary?
- Alternatively, 'Cleopas' is Greek for 'Proclaimer'. The character may be **symbolic** in which case the reader is supposed to put themselves in the place of the unnamed disciple and imagine themselves in the story.

The two disciples are discussing the events of the last week. The Risen Jesus approaches them, appearing to be another traveller. They are *kept from recognising him*. Jesus asks them what they are talking about and they explain:

> "About Jesus of Nazareth," they replied. "He was a prophet, powerful in word and deed before God and all the people. [20] The chief priests and our rulers handed him over to be sentenced to death, and they crucified him; [21] but we had hoped that he was the one who was going to redeem Israel. And what is more, it is the third day since all this took place. [22] In addition, some of our women amazed us. They went to the tomb early this morning[23] but didn't find his body. They came and told us that they had seen a vision of angels, who said he was alive. [24] Then some of our companions went to the tomb and found it just as the women had said, but they did not see Jesus."

> *The story of the empty tomb is re-told here; the mysterious men are confirmed to be angels but the disciples describe what the women experienced as "a vision of angels". A vision, rather than actual angels. Is this Luke toning down the supernatural and eschatological material he has inherited from* **Mark**? *Or is it another example of diminishing the importance of the female witnesses to the Resurrection?*

Notice that these disciples have a faulty understanding of Jesus. They think of him as a *mighty prophet* and they hoped that he would *redeem Israel*. In other words, they saw Jesus as purely a Jewish prophet and thought he offered a political solution to the **Roman occupation**.

> *Still thinking in terms of national liberation, they have not yet realised that this Messiah redeems Israel and the nations from the rule of Satan and the burden of sins* **– Frank Matera**

The Risen Jesus tells them that they have misunderstood things. He explains the true meaning of the **Messiah**, arguing from *Moses* (i.e. the Torah followed by the **Sadducees**) and the *Prophets* (i.e. the Oral Law of the **Pharisees**). Luke calls this *opening the Scriptures* which had previously been closed by misunderstanding.

When they arrive at Emmaus, the disciples beg this stranger to stay and dine with them.

> 30 When he was at the table with them, he took bread, gave thanks, broke it and began to give it to them. 31 Then their eyes were opened and they recognized him, and he disappeared from their sight. 32 They asked each other, "Were not our hearts burning within us while he talked with us on the road and opened the Scriptures to us?"

Their *eyes were opened* at the moment Jesus *took bread, gave thanks, broke it* – this is the formula for the **EUCHARIST**, the central act of Christian worship that Jesus modeled at the **Last Supper (Luke 22: 19-23)** and in the **Feeding of the 5000 (Luke 9: 16,** *c.f.* **Topic 2).**

The two disciples have been on a spiritual journey as much as a physical one. They started off *downcast* and confused about the meaning of Jesus' teachings and the empty tomb. They did not understand the true meaning of the Jewish scriptures or the Messiah. By the end of the journey, they have been educated intellectually but they still do not recognise Jesus. However, they show kindness and hospitality to a stranger, so the teachings have touched their hearts as well as their intellects.

They recognise Jesus when they share the meal. Psychologically, this might be because his characteristic gesture of breaking bread was so recognisable no disguise could conceal Jesus' identity. Mystically, it refers to Christ's continued presence in the bread and wine of the Eucharist that believers share.

If this passage is an **allegory** (p19) for encountering Christ in the Eucharist, it's not a historical account of a Resurrection experience. **Form Critics** would call it a *PERICOPE* (textual unit) reflecting the beliefs and rituals of Christians later in the 1st century CE

The disciples' response to this new-found faith is that they want to share it. They return to Jerusalem, the place they had been escaping from, and join the Christian community there. Like Cleopas, they become 'proclaimers' who bear witness to the Resurrection.

> 33 They got up and returned at once to Jerusalem. There they found the Eleven and those with them, assembled together 34 and saying, "It is true! The Lord has risen and has appeared to Simon." 35 Then the two told what had happened on the way, and how Jesus was recognized by them when he broke the bread.

Notice that the passage refers to Jesus appearing to Simon Peter. We last saw Peter wandering away from the tomb and *wondering*. The tradition that Peter was the first of the Disciples to meet the Risen Jesus is recorded in by **Paul** who refers to Peter by his Greek name *Cephas*:

> *He was raised on the third day according to the Scriptures, and that He appeared to Cephas [Peter] and then to the Twelve* **– 1 Corinthians 15: 5**

> *It's odd that Luke doesn't describe Simon Peter's solo meeting with the Risen Jesus (in fact, none of the Gospels do). Yet Peter clearly had that reputation and was looked to as the authority on Jesus' Resurrection by later Christians (except of course by the **Johannine Community**, who looked to their 'Beloved Disciple').*

Future of the Church: The Emmaus passage is an extended metaphor for the future development of the Church, growing from scattered and fleeing former-disciples who acquire a new hope and sense of purpose because of the Resurrection. They boldly reinterpret the Jewish Scriptures in new ways, celebrate their faith with the Eucharist where they continue to experience Christ's presence and go back to the Synagogues of the Jewish community, preaching Jesus Christ as a suffering Messiah who rose from the dead.

Power of God: This passage again shows the *"veiled and secret"* power of God that is only revealed in love, generosity and sharing. Even the Scriptures are *veiled and secret* and need to be *opened* by inspired interpretation. God's power is the power of INSPIRATION: the disciples feel their *hearts burning* as the truth about Jesus dawns on them and the meaning of the Scriptures becomes clear.

> *This is similar to the concept of being 'Born Again' that is so important in **John's Gospel**. In fact, the rich symbolism of the **Road to Emmaus** would fit very well in John's Gospel too.*

Sacrifice: Luke doesn't specify which passages Jesus used to *open the Scriptures* to the two disciples. However, it seems likely that **Isaiah**'s **Suffering Servant** (*c.f.* **Topic** 1) would have featured along with the passages from the Psalms that were fulfilled at the Crucifixion (especially **Psalm 22**). Jesus corrects their expectation that the Messiah would be a **Kingly Messiah** who conquers through force and introduces them to a **Suffering Messiah** who is victorious through sacrificing himself.

The Risen Jesus perhaps also interprets the festivals and sacrifices at the Temple as referring to his own perfect sacrifice of himself to God (the way John's Gospel interprets festivals as applying to Jesus).

Salvation: The passage is a metaphor for salvation as well. Although the two disciples followed Jesus, they weren't part of the Kingdom of God. They only enter the Kingdom when they understand Jesus properly, share his presence in the Eucharist and join other believers to form the Church. When Jesus *opens the Scriptures*, he introduces them to salvation-history: the idea that God's salvation is a long-term plan over the centuries, building up to Jesus' ministry, death and Resurrection, but then continuing into the future as the Christians go out to spread the word about the Resurrection.

Jesus Appears to the Disciples & the Ascension (Luke 24: 36-53)

Finally, there is a direct and literal appearance of the Risen Christ. He says *"Peace be with you"* (a phrase also used by the Risen Jesus in **John's Gospel**).

> *Shalom aleikhem* ("peace be upon you") is the tradition Hebrew greeting used by Jews all over the world. The traditional reply is *aleikhem shalom* ("unto you, peace").

Despite the Resurrection encounters so far, the Disciples still think they are seeing a ghost.

> [37] They were startled and frightened, thinking they saw a ghost. [38] He said to them, "Why are you troubled, and why do doubts rise in your minds? [39] Look at my hands and my feet. It is myself! Touch me and see; a ghost does not have flesh and bones, as you see I have."
>
> [40] When he had said this, he showed them his hands and feet. [41] And while they still did not believe it because of joy and amazement, he asked them, "Do you have anything here to eat?" [42] They gave him a piece of broiled fish, [43] and he took it and ate it in their presence.

Jesus demonstrates that he has risen to full, physical life: he is not a disembodied spirit. He invites them to touch him and proves his physicality by eating some fish. **John 20: 24-29** has a similar passage, but includes the detail of 'Doubting' Thomas being absent and, on returning, claiming that only by touching the nail wounds in Jesus' hands will he believe. Jesus then reappears and shows Thomas his wounds.

This passage clashes with the mystical and spiritual appearance of Jesus in the **Road to Emmaus** (p149). It's possible that Luke inserted it deliberately to counter a belief in some 1st century Christians that Jesus had been raised from the dead only as a spirit or only in some metaphorical sense.

Jesus then treats the Eleven Disciples in the same way he taught the disciples in Emmaus: he *opens their minds* so that they can understand how the Jewish Scriptures predict him. This can be summed up like this:

> "This is what is written: The Messiah will suffer and rise from the dead on the third day, [47] and repentance for the forgiveness of sins will be preached in his name to all nations, beginning at Jerusalem. [48] You are witnesses of these things.

In fact, this passage works as a simple summary of the entirety of Luke's Gospel!

Jesus instructs them to remain in Jerusalem until he sends them *"what my Father has promised"* and they are *"clothed with power from on high"*. **John's Gospel** calls this the *Paraclete* ('Helper' or 'Advocate') and Christians term it the HOLY SPIRIT.

> *At the time that Luke is writing, Christians haven't worked out the details of the Trinity or consistent terms for things, which is why Luke uses different phrases like "clothed with power" to describe the Holy Spirit.*

Luke goes on to write the **Book of Acts** about how the Disciples (now Apostles) spread the Christian faith. **Acts 2: 1-4** describes the arrival of the Holy Spirit at the Festival of Pentecost, causing the Apostles heads to burn like fire and empowering them to speak in tongues that can be miraculously understand by all listeners. Christians today regard Pentecost as the true 'birthday' of the Church.

Luke's Gospel ends with a description of Jesus' ASCENSION.

> [50] When he had led them out to the vicinity of Bethany, he lifted up his hands and blessed them. [51] While he was blessing them, he left them and was taken up into heaven. [52] Then they worshiped him and returned to Jerusalem with great joy. [53] And they stayed continually at the temple, praising God.

Luke describes this event again in **Acts 1: 9-11**, adding the detail that Jesus was with them for forty days before ascending.

'Forty days' might be a symbolic number because '40' is often used in the Bible to represent a period of trial or revelation:

- Noah was in the ark for forty days
- Moses spent forty days on Mount Sinai receiving the **Law** from God.

In the same way, the disciples are with Jesus for forty days while God is starting a *"new creation"* and *opening their minds* to a new interpretation of the Law of Moses.

Rudolf Bultmann (p33) argues that the story of the Ascension is rooted in the mythological 'triple-decker' view of the universe (with heaven above the clouds and hell below the ground) that is completely unacceptable to modern minds.

However, **C.S. Lewis** argues *"there is no possibility of isolating the doctrine of the Resurrection from that of the Ascension"* because *"a phantom can just fade away; but an objective entity must go somewhere –something must happen to it"*. Lewis argues that the Risen Jesus left our reality for a new mode of existing but that this is inexplicable in normal language: Luke describes it as best he can with mythological pictures of Jesus rising into the air, but it's the idea **behind** this picture that matters. Something supernatural occurred when the Risen Jesus ascended, but exactly what it was cannot be explained.

> *Notice that Luke ends his Gospel with Jesus' followers worshiping at the Temple. You can't imagine John ending his Gospel like that! This goes to show that Luke does not see Christianity as incompatible with Judaism the way that John does.*

Atonement: The ransom, satisfaction and penal substitution theories of atonement are all based on a 'Christological' interpretation of the Scriptures – the idea that the Old Testament is *really* all about Christ. For example, the sin of Adam and Eve unleashes death upon the world and all their descendants live under Original Sin. This is why humans need to be **ransomed** from the Devil, or why God's demand for justice needs to be **satisfied**, or why individuals deserve to be punished but Jesus can take their place as a **substitute**. These ideas of atonement could be what Jesus explained when he *opened the Scriptures* and *opened the disciples' minds*.

Forgiveness of Sins: The Risen Jesus claims that *"repentance and the forgiveness of sins"* are the key messages of the Scriptures and the point of his suffering and Resurrection. Luke seems to suppose that forgiveness of sins is offered as soon as people sincerely repent and that Jesus' suffering, death and Resurrection trigger people's awareness of guilt and desire to repent (**moral influence** theory of atonement).

Future of the Church: The **Road to Emmaus** (p149) episode works as an **allegory** (p19) for the formation of the Church. The disciples leave behind a Jewish understanding of the Messiah once Jesus *opens the Scriptures* and they encounter the Resurrected Christ by sharing the Eucharist of bread (and, presumably, wine). Later, Jesus promises the Holy Spirit will come to guide and empower Christians (he calls this being *"clothed with power from on high"*). The arrival of the Holy Spirit at Pentecost is described by Luke in **Acts 2: 1-4** and is the 'birthday' of the Church.

Power of God: The *"veiled and secret"* power of God gives way to the power of God in strength. At first, God's power is still secretive: the body of Jesus vanishes, the Risen Jesus is disguised and, once recognised, disappears. However, when the Risen Jesus appears to all the Disciples, God's power is revealed to everyone. When the Ascension happens, the power of language to describe the event is inadequate to convey the power of God. God's power becomes *"veiled and secret"* again as Jesus withdraws from sight and the Holy Spirit comes to guide the Church until his return at *Parousia*. When Christ returns on Judgment Day, God's power will no longer be secret but revealed to everyone.

> *By raising Jesus from the dead, God asserted his power in a definitive way over every malevolent power, whether on earth or in heaven* **– Frank J. Matera**

Salvation: Salvation is linked to the message of *"forgiveness of sins … preached in [Jesus'] name to all nations, beginning at Jerusalem"*. This sums up the idea of salvation-history, with the Ascension starting a new phase in history. The Church will start its message of salvation in Jerusalem – this is referring to a geographical starting point but also symbolizes the message being preached to Jewish audiences. Later, the message of salvation will be preached to *all nations* i.e. to the Gentiles.

Evaluating the Resurrection in Luke

All the Gospels describe the empty tomb in broadly similar ways. **Source Criticism** claims that Luke has taken the basic text from **Mark's Gospel** but altered it in several ways:

- Luke has **removed** material from Mark; e.g. the young man (or angel) in the tomb tells the Disciples that they will meet the Risen Jesus in Galilee; the women meeting the Risen Christ himself
- Luke **changed the order** of material in Mark; e.g. in Mark and Matthew, **Mary Magdalene** is the first to meet the Risen Christ, followed by the Eleven Disciples
- Luke has **added** new material that wasn't in Mark; e.g. two angels rather than one, the encounter **on the road to Emmaus**, touching Jesus' hands and feet, the Risen Jesus eating fish

Redaction Criticism argues that these alterations reveal Luke's theological agenda and social setting.

- Luke removes the instruction to go to Galilee because he will describe in the **Book of Acts** how the Christian movement spread out from Jerusalem. He perhaps removes the women's encounter because female testimony was not persuasive in the 1st century and Luke wants to provide more convincing evidence.
- Luke refers to (but doesn't describe) **Simon Peter** being the first to meet the Risen Jesus, because Peter is the hero of the early Christian movement that Luke goes on to describe in the **Book of Acts**.
- Luke adds material to emphasise his belief that the Resurrection can only be understood through (i) the correct 'Christological' interpretation of Scripture and (ii) the celebration of the Eucharist as part of a community of Christian believers

Resurrection faith is possible for all whose minds have been opened to the Christological meaning of Scripture and share in the community's Eucharistic celebration **– Frank J. Matera**

But how accurate is Luke's description of the Crucifixion?

a. Luke's Resurrection is HISTORICALLY ACCURATE. The empty tomb was a historical fact and the Resurrection appearances actually happened as they are described. This is a conservative/traditionalist view that is shared by **Frank J. Matera** and **I. Howard Marshall**.

b. Luke's Resurrection is SYMBOLIC. The Resurrection appearances are **allegories** (p19) for faith, the indestructibility of love, the importance of the Eucharist and the unity of the Christian community. This is a liberal/modernist view that would be shared by **Albert Schweitzer** (p162) and **Rudolf Bultmann** (p33).

There are problems with reading the Resurrection as historical. Luke's Gospel is not internally consistent:

- The women encounter two men, but later this is described as a *"vision of angels"*

- **Simon Peter** goes alone to the tomb but later the disciples say *"some of our companions went to the tomb"* suggesting a group of them went
- Simon Peter finds nothing at the tomb but later the Eleven claim that *"the Lord has risen and appeared to Simon"*

Moreover, Luke's Gospel is not consistent with the other Gospels:

- The identities of the women change in each Gospel (but **Mary Magdalene** is consistent)
- The number of angels in the tomb varies (only one in Mark, one **outside** the tomb in Matthew, none in John)
- There is a squad of Roman guards in Matthew but not in the other Gospels
- The women encounter the Risen Jesus first in the other Gospels but not at all in Luke
- The Resurrection appearances are in Galilee in the other Gospels but they are around Jerusalem in Luke

However, there are some consistent features of the Resurrection appearances:

- The Risen Jesus can change his appearance (or at least *keep people from recognizing him*); this also happens in **John 20: 14-15** when Mary Magdalene mistakes the Risen Jesus for a gardener
- The Risen Jesus can disappear from sight and appear inside locked rooms
- However, the Risen Jesus is still physical: he can be touched, he can eat solid food
- The Risen Jesus continues to teach his Disciples the true meaning of Scripture and gives them instructions for converting others
- At some point, the Risen Jesus ascends into Heaven and is not seen again

Conservative Christians argue that the Resurrected Jesus has a different *sort* of existence to the old physical existence:

> *He now enjoys a bodily existence that transcends the corporeal existence with which human beings are familiar* – **Frank J. Matera**

and

> *Christians thought of the body as being raised. But also transformed so as to be a suitable vehicle for the very different life of the age to come* – **Leon Morris**

The Ascension is a difficult passage for modern readers to take literally (especially the full levitating-into-the-sky version in **Acts 1: 9-11**).

However, Christians like **C.S. Lewis** respond that the Disciples observed a transformation that could not be expressed in conventional language, so they used the mythological symbols of the 1st century, with Jesus going "up" into a Heaven overhead.

> *If you study **Philosophy of Religion (Unit 1)**, this is a good example of **religious language** being ineffable or analogical.*

The point is that they saw Jesus leave our world and become part of God in some more complete sense. If we saw something like that happen, we would have to use **myth** and **symbolism** to describe it too.

Liberal Christians who treat the Resurrection as symbolic have to deal with **Paul**'s criticism:

> *if Christ has not been raised, our preaching is useless and so is your faith* – **1 Corinthians 15: 14**

This is the idea that the Resurrection is the essential belief of Christianity: without it, Christianity is just a collection of charming ethical ideas about love, forgiveness and the importance of community. Paul goes even further, arguing that the Resurrection is **supposed** to be a nonsensical idea:

> *For since in the wisdom of God, the world through its wisdom did not know Him, God was pleased through the foolishness of what was preached to save those who believe* – **1 Corinthians 1: 21**

The Resurrection sounds like *foolishness* to the *wisdom of the world*, which includes liberal Christians. **Bultmann** (p33) argues that modern scientific people cannot make the *sacrificium intellectum* ('sacrifice of the intellect') to believe in something that doesn't make logical sense, but Paul argues this sort of faith is exactly how God *saves those who believe*.

Challenges to the historical truth of the Resurrection are considered in more detail in **Topic 6** (p172).

Does Luke's Gospel describe the Resurrection as a historical event?

YES	NO
Luke records details like the empty tomb and the appearance of the Risen Christ to Simon Peter and the other Disciples that are backed up by the other Gospels and by Paul's account of the Resurrection. His account can be HARMONISED with the other Gospels.	Luke is too inconsistent in his accunt. He contradicts himself about what the women saw at the tomb, who investigated it and who saw the Risen Jesus first. He contradicts the other Gospels about the instruction to meet the Risen Jesus back in Galilee.
Luke is clear that, although there is a lot of symbolism to the Resurrection, it is also a physical fact. He describes the Disciples touching Jesus' hands and feet and Jesus eating fish. Although it is described in the mythological language of the 1st century, the Ascension is also a historical event. **Paul** is right to declare that preaching and faith are *useless* without a belief in these facts.	The Resurrection appearances are *pericopae* (textual units) reflecting the beliefs of 1st century Christians in the Eucharist and the Holy Spirit; they are not meant to be historical and barely pretend to be. The 'levitating Jesus' of the Ascension is clearly a fantasy, though it has a powerful symbolic value if it is de-mythologized first, as **Rudolf Bultmann** explains.

KEY SCHOLARS

R. Alan Culpepper

Topic: 5.2 Why Did Jesus Have to Die?

R. Alan Culpepper is a Christian minister and a professor of theology. He is a Southern Baptist, which is a fairly conservative branch of Protestant Christianity. However, his main book *The Anatomy of the Fourth Gospel* (1983) is a work of narrative theology (p161).

Culpepper approaches **John's Gospel** as if it were a novel, identifying the narrative style, how characters are represented, symbolism, irony and how the author communicates his message to the reader. To be clear, Culpepper is *not* saying that the Gospel is a piece of fiction. He is arguing that the author of John's Gospel uses the same techniques as a novelist to communicate his message and that we can understand the Gospel better by reading it *as if* it were a novel.

For example, Culpepper treats Jesus as the 'hero' of the story and compares him to heroes in myths and romances. He recognises there is *conscious plotting* in John's Gospel, with the narrative shifting between Galilee and Jerusalem and making use of flashbacks and ironic contrasts (such as when people misunderstand Jesus or say things that are true in a way they didn't intend). Jesus' discourses, Signs and confrontations are placed at symbolic times (such as the major Jewish Festivals) or locations (such as the Temple).

> *Jerusalem is established as the locus of Jesus' sharpest conflict with unbelief which has been hardened by misunderstanding of the scriptures* – **R. Alan Culpepper**

The idea of 'unbelief' is personified by *the Jews*. Since the main plot is about belief/unbelief, the Jews function as the antagonists in the story. However, Culpepper does not think John's Gospel is making a historical point about who killed Jesus:

> *The Jews carry the burden of the unbelief of 'the world' in John* – **R. Alan Culpepper**

For Culpepper, unbelief is Jesus' enemy and the force responsible for killing him. The *Jews* merely symbolise this unbelief.

Culpepper shares certain ideas with **Rudolf Bultmann** (p33). He thinks that ancient readers were able to respond to the message of the Gospel without having to separate it into material that is literally true and material that is symbolic. Modern readers can't help making these distinctions and that makes it hard for us to read John's Gospel the way it was meant to be read (neither literally nor symbolically, but with elements of both).

> *When art and history, fiction and truth, are again reconciled, we will again be able to read the gospel as the author's original audience read it* – **R. Alan Culpepper**

Culpepper thinks that treating John's Gospel as a novel helps get modern readers into the mindset to appreciate the Gospel without being distracted by questions like, *Is this historical?* or, *Is this meant to be symbolic?*

I. Howard Marshall

Topic: 5.1 The Kingdom of God in Luke; Topic 5.3 Crucifixion & Resurrection Narratives in Luke

I. Howard Marshall is a Scottish professor of theology. He is a Methodist (like **Morna Hooker**) but leans towards a conservative position. His area of specialism is **Luke's Gospel** and the **Book of Acts**; he made his reputation with *Luke: Historian & Theologian* (1970) but his popular work was *I Believe in the Historical Jesus* (1977). He is also a key scholar for **Topic 6.2 How Should We Live?**

As the titles of Marshall's books suggest, he argues the position that Luke is broadly historically accurate (Marshall his not a fundamentalist: he accepts there may be mistakes, symbolism and exaggerations in the Bible). He argues against a type of liberal scholarship that presents Luke as dramatically altering the Christian message by taking out crucial (apocalyptic) material and adding in new material. You could view Marshall as an opponent of **Redaction Criticism**.

A particular target of Marshall's arguments is the scholar **Hans Conzelmann**, who proposes the theory of salvation-history. Most scholars accept the broad idea of **salvation-history**: Luke has a particular focus on putting Jesus' ministry into a historical context and presenting him as a role model for future Christians. Conzelmann goes further, arguing that the original idea of the **Kingdom of God** was that Jesus believed the world was ending in his lifetime (an **immediate** or perhaps **imminent** apocalypse) but Luke has changed this to show Jesus preaching the idea that the world would end in the far **future** or else that the eschatological themes really describe what happens in the **afterlife**.

Marshall argues that Luke is faithful to his original sources and does not significantly change them.

> *Jesus believed and taught that God was already acting in his ministry powerfully but secretly to establish that realm and to initiate a chain of events that would lead up to and include the End* **– I. Howard Marshall**

The idea that God's power (and the Kingdom of God) is *"veiled and secret"* is important for Marshall. He argues that Luke's Gospel describes the subtle beginnings of the Kingdom of God, which will grow more unmistakeable with time.

> *Jesus used one and the same term, 'the Kingdom of God', for the present and the future of God's rule* **– I. Howard Marshall**

Marshall admits that Luke has put his own distinctive spin on the concept of the Kingdom of God. For example:

> *Jesus purged the concept of its nationalistic associations* **– I. Howard Marshall**

In other words, Jesus reinterpreted the Kingdom, not as a political hope for the Jewish nation but as a spiritual hope for all people, including Gentiles. However, even this is an idea that is found in the earlier **Gospel of Mark**, just less explicitly.

.

Frank J. Matera

Topic 5.3 Crucifixion & Resurrection Narratives in Luke

Frank J. Matera is an American Catholic priest and professor of theology. Like **I. Howard Marshall**, he leans towards a conservative position but, as a Catholic, he feels free to interpret the Bible rather liberally. His area of specialism is **Paul's Epistles** but, since **Luke's Gospel** is very close to Paul in thought, he has written on **Luke-Acts** as well. He is also a key scholar for **Topic 6.2 How Should We Live?**

> *Or he seems to be, since the Specification refers to a "L. Matera" that I cannot identify.*

In *Passion Narratives & Gospel Theologies* (1986), Matera links the way Luke describes Jesus' crucifixion to the underlying theology of the Gospel. Unlike **Marshall**, he doesn't oppose the liberal scholarship of Conzelmann. Matera regards Luke as a *"creative writer"*, which means someone who *"edits and arranges his traditions in a manner which expresses his theological convictions"*. This has a lot in common with the views of **Redaction Criticism**.

However, Matera is not a REVISIONIST – he is not advancing a new or unusual interpretation of Luke because he sees Luke as working within a traditional framework of Christian belief. This is a very 'Catholic' approach to Bible scholarship which views the Bible as a human document but sees the tradition surrounding it as divinely inspired. **Raymond E. Brown** takes the same view.

Matera identifies four key themes in Luke:

- **The destiny of Jesus:** Matera draws attention to the number of times Jesus says *"it is necessary"* to argue that Luke has a clear sense of Jesus fulfilling his destiny by dying on the cross
- **Model for discipleship:** Matera argues that Luke presents Jesus as a role model for future Christians to be disciples by imitating his patience and forgiving nature
- **Rejection of God's prophet:** Matera analyses Jesus as a prophet who is rejected by Judaism and sees Jesus' ministry as a return of the 'Age of Prophecy' that was thought to be dead
- **Death of God's royal Son:** Matera argues that Luke presents Jesus as a King who is rejected by his own subjects (as in the **Parable of the Ten *Minas***, p93); Jesus receives a royal burial and, after the Ascension, becomes a king in Heaven

In *Resurrection: The Origins & Goals of Christian Life* (2015), Matera explores all the Resurrection narratives and their impact on how Christians should live today. He identifies 3 distinctive features of Luke's Resurrection narratives:

1. People can be in the presence of the Risen Christ and not recognize him if they are spiritually unprepared.
2. This spiritual preparation comes from a correct understanding of the Scriptures that is 'Christological' (i.e. understanding that they refer to Christ)
3. When spiritually prepared, believers will encounter the Risen Christ in the **Eucharist**, specifically the breaking of bread.

Ellis Rivkin

Topic: 5.2 Why Did Jesus Have to Die?

Ellis Rivkin is unusual for the scholars in this course for not being a Christian (although that could perhaps be said of **Albert Schweitzer** too). Rivkin is Jewish and usually writes about Jewish history. However, *What Crucified Jesus?* (1984) is an important contribution to the debate about why Jesus had to die.

> *It's a slim book (well under 100 pages) and very readable – students would benefit from reading it themselves. Second-hand copies are sold online for about £3 (including postage).*

Ellis argues that the different sects in **1st century Palestine** shared a common cultural attitude towards religious differences:

- **Two Realms:** Jewish sects accepted the idea of the religious realm and the political realm being separate. They respected the right of the Romans to tax them, rule them and raise armies so long as, in return, they were left free to practice their religion without interference. However, if the Romans interfered with Jewish worship, there would be rebellion.
- **Live-and-Let-Live:** The Jewish sects limited their hostility towards each other to argument and insults. They did not try to use force to silence each other or force other sects to follow their religious codes. Therefore the **Pharisees** and the **Sadducees** could manage worship in the Temple together and the **Essenes** would be left alone in their desert monasteries.

Rivkin points out that the **Zealots** did not respect the doctrine of the Two Realms, so the Pharisees and the Sadducees cooperated to help the Romans capture and kill them.

Rivkin also draws a distinction between two types of Jewish 'council':

- **Bet Din:** A religious council that settled theological questions and punished religious lawbreaking. However, Rivkin insists that the Bet Din only had authority over its own members, so the Pharisees had no power to punish Sadducees or Essenes for breaking their rules – and therefore no power over Jesus and his followers.
- **Sanhedrin:** A political council that settled matters of national security. Rivkin argues that the Sanhedrin was assembled by the High Priest to collaborate with the Romans. It had no interest in religious questions like the **Sabbath regulations**.

According to Rivkin, Jesus threatened the peace because he drew large and volatile crowds. A political Sanhedrin judged him to be a menace but this had nothing to do with Jesus' religious claims to be the **Son of God**. Pontius Pilate executed Jesus as a political menace on the advice of the Sanhedrin. However, Jesus' naïve disciples misunderstood what had happened as Jesus being punished for **blasphemy**.

The title of Rivkin's book sums up his conclusion. Jesus was not killed by a person or a group of people, but by *"the Roman imperial system"* with its *"cruelty and ruthless disregard for the human spirit"*. He argues the Jews were as much victims of this system as Jesus.

Albert Schweitzer

Topic: 5.1 The Kingdom of God in Luke

Albert Schweitzer (1875-1965) is a massively influential Bible scholar. He is also a philosopher, doctor and musician who won the Nobel Peace Prize in 1952.

Schweitzer's classic overview of the research into Jesus was published in 1906. The brilliantly titled English edition, *The Quest of the Historical Jesus*, came out in 1910. Schweitzer offers a 400 page survey of historical Jesus research down to his own time, starting with **Hermann Reimarus** (1778) and ending with **William Wrede** (1901). He argues that Jesus' image has changed with the times and different scholars tend to make Jesus reflect their own values and concerns. Schweitzer's own position is that Jesus must be interpreted as a 1st century Jew with beliefs that were very much 'of his own time'.

Schweitzer identifies *"three great alternatives"* in historical research on Jesus: (1) whether Jesus should be viewed as historical (Schweitzer things he should), (2) whether the Synoptic Gospels represent an earlier tradition than John's Gospel (Schweitzer thinks they do) and (3) what Schweizer calls the *"eschatological question"* raised by **Johannes Weiss** in 1892. This is the idea that Jesus preached an apocalyptic message, thoroughly convinced that the world was coming to an end in his lifetime.

Schweitzer describes Jesus' false hopes for an apocalypse; he suggests that Jesus believed that, if he encouraged his enemies to execute him, this would trigger God's apocalyptic intervention in the world. They did execute him, but still the apocalypse did not happen:

> [Jesus] *lays hold of the wheel of the world to set it moving on that last revolution which is to bring all ordinary history to a close. It refuses to turn, and he throws himself on it. Then it does turn; and crushes him* – **Albert Schweitzer**

Schweitzer calls Jesus a *"failed messiah"* who died on the cross a disappointed and disillusioned man – Schweitzer draws attention to Jesus on the cross crying out *"My God, my God, why have you forsaken me?"* which is in **Mark 15: 34** and **Matthew 27: 46**). Yet even though Schweitzer regards the historical Jesus as a failure and Christian theology based on him as deeply mistaken, he finishes his book with a chapter titled *Results*.

> *Jesus means something to our world because a mighty spiritual force streams forth from him and flows through our time also* – **Albert Schweitzer**

Jesus reflects Schweitzer's own philosophy of 'Reverence for Life'. For Schweitzer, it's what Jesus **stands for** that matters: love, forgiveness and moral courage:

> *it is not Jesus as historically known, but Jesus as spiritually arisen within men, who is significant for our time and can help it* – **Albert Schweitzer**

Schweitzer regards the symbolism of Jesus as much more valuable than anything the historical Jesus did or believed. In this way, he is very similar to **Rudolf Bultmann** (p33) who believes in de-mythologizing Jesus for the modern age.

TOPIC 6: CHALLENGES TO THE RESURRECTION & ETHICAL LIVING

Scientific and historical-critical challenges – faith and history: the death and resurrection of Jesus in modern scholarship

- Context of scientific challenges to the resurrection as miracle; the challenge of the Enlightenment – resurrection as a fictional event, the resurrection as myth, the resurrection as an event in the experience of the disciples.

- The work of Ian Wilson and Frank Morison on the historical evidence for the resurrection of Jesus based on analysis of the different Gospel narratives and alternative explanations for the empty tomb.

- Context, comparison and the strengths and weaknesses of these views. Their significance for understanding the texts and their impact on other areas of study over time.

How should we live?

- Christian life: the ethical teaching of Jesus from the Sermon on the Plain in Luke 6 and other texts on the poor, outcasts, wealth and forgiveness, including the parables of the Lost (Luke 15), the Good Samaritan (Luke 10), the Rich Man and Lazarus (Luke 16).

- The relationship of the teaching of Jesus to that of Judaism at the time. Interpretations of this material for today, including religious and secular views, and the impact on Christian codes of living, including equality and pluralism.

- With reference to the ideas of I H Marshall and L Matera [sic].

SCIENTIFIC & HISTORICAL-CRITICAL CHALLENGES, ETHICAL LIVING AND THE WORKS OF SCHOLARS

What's this topic about?

What are the implications of the Resurrections? Can modern people still believe in it as a miraculous event or must it be viewed symbolically? What are the implications for ethical living in a multi-faith society?

SCIENTIFIC & HISTORICAL-CRITICAL CHALLENGES

This topic looks at the death and resurrection of Jesus in modern scholarship, including Enlightenment challenges to the resurrection as a miracle and views of it as a fiction, a myth or a subjective experience. There are no key scholars but **Frank Morison** and **Ian Wilson** feature in the Anthology.

HOW SHOULD WE LIVE?

This topic covers Jesus' **sermon on the plain** in Luke's Gospel and 3 Parables (**Good Samaritan, Lost Sheep//Coin/Son** and **Rich Man & Lazarus**) as well as Jesus' teachings in **relation to Judaism**. Key scholars are **I. Howard Marshall** and (*we suppose*) **Frank J. Matera**.

Before you go any further...

... there are some things you need to know.

THE RESURRECTION IN THE GOSPELS

The Resurrection is Jesus being raised from the dead. The Gospels provide other examples of persons being raised from the dead (the son of the widow of Nain in **Luke 7: 11-15**, Jairus' daughter in **Luke 8: 41-55**, Lazarus in **John 11: 1-44** and *many holy people who had died* when Jesus is crucified in **Matthew 27: 50-53**). However, these are not 'resurrections'. These people are *restored* to life but to the old life that they had before, which will inevitably end again in death. The Resurrection is Jesus being raised to a NEW KIND OF LIFE.

- It is a life **not restricted by the laws of nature** (the Risen Jesus can appear and disappear)
- It is a **physical life** (the Gospels describe the Risen Jesus being touched and eating food)
- It is a life in a **different sort of body** (the Risen Jesus is not always recognised, even by people who knew him well, until he does or says something distinctive)
- It is a life that **continues in a new heavenly reality** (the Risen Jesus ascends into Heaven, after which the Resurrection-appearances stop)

It is worth examining how each Gospel presents the Resurrection.

The Resurrection in Mark

According to the theory of **Markan Priority** (c.f. **Topic 3**), Mark is the earliest Gospel so Mark's description of the Resurrection holds particular interest. However, the earliest surviving texts of Mark's Gospel end at **Mark 16: 8** with the women discovering the empty tomb, receiving a message from a mysterious young man (or angel) and fleeing in fear: *"they said nothing to anyone, because they were afraid."*

- Some scholars think that the women did in fact go to the Eleven Disciples (eleven since the departure of Judas the betrayer) and tell them about the empty tomb; they just *said nothing to anyone* on the way back from the tomb. Logically, since Mark narrates what the women experienced, they **must** have told someone.
- Other scholars think Mark deliberately ends the Gospel here in this unsatisfactory way in order to encourage the reader to do what the women failed to do: to go out a bear witness to the Resurrection themselves. This interpretation is linked to a **literary interpretation of Scripture** (p61), because Mark ends his Gospel they way he does, not to describe the facts of what happened, but to produce an emotional and imaginative effect on his readers.

Later, two endings were added on to Mark's Gospel. The 'shorter ending' reads like this:

> *Then they quickly reported all these instructions to those around Peter. After this, Jesus himself also sent out through them from east to west the sacred and imperishable proclamation of eternal salvation. Amen.*

This ending clears up the facts that the women **did** tell **Peter** and the other Disciples about the empty tomb and it emphasises the Resurrection is a message for everyone in the world, not just Jews. However, it still doesn't include any Resurrection appearances.

The 'longer ending' features in modern Bibles as **Mark 16: 9-20** and seems to have been added by the end of the 2nd century, if not earlier. It contains four episodes:

1. Jesus appears to **Mary Magdalene** (the leader of the group of women) but no one believes her.
2. Jesus appears *in a different form* to two unnamed disciples *while they were walking in the country*. This links to the passage in **Luke** describing the Risen Jesus' appearance **on the road to Emmaus** (*c.f.* **Topic 5**). Unlike in **Luke**'s version, these disciples are not believed either.
3. Jesus appears to the Eleven while they are eating (perhaps a reference to the Christian celebration of the **Eucharist**), criticises their lack of faith and commissions them to spread the word of his teachings and Resurrection.
4. Finally, Jesus ascends into Heaven.

This ending also emphasises the Resurrection being a message for the whole world and maintains a typical Markan theme of the Disciples lacking faith. It also preserves the tradition that Mary Magdalene was the first witness to the Resurrection.

The Resurrection in Matthew

According to **Source Criticism** (*c.f.* **Topic 3**), Matthew's Gospel drew heavily on Mark's account, supplementing it with extra details from "***Q***" and perhaps other sources. Matthew closely follows the story from the 'longer ending' to Mark:

1. The women (including **Mary Magdalene**) are the first to encounter the Risen Jesus, meeting him on the way back from the empty tomb
2. The Eleven Disciples meet the Risen Jesus in Galilee and, once again, *some doubted* but Jesus gives them the 'Great Commission' to *go and make disciples of all the nations* (i.e. the Gentiles). The Ascension is ***not*** described.

Matthew also includes a detail missing from the other Gospels that Roman soldiers were set to guard the tomb but were knocked unconscious by an angel. The solders are bribed by the Jewish leaders to spread a false story that the Disciples stole Jesus' body, a story *"which has been widely circulated among the Jews to this very day"* according to **Matthew 28: 15**.

The Resurrection in Luke

You covered this account in depth in **Topic 5** (p134). These are the main points:

1. The women do ***not*** encounter the Risen Jesus
2. Jesus appears to two disciples **on the road to Emmaus** but they do not recognise him until he breaks bread with them
3. Luke claims (but does not describe) **Peter** as being the first to meet the Risen Jesus.
4. The Eleven Disciples think the Risen Jesus is a ghost but he invites them to touch him and he eats food in front of them
5. The Ascension is described but not the commission to take the message to the Gentiles (although Luke does describe this in his second volume, the **Book of Acts**).

The Resurrection in John

As you would expect, **John**'s account is different from the Synoptic Gospels but includes some striking similarities:

1. **Mary Magdalene** is the first to encounter the Risen Jesus; at first she does not recognise him (and takes him to be the gardener outside the tomb) but she does recognise him when he calls her by name
2. Jesus next appears to the Eleven Disciples and instructs them to touch his hands and feet
3. Jesus appears again when **'Doubting' Thomas** is present and Thomas touches the nail wounds in Jesus' hands and the spear wound in his side

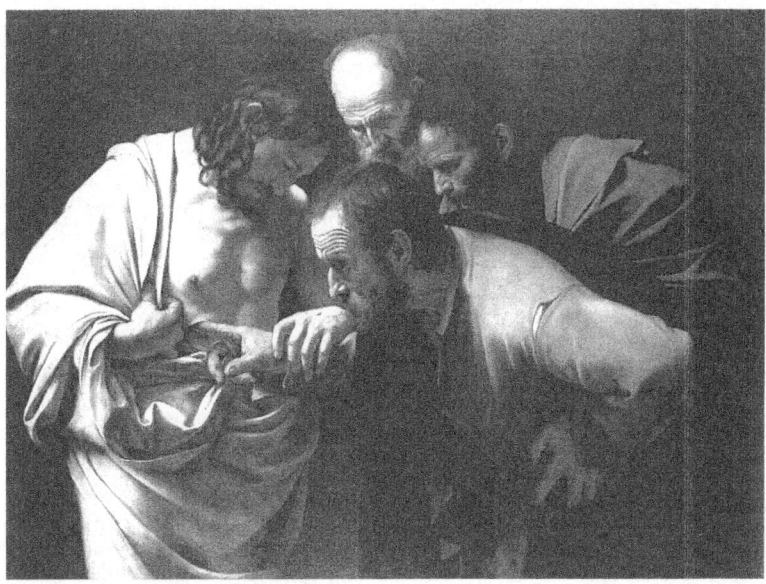

Doubting Thomas investigates Jesus' wounds in Caravaggio's painting of John 20: 24-29

John's Gospel seems to end at **John 20: 31** in its original form, but **John 31** describes more Resurrection appearances:

4. The Disciples meet Jesus in Galilee while they are fishing; they do not recognise him at first but when they do they land a miraculous catch of fish (with the 153 fish perhaps **symbolising** the members of the **Johannine Community**). Jesus reinstates **Peter** as the leader of the Disciples. There is no Ascension scene but it is implied because Jesus talks about a period of delay *"until I return"* (meaning *Parousia* or the 'Second Coming').

The Resurrection according to Paul

Paul's **epistles** (letters) make up 28% of the New Testament. Paul was not one of Jesus' original Disciples: he was a **Pharisee** who persecuted the first Christians. However, he converted to Christianity after a vision of the Risen Christ. He passes on his understanding of the Resurrection as he claims to have *received it* from others:

> *he appeared to Cephas* [i.e. Peter] *and then to the Twelve. After that, he appeared to more than five hundred of the brothers and sisters at the same time* – **1 Corinthians 15: 5-6**

Paul's account makes no mention of the women (or the empty tomb, for that matter) and agrees with Luke in that Cephas/Peter was the first witness to the Resurrection.

Remember that Paul wrote in the 50s CE when Christianity was just beginning; his account is 10-15 years earlier than Mark and 30 years earlier than Matthew or Luke.

Paul also describes his **own** Resurrection experience, which is both similar to and different from the other Disciples.

Paul (at that time named Saul) was a servant of the High Priest in Jerusalem who assisted in the stoning to death of Stephen, the first Christian martyr.

Around 33-36 CE, Saul travelled to Damascus to persecute the Christian community there, but has a dramatic encounter on the road:

> *I saw a light from heaven, brighter than the sun, blazing around me and my companions. We all fell to the ground, and I heard a voice saying to me in Aramaic, 'Saul, Saul, why do you persecute me?'* **– Acts 26: 13-14**

Saul asks who is speaking to him and hears the reply: *"I am Jesus, whom you are persecuting."*

Paul is struck blind by this **numinous religious experience** (termed a CHRISTOPHANY, an encounter with the Risen Christ), Saul converts to Christianity, changes his name to Paul and becomes an enthusiastic missionary for the very faith he had been persecuting. When Paul converts, his blindness disappears.

Evaluating the Resurrection Accounts

There are striking DISSIMILARITIES between these accounts:

- Who is first to encounter the Risen Jesus? **Mark** (in the 'longer version'), **Matthew** and **John** claim it is the women, specifically **Mary Magdalene**; **Luke** and **Paul** claim it is **Peter**
- Where do the Resurrection appearances take place? **Mark** implies and **Matthew** explicitly states they are in Galilee; **Luke** is clear that they are in and around Jerusalem; **John** describes Jerusalem *and* Galilee
- When do the Resurrection appearances end? **Mark** (in the 'longer version') and **Luke** describe the Ascension; **Matthew** and **John** do not

Some critics emphasize these dissimilarities to cast doubt on the Resurrection. However **E.P Saunders** points out that the accounts possess many of the confusions of actual eyewitnesses to dramatic events (like disasters); if the Resurrection was a hoax created by the disciples, you would *expect* the accounts to be much more consistent. Furthermore, there are basic SIMILARITIES between the accounts:

- Jesus' body disappears. The women are the first witnesses to the empty tomb but are not believed
- The Risen Jesus is not always recognised at first: this happens in **Luke** and in **John** (twice: first for **Mary Magdalene** and then for the Eleven Disciples)
- **Luke** describes the mystical encounter **on the road to Emmaus** and **Mark** (in the 'longer version') seems to refer to this too
- Jesus appears to the Eleven Disciples; **Luke** and **John** both describe their disbelief and Jesus offers himself to them to be touched and eats food
- Jesus gives the Disciples a 'commission' to preach to the Gentiles; in **Mark** and **Matthew** this is explicit; **Luke** makes it explicit in his sequel, the **Book of Acts**; in **John** it is only implied

There are also AMBIGUITIES (details that can be interpreted in different ways):

- Some of the encounters seem to be very **symbolic** and may be **allegories** for encountering Christ in the Eucharist celebration (i.e. a **mystical** experience) rather than literal descriptions of meetings (e.g. the **road to Emmaus**, p149)
- The encounters, especially **Paul**'s Christophany, seem more like **visions** – except that **Luke** and **John** both go out of their way to establish that the Risen Jesus is physical
- The time frame is very unclear and almost dream-like: **Luke** presents the encounters as all happening on the same day but in **Acts 1: 3** he states that the appearances happened over 40 days; **Matthew** and **John** flash from Jerusalem to Galilee; **Mark** is completely non-specific about where and when the encounters take place.

These ambiguities lead some scholars to suppose that the Gospel accounts are not *supposed* to be interpreted **literally**. If this is the case, then the original readers of the Gospels might have understood that these descriptions to be **allegories** (p19). Liberal scholars today interpret the Resurrection in this way, but conservative (and especially fundamentalist) Christians insist on a literal interpretation and often quote **Paul** in support:

> *if Christ has not been raised, our preaching is useless and so is your faith* – **1 Corinthians 15: 14**

Whatever ambiguities might be present in the Gospels, Paul is the earliest Christian commentator on the Resurrection and seems to treat it as a historical event, not an allegory.

However, Paul's own Christophany is not an encounter with the physically resurrected Christ. It is more like a **vision** (although Paul's companions seem to experience it too). This leads some scholars to wonder if Paul (who never mentions the empty tomb) really believed in a physical, bodily Resurrection of Jesus.

How did Christianity begin: with an allegory about Jesus' message surviving his death, a vision of the dead Jesus or Jesus rising back to physical life?

BELIEF & DISBELIEF IN THE GOSPELS

It is significant that the Gospels do **not** present the response to the Resurrection as being immediate belief, even when the Risen Jesus physically appears.

- The Disciples disbelieve the women's testimony
- The Disciples think Jesus is a ghost at first (e.g. in **Luke** and **John**)
- **Paul**'s letter to the **Corinthians** shows that some of them doubted the Resurrection, which is why he argues that it is central to Christian faith

The episodes where some disciples recognise the Risen Jesus but others don't might represent the different reactions of belief and disbelief among Jesus' followers.

However, the reaction of the disciples is important because it shows they were not gullible fools or naturally inclined to believe people could come back from the dead.

> that Jesus of Nazareth was raised from the dead was just as controversial nineteen hundred years ago as it is today– **N.T. Wright**

The Priestly Plot in Matthew

Matthew 28: 11-15 describes how the Jewish leaders bribe the Roman soldiers to spread the story that the disciples stole Jesus' body to fake the Resurrection. This shows that there were disbelievers making these claims at the time Matthew was writing (around 85 CE perhaps).

> *Who to believe? It's interesting (and a bit sad) that there was a problem with 'Fake News' two thousand years ago, just like today*

However, the important point is that, right from the beginning of the Christian religion, there were doubts about the Resurrection and people were suggesting NATURALISTIC (non-supernatural) explanations for what had happened.

Hellenic vs Jewish conceptions

The Gentiles in the **Hellenic culture** of the Roman Empire mostly followed a DUALIST philosophy: they believed body and spirit were separate, that bodies were mortal and died but spirits could be immortal and might live on without the body. For people like this, it would be understandable (although still surprising) if Jesus returned from the dead as a spirit.

> *Some Gentiles interpreted the Resurrection that way. Paul's letter to the Corinthians seems to address Gentile converts who believed in a 'spiritual' rather than a physical Resurrection. The passages in Luke and John where the Disciples touch Jesus oppose this belief.*

Most 1ˢᵗ century Jews did **not** follow a dualist philosophy: they believed body and soul were one. The **Pharisees** believed in a general resurrection of the dead at the end of time but the **Sadducees** believed there would be no resurrection of the dead. The idea of **one particular person** being raised from the dead by God would not have fitted in with their beliefs either.

Therefore, from a philosophical standpoint, the Resurrection of Jesus would be difficult for 1ˢᵗ century Gentiles AND Jews to accept; perhaps just as difficult as for 21ˢᵗ century secular people.

Seeing is *not* Believing

A feature of the Gospel accounts is that the disciples do not believe in the Resurrection **even when** they encounter the Risen Jesus.

> *When they saw him, they worshiped him; but some doubted* – **Matthew 28: 17**

Matthew's Gospel doesn't explain why *some doubted* but we can assume that these disciples suspected this was a hallucination or a hoax. **Luke** gives more detail:

> *They were startled and frightened, thinking they saw a ghost* – **Luke 24: 37**

Luke's Gospel clarifies that people only believe fully in the Resurrection when they correctly understand the Scriptures. For example, the Risen Jesus says:

> *Everything must be fulfilled that is written about me in the Law of Moses* [i.e. the Torah], *the Prophets and the Psalms* – **Luke 24: 44**

In other words, believing in the Resurrection isn't just factually accepting that a dead person is once again alive. It's a complete interpretation of life and death based on a correct understanding of the Bible. **John's Gospel** makes a similar point when the Risen Jesus says to the Disciples:

> *Because you have seen me, you have believed; blessed are those who have not seen and yet have believed* – **John 20: 29**

The point seeing to be that encountering the Risen Jesus is only valuable insofar as it leads to believing in the Word of God revealed in the Scriptures; other Christians can believe in the Word of God without meeting the Risen Jesus and that is, if anything, better still.

TOPIC 6.1 SCIENTIFIC & HISTORICAL-CRITICAL CHALLENGES TO THE RESURRECTION

The first systematic challenge to the Resurrection came from pagan philosophers in the Roman Empire, criticising the rose of Christianity. Much later, these challenges were re-stated by the philosophers of the Enlightenment.

Celsus vs Origen

Although the Edexcel Specification invites candidates to consider challenges to the Resurrection made during and after the Enlightenment, most of these arguments were framed much earlier, back in 180 CE by a pagan philosopher named **Celsus** in a book called *The True Word* (*Alethes Logos*).

Celsus launches two attacks on Christianity: he writes one section from the perspective of a Jew, interpreting Christianity as a corruption of Judaism and a misunderstanding of the Jewish Scriptures; in the second part, Celsus challenges Christianity head on by ridiculing the Resurrection of Jesus.

For half a century, Celsus went unanswered until the brilliant Christian scholar **Origen** (184-253 CE) took on the task of replying.

> *Origen's 'Against Celsus' (248 CE) is not just masterful debating but also preserves Celsus' original text (which otherwise would be lost to history) because Origen reproduces it word-for-word in order to reply to it.*

Celsus suggests that Jesus' Resurrection appearances may have been hallucinations produced by *"wishful thinking"*.

Origen [*right*] replies that the appearances were in broad daylight to groups of people and that there is no evidence in the Gospels that the witnesses were *"mentally unbalanced nor delirious"*.

Celsus suggests that Jesus' Resurrection was just a poor copy of the *fantastic tales* (*terateias*) of pagan heroes descending into the Underworld and returning (an argument used in the 20th century by **Sir James Frazer** and the **sociological approach** to interpreting Scripture (p55).

Origen replies that, unlike the myths of gods like **Osiris**, Jesus dies publicly in a known place under a known Roman official. It is history, not mythology.

Celsus suggests that the Resurrection is a hoax and that the Disciples lied about meeting the Risen Jesus.

Origen argues that the *"the clear and certain proof"* for the Resurrection is the CHANGED LIVES of the disciples, going from frightened fugitives to brave martyrs who gained a *"power of endurance and resolution continued even to death"*. Why would anyone **invent** the story that Jesus had risen from the dead and then be willing to die for it themselves? A later Christian writer, Eusebius (311 CE), puts it like this:

> *Why would they die for him when he was dead, after they had deserted him when he was alive?* – **Eusebius**

This view was restated in by **Jacques Abbadie** (1698):

> *no one dies for a fiction which they have invented* – **Jacques Abbadie**

Origen's replies to Celsus were considered to be the last word on the subject for several centuries, but versions of Celsus' arguments returned, strengthened with scientific evidence, during the Enlightenment.

> *In drawing attention to the discrepancies in the resurrection narratives, Celsus has grasped the end of a thread that would eventually threaten to unravel the whole fabric of the accounts* – **William Lane Craig**

The Challenge of the Enlightenment

You have already looked at Enlightenment challenges to Scripture as part of **Topic 4** *(p41) but I'll summarise those ideas here very briefly.*

The **Enlightenment** is often referred to as the "Age of Reason". This period begins with the ideas of Descartes in the 17th century and ends with the American and French Revolutions in the 18th century. Thinkers in France, Germany and Britain (especially Scotland) rejected many of the beliefs and traditions of previous generations and developed new ways of looking at the world based upon:

- **Rationalism:** truth comes from the use of reason, rather than accepting tradition or the authority of others
- **Empiricism:** all knowledge comes from our experience of the world using the 5 senses and is explored using scientific methods
- **Scepticism:** the reasonable starting position is to doubt the truth of all knowledge claims

These three factors combine together in the SCIENTIFIC WORLDVIEW that emerged during the Enlightenment and it was this worldview, rather than any particular scientific discovery, that undermined the plausibility of the Resurrection for many people.

> *The success of science encouraged people to believe that the world was governed by rational universal laws, discoverable by the human mind. Whether or not God was the author of such laws became increasingly irrelevant* – **Murray Rae**

Enlightenment scholars like **Thomas Hobbes** (1651) and **Jean Astruc** (1753) questioned the age and the authorship of the Old Testament.

Baron D'Holbach (1761) uses contradictions between the four Gospels to question whether they really could be **inspired** by God.

Hermann Reimarus (1774, p44) went even further, arguing that the historical Jesus was a Jewish prophet-turned-political-revolutionary who never claimed to be the **Son of God** and whose disciples stole his body to fake the Resurrection.

Challenges like those of Reimarus were essentially the same arguments as the ones posed by Celsus centuries earlier, but this time they were strengthened by:

- a new **scientific world-view** that was deeply sceptical about miracles
- a **scientific approach to analyzing the Bible** which weakened confidence that the Gospels really were eyewitness accounts of the events they describe

Because of this, these challenges could not be countered with Origen's arguments quite so easily.

For example, **Thomas Woolston**'s *Six Discourses on the Miracles of Our Saviour* (1730) calls the Resurrection *"a monstrous fraud"*. Woolston proposes that the disciples stole Jesus' body, perhaps by bribing the guards or getting them drunk. Woolston echoes **David Hume**'s argument that, even if this is unlikely, it's a better explanation than the impossible idea of a resurrection:

> *Because the resurrection violates the course of Nature, no human testimony could possibly establish it, since it has the whole witness of Nature against it* – **Thomas Woolston**

In answer to Origen's view that the Disciples' willingness to die for the Resurrection was evidence they had not faked it, Woolston replies: *"Many other criminals and cheats have gone to their death proclaiming their innocence."*

What do you think? Is a willingness to die for your beliefs proof of your sincerity? Or will liars and fantasists stick to their crazy stories right to the end rather than admit the truth?

The Resurrection as a Miracle

If naturalistic solutions (like a hoax or the Swoon Hypothesis – see p178) are rejected, then the Resurrection must be accepted as a miracle. This type of inductive logic is famously summarised by **Arthur Conan Doyle**'s fictional character Sherlock Holmes in the context of solving crimes:

> *when you have eliminated the impossible, whatever remains, however improbable, must be the truth* **– Arthur Conan Doyle**

This quote is widely misused. Sherlock Holmes was a (fictional) superhuman genius who could consider and eliminate all the possible alternatives, whereas ordinary humans (and Bible scholars) cannot consider every possible alternative. Nevertheless, the quote illustrates an important point that many of the naturalistic explanations of the Resurrection are deeply improbable whether or not God exists, whereas, *if* God exists and *if* God performs miracles, the Resurrection might not be that improbable at all.

> *That Jesus rose naturally from the dead is fantastically improbable. But I see no reason whatsoever to think that it is improbable that God raised Jesus from the dead* **– William Lane Craig**

But does God perform miracles? The Enlightenment brought about increasing scepticism regarding miracles and an interventionist God who would perform them.

- Enlightenment scientists building on **Isaac Newton's laws of motion** constructed a view of the universe operating according to unvarying laws. This world-view made the idea of those laws being suspended or broken seem less likely
- **Enlightenment Deism** (p44) proposed a God who created the universe but does not intervene in it

Part of the Deist argument was that miracles are simply impossible: the God of Deism does not perform miracles because that would be to go against the very laws that he himself has created. **Hermann Reimarus** (1754) summed up the Deist objection to miracles like this:

> *miracles contradict the order of creation and that therefore it is impossible for a rational man to believe in them* **– Hermann Reimarus**

Reimarus' view assumes that the *order of creation* does not allow for miracles. However, if the interventionist God of the Bible is real, then the *order of creation* is **supposed** to be contradicted on occasions – and the Resurrection would be one of those occasions.

David Hume *Of Miracles*

David Hume (1748) wrote an influential attack on miracles. However, Hume is clearly targeting the Resurrection in particular. He writes that we don't regard unusual events as a miracle because, despite being unusual, unusual events are **sometimes** observed to happen, but:

> *it is a miracle, that a dead man should come to life; because that has never been observed in any age or country* – **David Hume**

Hume argues that a miracle (of any sort) is, by definition, ***the most improbable thing*** that can happen. Therefore, if a miracle is reported, it is ***always*** more probable that the witness is lying or mistaken:

> *When anyone tells me, that he saw a dead man restored to life, I immediately consider with myself, whether it be more probable, that this person should either deceive or be deceived* – **David Hume**

Hume is not arguing that miracles CANNOT happen; he's arguing that a rational person should always prefer a naturalistic explanation of an apparent miracle, even if it's very unlikely, to the miracle itself, which is by definition ***even more*** unlikely.

Hume's argument has been criticised for being a CIRCULAR ARGUMENT. He starts with the assumption that the laws of nature are supported by exceptionless testimony, but this testimony is only exceptionless if we discount all reports of miracles. For example, Hume says that a dead man coming to life *"has never been observed in any age or country"* but the Resurrection ***is*** exactly such an observation.

Hume goes on to make a series of criticisms of testimonies about miracles that are clearly aimed at the Resurrection in particular:

- People enjoy incredible stories, which excite *"surprise and wonder"*
- Miracle stories tend to come from "*ignorant and barbarous nations*"
- These stories belong in the past, because over time societies progress out of believing in supernatural events

There's a very clear Enlightenment outlook here: scientific progress is curing European societies of belief in the supernatural, but religions are rooted in the pre-scientific past when people were more gullible.

Hume probably exaggerates how gullible people in the past really were. We have seen that disbelief and proposing naturalistic alternatives were the first responses to the accounts of the Resurrection, even in 1st century Palestine. This leads **N.T. Wright** (2003) to point out:

> *The discovery that dead people stay dead was not first made by the philosophers of the Enlightenment* – **N.T. Wright**

In other words, people in the 1st century knew perfectly well that dead men don't come back to life. It was just as improbable to them as it was to Hume 1700 years later.

Hume tackles the question of why a Disciple might invent a fiction that he was prepared to die for by suggesting that:

> *he may know his narrative to be false, and yet persevere with it, with the best intentions in the world, for the sake of promoting so holy a cause* – **David Hume**

Hume means that religious fanatics are prepared to die for a *holy cause* and they are also prepared to lie for that cause as well. If the Disciples were determined to spread Jesus' message of love and forgiveness of sins, they might have been prepared to invent the Resurrection to help spread the message.

Hume is certainly right that fanatics can tell lies for their cause with a clean conscience. This invites two responses:

1. Were the Disciples *really* fanatics of that sort? The New Testament presents them as rather simple men without great conviction: they run away when Jesus is arrested and Peter, the bravest, denies Jesus three times; they disbelieve in the Resurrection at first and they don't go to much effort to make their accounts of the Resurrection agree

2. Would the story of the Resurrection have made their *holy cause* more persuasive? In the Bible, most people disbelieve in the Resurrection when they first hear about it. Jesus' message of love and forgiveness could have been taught very effectively without the story of the Resurrection, so why invent an implausible story to support a moral teaching that is already appealing to most people?

Did the Enlightenment successfully challenge the Resurrection as a miracle?

YES	NO
The Enlightenment saw the birth of science which shows us how the universe works according to fixed laws that do not require God to explain them. The Resurrection goes against our understanding of how the universe works.	The scientific laws describe how the universe is supposed to work on average, but if God exists then he is the source of those laws and can suspend or reverse them if he chooses. Science doesn't show that a miracle is impossible or even unlikely.
Hume demonstrated that a miracle is so improbable that it's always reasonable to assume the witness is mistaken or lying. Jesus' Disciples came from an *"ignorant and barbarous"* time and were motivated to invent the Resurrection to promote their *"holy cause."*	Hume's argument is circular, because he assumes that dead men never come back to life then uses this to argue that one should never believe a report of a dead man coming back to life. Hume's cynical view of people in the past as gullible or fanatical does not match the descriptions in the Gospels.

The Resurrection as a Fictional Event

In place of miracles, scholars of the Enlightenment offered NATURALISTIC explanations of the Resurrection. One of these is the "Theft Hypothesis" that Jesus' Disciples stole his corpse to fake the Resurrection (perhaps not intentionally: they might merely have moved the body then the women arrived and, finding the empty tomb, leapt to conclusions that Jesus had risen from the dead).

The Theft Hypothesis seems to be as old as Christianity itself, since **Matthew 28: 11-15** references it being spread around by the Jewish leaders and **Celsus** brings it up as well. The standard objection was given by **Origen**, that the Disciples would not embrace suffering, persecution and death for the sake of a lie.

A different argument that the Resurrection is fictional is the "Swoon Hypothesis", which argues that Jesus did not really die on the cross but that his Disciples misinterpreted his reappearance as a miraculous resurrection.

The Swoon Hypothesis

This is the suggestion that Jesus passed out ('swooned') on the cross but did not die. He later recovered consciousness in the tomb.

The main support for this argument is medical. Jesus died after 6 hours on the cross, which is a very short time. **Mark 15: 44** records Pontius Pilate being surprised to learn that Jesus had died so soon. **Justus Lipsius** (1629) argues that healthy adults would suffer crucifixion for 2-4 days, up to 9 days in some cases. This lends support to the idea that Jesus might have 'swooned'.

Karl Friedrich Bahrdt (1741-1792) proposes a conspiracy theory, that Jesus' followers gave him a drug that brought on a near-death state so that he would *appear* to die on the cross then later recover in safety. Bahrdt thought that Jesus pretended to be a spiritual Messiah to encourage the Jews to abandon their belief in a violent Kingly Messiah. The creation of a completely separate religion ('Christianity') was not part of the plan.

Scholars like Bahrdt argue that Jesus was a member of a secret society and that the man or men in white robes described in the Synoptic Gospels (e.g. **Mark 16: 5**) were conspirators who had opened the tomb and helped Jesus revive. The women arrived at the tomb and surprised them in the act, but mistook them for angels. Since the **Essenes** wore white robes, this theory often proposes that Jesus was an Essene and that the Essenes revived him and helped him recover at one of their desert monasteries.

Not all supporters of the Swoon Hypothesis agree with this conspiracy theory. **Heinrich Paulus** (1761-1851) supposes that Jesus went into a coma on the cross but awoke naturally because of the cold air of the tomb.

Critics of the Swoon Hypothesis point out that Jesus had been beaten several times and flogged by the Roman soldiers before the Crucifixion. He was too weak to carry his own cross so **Simon of Cyrene** was made to carry it for him. Given his physical state, it's quite possible he would have died quickly.

Moreover, Roman soldiers who had carried out hundreds of crucifixions would not have allowed prisoners to be taken down if there was any reason to suppose they were still alive.

> *These executioners knew what they were doing, and theories that Jesus somehow physically survived the cross represent a combination of fantasy, revisionism, and half-baked science* – **Bruce Chilton**

More important, the wounds resulting from crucifixion would have been traumatic. **Flavius Josephus** (99 CE) describes friends who were crucified but rescued and says two of the three died from their injuries despite the best medical care on offer. **David Strauss** (1865) argues that it's impossible to believe that *"a being who had stolen half dead out of the sepulcher* [i.e. tomb]*"* could have convinced the Disciples that he had returned to full and supernatural life.

> *The suggestion that a man so critically wounded then went on to appear to the disciples on various occasions in Jerusalem and Galilee is pure fantasy* – **William Lane Craig**

The Swoon Hypothesis is popular with some Muslims because the Qur'an states that Jesus did not die on the cross. Some believe that a substitute replaced the real Jesus.

Is the Resurrection a fictional event?

YES	NO
Naturalistic solutions should always be preferred to supernatural ones. This is the 'Principle of Parsimony' (also known as OCCAM'S RAZOR). We know that hoaxes occur and that people who seem to be dead sometimes recover. It makes more sense to suppose that something like this explains the apparent 'Resurrection'.	These naturalistic solutions are not 'parsimonious' at all: they just involve more speculation. Why would the first Christian disciples be prepared to suffer and die for what they knew to be a hoax? How could the crucified Jesus recover from his wounds enough to get out of a tomb with a stone rolled across the exit?
A conspiracy theory would explain the disciples' beliefs and Jesus' escape from the tomb. If an Essene sect drugged Jesus then later revived him it would explain his suspiciously quick 'death' on the cross and the appearance of the white-robed men at the empty tomb. The disciples mistook them for angels because they weren't "in on it". The conspiracy hoped to change Jewish beliefs, but did not intend to start a new religion.	Enlightenment scholars did love their conspiracy theories and other people still do, but these theories involve large groups of people working in absolute secrecy and no one telling what they know. How could Jesus have been part of an Essence secret plot that his closest disciples knew nothing about? How could the Essenes have healed him of his wounds enough to pose as the Resurrected Son of God in front of people who knew him?

The Resurrection as a Myth

In the 19th century, the view of the **Resurrection as a fiction** (p178) lost popularity, but sceptics continued to propose naturalistic alternatives. One is the idea that the resurrection is a **myth** and that 1st century beliefs about pagan gods and Jewish prophets got 'attached' to the story of Jesus.

This is another view that was first proposed by **Celsus** in the 2nd century. Celsus noticed the similarity between Jesus' death and resurrection with the character of certain pagan gods.

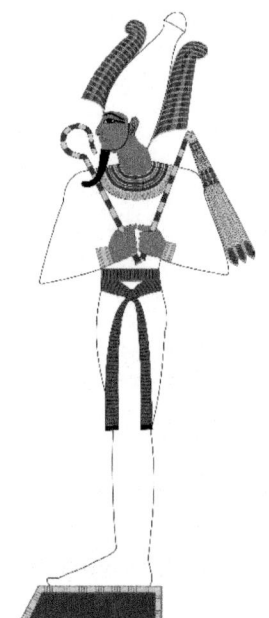

The Egyptian god **Osiris** is a good example. Osiris' birth was heralded by a star in the heavens. Osiris was a healer and a prophet but he was betrayed by someone close to him and murdered; his body was hidden away — though not for long, as he returned in a miraculous resurrection to reign in heaven as the god who judges the dead and assigns rewards in paradise or punishments in hell

Anthropologists (who study ancient cultures, see p57) describe this sort of being as a DYING-AND-RISING GOD. There are a lot of them in different mythologies all around the world. Although Jesus is the best-known example of a resurrected figure, he is far from the only one.

The Ancient Jews did not have myths about a dying-and-rising god, but they had myths about comparable figures. In **Unit 1 (Context of the New Testament)**, you studied the **Suffering Servant** in **Isaiah** who is supposed to suffer and die and then be restored to life by God. The prophet **Elijah** did not die a mortal death but was taken up into heaven in a fiery chariot; it was widely believed by 1st century Jews that Elijah was immortal and would return to Earth one day.

According to the "Mythicist Theory", after Jesus' death, pagan myths (such as **Osiris**) and Jewish myths (such as the **Suffering Servant** and **Elijah**) became mixed up with Jesus' story, including the all-important dying-and-rising motif. This happened gradually over many re-tellings (rather like 'Chinese Whispers' where the original message gets changed out of all recognition).

A crucial part of this argument is that the Disciples originally believed in a SPIRITUAL RESURRECTION – that Jesus had risen as a spirit – but that over time the myth took over that Jesus had returned to physical life. There are details that support this view:

- The earliest Christian writer is **Paul** and his encounter with the Risen Jesus is more like a spiritual vision. Paul never mentions the empty tomb or the physical appearances of Jesus.
- **Mark's Gospel** (which originally seems to lack Resurrection scenes) was written perhaps 10-20 years after Paul's letters and the other Gospels (which *do* feature Resurrection scenes) perhaps 10-20 years after Mark.

Even in the later Gospels, there are tensions between the scenes that show a belief in a physical Resurrection (e.g. touching Jesus' hands and feet) and more mystical encounters (e.g. the **road to Emmaus**, p149). This makes sense if the physical Resurrection scenes have been added in later but the mystical scenes are older and more authentic.

Jewish followers added to this vision all sorts of details from **Isaiah's Servant Songs** and legends about **Elijah**. When Gentiles joined the Church they added details from their pagan culture, such as a dying-and-rising god like **Osiris** who physically comes back to life.

David Strauss, *The Life of Jesus Critically Examined*

David Strauss (1835), one of the most influential Bible scholars of the century, refuted the "Theft" and "Swoon" Hypotheses and proposed the view that the Resurrection was really a **myth**. Strauss' wrote *Das Leben Jesu* when only 27 and argued that the disciples attributed to Jesus all the miracles that Jewish myths had said that a Messiah would do. By 'myths', Strauss means:

> *the expression of primitive Christian ideas formulated in unintentionally poeticizing sagas and looking very like history* – **David Strauss**

In other words, a myth is UNINTENTIONAL POETRY that looks like HISTORY. Strauss admits there is spiritual truth in these myths – in that sense, they are not *false* – but they are not *history* either. Strauss thinks of a myth as a sort of dream that humans naturally come up with to express feelings that are important to them.

Strauss' book caused an uproar across Europe. The **Earl of Shaftesbury** called it "*the most pestilential book ever vomited out of the jaws of hell!*" Strauss lost his job at the University of Zürich due to the controversy and never worked as a teacher again.

There are problems with Strauss' theory. As you noted when studying **Topic 1.1 (Prophecy Concerning the Messiah)**, there are many ways in which Jesus does *not* fit the template for the Jewish **Messiah**, the **Suffering Servant** or the **son of David**. If a mythic detail like the Resurrection was added to Jesus' story by later Christians, why were awkward details like his being from Galilee rather than Judea not removed while they were at it?

The Gospels do not read like pagan myths or psychological wishes. They contain very specific times (e.g. 23 April, 33 CE for the Resurrection) and places (Jerusalem) and psychological motives (blasphemy, political expediency). **Julius Müller** (1844) argues that *real* myths take place in "*the mysterious gloom of grey antiquity*" but the Gospels are not set in 'ancient times' but in recent memory of the first believers.

> *One cannot imagine how such a series of legends could arise … if eyewitnesses were still at hand who could be questioned respecting the truth*– **Julius Müller**

Many scholars argue that the 30 years between the Crucifixion and the appearance of the first Christian writings is not long enough for the process of myth-making to take place.

Nonetheless, Strauss' theory does show how a belief in the Resurrection could come about without the Disciples of Jesus behaving deceitfully or insincerely or even particularly gullibly, which makes his theory an improvement on the "Theft" and "Swoon" Hypotheses. He also introduced the idea of a 'myth' as a story which is not historically true but which is not a simple falsehood or fiction either – myths can express true ideas in story form.

> *The Mythicist Hypothesis is not to be confused with the 'Christ Myth Theory' that argues that the ENTIRETY of Jesus' life is a myth, not just the Resurrection. This isn't Strauss' position: he thinks the historical really Jesus existed. The Christ Myth Theory doesn't carry much weight among Bible scholars – but it's popular online (of course!) and you'll find a lot of websites dedicated to the idea that Jesus is a made-up person.*

Is the Resurrection a myth?

YES	NO
People in the 1st century viewed the world in a mythological way and expected their heroes to live mythic lives. By adding mythic details to Jesus' story, they wouldn't have thought they were deceiving anyone. Jewish-Christians would re-tell Jesus' story to make him more like Elijah (going up to heaven but then returning to Earth) and Gentiles would make him more like the dying-and-rising pagan gods.	Myths do not 'pop up' like mushrooms; they take lifetimes to develop and evolve. However, the first Christian writings appeared within a couple of decades of Jesus' life, death and resurrection and in a community where the original witnesses were still on hand to describe their experiences. This cannot be said of Elijah or Osiris who lived in "*the mysterious gloom of grey antiquity.*"
The 1st century Christians lived in a world before the study of history had been discovered. It was natural for them to create "*unintentionally poetic sagas*" to communicate their intense love and reverence for Jesus: they exaggerated his achievements in the only way they knew how, by making him resemble the great figures of mythology, including coming back to life.	The Ancient Greeks and Romans had their historians too and they knew enough to be sceptical about myths and legends. The idea that Christians started with a belief in a purely spiritual Resurrection than mythologized it into a physical Resurrection fails to account for the historical details: the Empty Tomb, the testimony of the women, the meetings with the Risen Jesus who can be touched and eats.

The Resurrection as an Event in the Experience of the Disciples

As anthropology developed in the 20th century, the view of the **Resurrection as a myth** came to seem less plausible. A different naturalistic interpretation was that the Resurrection appearances were in fact hallucinations or visions. This idea was also put forward by **David Strauss** (1835) who argues the Disciples hallucinated Jesus' return from the dead because:

> *incapable of thinking of Jesus as dead, they were deluded into thinking that he had risen and appeared to them* **– David Strauss**

Celsus had suggested this back in the 2nd century and **Origen** rejected it on the grounds that the Disciples were *"neither mentally unbalanced nor delirious."* However, the development of Psychology shows that otherwise-healthy people under conditions of great emotional stress can show psychotic symptoms (such as hallucinations) while appearing normal in other respects.

Reports from Singapore General Hospital following the tsunami tragedy in Thailand (2004) describe accounts of "ghost sightings" among survivors who had lost loved ones. There may well be cultural or religious factors since many Thais believe that spirits may be put to rest only by relatives. Neurologist **Oliver Sacks** explains how such hallucinations can be psychologically comforting:

> *seeing the face or hearing the voice of one's deceased spouse, siblings, parents or child... may play an important part in the mourning process* **– Oliver Sacks**

Christian Weisse (1838) writes that the Resurrection *"has its source in the disciples' experience of the presence of Christ"* – but all the precise details were from their imaginations. **Ernest Renan** (1863) claims that the Resurrection was created by the imagination of **Mary Magdalene** and passed on to the Disciples as a sort of MASS HYSTERIA:

> *The little Christian society ... resuscitated Jesus in their hearts by the intense love which they bore toward him* **– Ernest Renan**

Jack Kent, *The Psychological Origins of the Resurrection Myth*

Jack Kent (1999) makes a contribution to the **'Habermas-Flew Debate'** between **Gary Habermas** (theist) and **Antony Flew** (sceptic) concerning the Resurrection. Kent offers a psychiatric interpretation of the 'Resurrection experiences' of the early disciples, based on current medical knowledge.

Kent argues that the women at the tomb and later the Disciples experienced *"normal, grief-related hallucinations."* **Peter** experienced additional guilt over denying Jesus before the Crucifixion; **Paul** experienced inner conflict over his part in the stoning to death of Stephen and his persecution of Christians.

Kent proposes these men suffered a *"conversion disorder,"* a recognized psychiatric illness that can occur in times of great anxiety and self-doubt. Paul's blindness after his vision of Jesus might have been PSYCHOSOMATIC (it existed only in his mind).

However, **Gary Habermas** points out that conversion disorder usually occurs in women (up to five times more often), adolescents and people with poor education or low socioeconomic status; it also occurs in former soldiers. None of this applies to Paul although the other Disciples seem to have been poor and uneducated. The women who visited the empty tomb were probably uneducated but they don't seem to have been poor (they helped fund Jesus' ministry and one is described as the wife of Herod's official).

The idea of 'holy hallucinations' avoids the idea of the Disciples or the later Christians fictionalising or carrying out a hoax: they are sincere witnesses, but mistaken.

However, there are three important questions unanswered:

- Why did the hallucinations stop? The Gospels report the Risen Jesus ascending into Heaven, which **Luke-Acts** claims took place 40 days after the Resurrection. Why didn't the mass hysteria continue to spread to other believers, just as the first hallucinations had?
- Why did the witnesses all experience the *same* hallucination? Hallucinations are SUBJECTIVE – they are unique to each person – yet the Disciples all seem to have shared the same hallucination. Even in the case of mass hysteria, individuals do not all experience the same thing
- Why was the tomb empty? Because the hallucination hypothesis does not explain the empty tomb, another naturalistic explanation is needed to cover this, such as 'Theft' or 'Swoon'.

The Objective Vision Hypothesis

Some Christian scholars argue that hallucinations might be genuine religious experiences. **Hans Grass** (1964) claims that Jesus' body remained dead and his Resurrection appearances were God-given **visions**; this is the "Objective Vision Hypothesis" in which the Resurrection appearances were genuine supernatural visions, but not physical encounters. **Theodor Keim** (1872) calls this sort of vision a *"telegram from heaven."*

The idea of 'objective visions' explains why a group of people could share the same hallucination. However, the problem is that such visions are DECEPTIVE. Why would God send a vision that fooled his followers into thinking a physical Resurrection had taken place? Moreover, why believe in a God who causes utterly realistic visions but not a God who can raise the dead to life?

William Lane Craig dismisses this sort of theory, arguing that:

> *[God] would have no conceivable reason for skipping the physical miracle of a resurrection and befuddling his earnest followers into the bargain* **– William Lane Craig**

This theory, just like the naturalistic Hallucination Theory, rejects the Gospel accounts of the Risen Jesus' bodily form (such as touching his hands and feet) as later inventions.

Is the Resurrection a hallucination or vision?

YES	NO
We know that people suffering bereavement can hallucinate their loved one is still alive and this might explain **Mary Magdalene**. Conversion disorder' can produce hallucinations in people like **Paul** and **Peter** who were suffering great guilt and moral confusion. Belief in the Resurrection began as visions, only later being changed to physical encounters.	Hallucinations are subjective, but those who met the Risen Jesus all experienced the same thing. **Paul** does not fit the profile for conversion disorder, being older and educated; we don't have enough information to know whether **Peter** and the other Disciples cud have suffered from this disorder but it doesn't fit with their words and behaviour in Luke-Acts.
We know that mass hysteria can be contagious, especially in a tightly-knit group of people under great stress with powerful beliefs. When one person starts hallucinating, it spreads to the others. The hallucinations might even be genuine visions, sent by God, to inspire the Disciples' faith.	Mass hysteria is still subjective and produces different hallucinations. Moreover, this doesn't explain why the hallucinations stopped after 40 days or why the tomb was empty. If God sent visions of Jesus, then the Disciples misunderstood those visions as a physical Resurrection, which brings into question God's wisdom and omnipotence.

Evaluating Challenges to the Resurrection

Naturalistic interpretations to the Resurrection are as old as accounts of the Resurrection itself. The Theft Hypothesis was proposed by Jewish critics of Christianity and **Celsus** (185 CE) proposed the Mythicist and Hallucination Hypotheses.

During and after the Enlightenment, the Theft Hypothesis was re-stated very forcefully. This was part of **rationalist interpretations** of Scripture (p144). The rationalists were **Deists** who were prepared to accept the moral value of Jesus' teachings about compassion and repentance, but believed Christianity had been distorted by a belief in miracles and the supernatural.

The Theft Hypothesis allows for Jesus to remain a wise and holy man who taught a simple lesson of goodness, but his fanatical disciples corrupted this by faking his Resurrection. By extension, the established churches which teach these miracles continue to betray Jesus' original moral message.

The Theft Hypothesis fell out of favour in the 19th century. Improvements in Bible criticism made it clear how sophisticated the early beliefs about the Resurrection were and how sincere the first Christians were in their faith. The related Swoon Hypothesis was demolished by **David Strauss** (1865) who argues that a survivor of crucifixion would have been too frail to have convinced the Disciples that he had been resurrected or produce such awe and worship in them.

The Mythicist Hypothesis became popular in the 19th and early 20th century. It is part of **sociological** (p55) and **literary interpretations** (p61) of Scripture and was given a huge boost by the popularity of **Sir James Frazer**'s *The Golden Bough* (1915) and the new field of anthropology, which studies ancient cultures and looks for common links across all religions. Anthropology tends to view religious beliefs as expressions of social situations, so this view regards the Resurrection as a way for early Christians to express their beliefs about Jesus in story form and make their new religion resemble their previous (pagan or Jewish) belief.

However, anthropology developed over the 20th century and the earlier views of Frazer and his admirers came to be seen as simplistic. Myths do not grow up like mushrooms in a short amount of time and the Gospels, when subjected to literary analysis, do not resemble myths.

The Mythicist Theory links to the views of **Rudolf Bultmann** (p33) who interprets the Gospel stories as myths that once made sense to pre-modern people but which cannot be accepted by scientific people today. He argues that the New Testament must be DE-MYTHOLOGIZED to understand the symbolic meaning of the Resurrection and make it relevant to today.

A slightly different view comes from **R. Alan Culpepper** (p158) who argues that we have to read the accounts of the Resurrection like a novel in order to *"read the gospel as the author's original audience read it"*. This is because, ever since the Enlightenment, modern readers automatically separate literal and symbolic meaning, but the 1st century readers of the Gospels did not make such a distinction.

In 1967, **Raymond E. Brown** pronounced naturalistic theories about the Resurrection as failures:

> *Serious scholars pay little attention to these fictional reconstructions* – **Raymond E. Brown**

However, the Hallucination Hypothesis is coming back into favour. This was first popularised by **David Strauss** as part of the **historical interpretation** of Scripture (p49) but it lapsed in the 20th century when Psychology took a more scientific, less speculative direction. According to **Gary Habermas**, the theory is growing in popularity again the 21st century.

The new popularity of the Hallucination Hypothesis is perhaps due to changes in the psychology of mental disorders, which increasingly focuses on the minor abnormal disorders that affect otherwise-normal people.

This makes it more plausible when psychologists like **Jack Kent** propose that the Disciples could hallucinate for a temporary period then fully recover, perhaps as a response to stress in their lives. However, not everyone is happy with loose and easily-applied diagnoses like *"conversion disorder"*. **Allen Frances** (2012) complains that the new medical textbook for mental disorders (**DSM-5**) *"medicalizes"* healthy experiences like grief, anger or forgetfulness, turning them into mental disorders. Writers like Jack Kent are 'medicalizing' the Resurrection in the same way.

Has the Resurrection been successfully disproved?

YES	NO
Naturalistic explanations of the Empty Tomb and the appearances of the Risen Jesus will always be more persuasive to scientifically-minded people than the idea of someone miraculously rising from the dead. In particular, we now understand false beliefs better than ever and can diagnose why the Disciples might have become convinced that their Lord had returned from the dead.	It's important to remember that Jesus didn't raise *himself* from the dead (which would be very improbable) – he was raised from the dead BY GOD. This is a very different proposition. If God exists and can perform miracles, then the idea that the Disciples suffered from strange, intense but temporary delusions doesn't look nearly as plausible as an explanation of the Resurrection.
Even though there are problems with individual naturalistic explanations, it remains the case that it is more likely that ONE of them is in fact the truth than that the laws of nature were violated by ringing a man back to life.	1st century Christians weren't gullible fools. It was clearly as difficult for them to accept the Resurrection as it is for so-called scientifically-minded modern people. They accepted the Resurrection as a fact because the weight of evidence pointed towards it.

Frank Morison, *Between Sunset and Dawn*

> *The Edexcel Anthology includes this passage as extract #8. Rather confusingly, it dates the extract from 2015. Take note: the passage is from Frank Morison's book* Who Moved The Stone?' *which was* **originally** *published in 1930!*

Frank Morison (real name: **Albert Henry Ross**, 1881-1950) is a journalist who wrote this classic piece of Christian APOLOGETICS (defence) nearly 100 years ago. Morison grew up agreeing with the then-new challenges to Christianity from *"the German critics"* (people like **David Strauss**) and decided to research a book exposing the Christian religion as a 'myth'.

However, while researching the book, Morison came to the opposite conclusion, that the evidence pointed towards the Resurrection being a historical fact.

> *it effected a revolution in my thought. Things emerged from old-world story that previously I should have thought impossible* – **Frank Morison**

Who Moved the Stone? goes through the final 24 hours of Jesus' life and the days that follow in the style of a lawyer sifting evidence, calling witnesses and discrediting them and arriving at a conclusion which is 'beyond all reasonable doubt'. It reads like a detective story, rather like *Sherlock Holmes*, with the sense of a mystery being unravelled through painstaking logic. It was a best-seller in its day and has been reprinted ten times since.

> *If you like Edwardian 'whodunnit?' detective stories like Agatha Christie then you should definitely read this slim book. You can read the full text on websites (e.g.* **www.gospeltruth.net**) *or buy a Kindle or second-hand print edition for under £3.*

Between Sunset & Dawn is the 8th chapter of Morison's book. Earlier in the book, Morison discusses the tangled motives for the chief priests in arresting Jesus on the Passover night (he agrees with the Synoptic Gospels' dating of this) and explores how Jesus' Disciples were split into two groups: **Peter** and **John** (Morison identifies the 'Beloved Disciple' as John son of Zebedee and follows John's Gospel's account here) follow the guards to the city and are left inside the city walls during the Sabbath; the other Disciples run away and Morison concludes they would have escaped to the village of Bethany nearby to warn the sisters Mary and Martha of what had happened.

Morison goes on to analyse the **trial before Pilate** in detail, exploring **Pontius Pilate**'s psychology as well as the complicated legal processes at work. Morison's technique is to focus on the things that are left unsaid and the details that are left unexplained.

For example, Morison argues that Pilate was under emotional pressure from his wife to free Jesus, based on **Matthew 27: 19** which reports that Claudia had a dream about Jesus and begged her husband: *"Don't have anything to do with that innocent man!"*

Morison produces a HARMONISATION of the four Gospels, blending their accounts together to produce a single, plausible narrative. He uses elements from the **rationalist approach** (p44 – he removes miraculous elements, such as the healing of Malchus' ear in **Luke 22: 51**) and the **historical approach** to interpreting Scripture (p49 – he applies knowledge of Jewish and Roman legal processes and the archaeological layout of Jerusalem to reconstruct events like a historian).

In chapter 8, Morison considers what happened to Jesus' body on Easter morning. Right at the outset, he dismisses the idea proposed by **Celsus** (p172) and later by **Herman Reimarus** (p178) that the Disciples stole Jesus' body from the tomb.

> no great moral structure like the Early Church, based as it was upon lifelong persecution and personal suffering, could have reared its head upon a statement which every one of the eleven apostles knew to be a lie.

Morison is repeating the objections made by **Origen** and later **Jacques Abbadie** (1698) that *"no one dies for a fiction which they have invented."* **Thomas Woolston** (1730) disagrees, pointing out *"criminals and cheats have gone to their death proclaiming their innocence."* There is also the possibility of a conspiracy that the Disciples might not have known about, such as a rival group of disciples (Woolston suggests the mysterious **Essenes**). However, most scholars agree with Morison's verdict on this.

Morison goes on to consider 6 possible explanations for the women discovering an empty tomb:

1. Joseph of Arimathea removed Jesus' body
2. The Roman authorities removed Jesus' body
3. The Jewish authorities removed Jesus' body
4. Jesus was not really dead and later recovered in the tomb
5. The women went to the wrong tomb
6. No one visited the tomb and the story is a myth

Joseph of Arimathea removed Jesus' body

All the Gospels agree that a Jewish leader named **Joseph of Arimathea** provided an unused tomb for Jesus' body. It is plausible that this was only a temporary arrangement and that Joseph then moved the body to a more permanent resting place.

Morison points out an initial problem with this explanation: why would Joseph remove the body in the middle of the night? This would be difficult and inconvenient and there was no need to hide what he was doing. Even if he arrived with workmen first thing on the morning after the Sabbath, the women would have encountered him there, rather than an empty tomb.

However, Morison admits that Joseph might have had *some* reason to want to avoid attention so it's possible he removed the body in the night. This would explain **Mary Magdalene**'s message that *"they have taken away the Lord and we do not know where they have laid him!"*

Morison considers Joseph's possible motives:

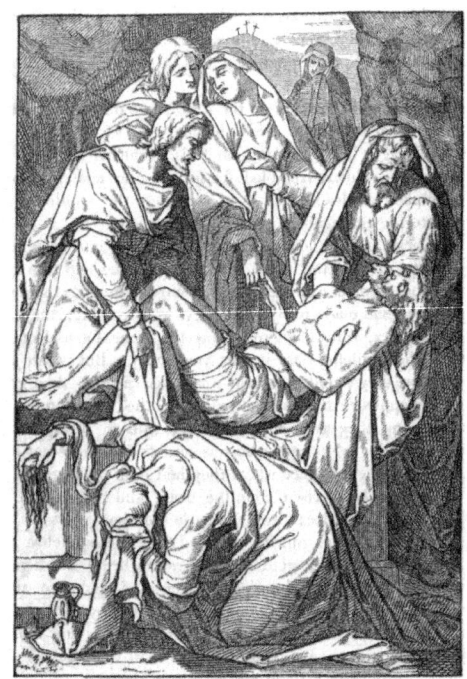

1. He was a pious Jew and did not want a body to remain hanging overnight (forbidden by **Deuteronomy 21: 23**)
2. He was a secret follower of Jesus and wanted to show his teacher a last respect

Morison rejects the first theory because no effort was made to bury the two thieves who all four Gospels describe as being crucified alongside Jesus.

However, if Joseph was a secret follower of Jesus, then he would have been pleased for Jesus' body to remain in his tomb: it would have been an honour – or, as Morison sums up the view that Joseph moved the body: *"overwhelmingly, psychology is against it."*

If Joseph moved the body to a better location, then *that* location would have become a *"tomb or shrine becoming the centre of veneration or worship."*

However, there were never any rumours of alternative resting places for Jesus' body.

> Strange though it may appear, the only way in which we can account for the absence of this phenomenon is the explanation offered in the Gospels, viz. that the tomb was known, was investigated a few hours after the burial, and that the body had disappeared.

Morison concludes that, although the empty tomb is unlikely, the idea of Joseph of Arimathea removing the body but concealing its new location is even more unlikely.

Evaluating Morison on the burial

Morison assumes that the story of Joseph of Arimathea providing a tomb for Jesus is historical in the first place but some critics suggest otherwise. **Bart Ehrman** argues that standard practice for the Romans was to bury crucified convicts together in an unmarked shallow grave where they would probably be dug up and eaten by animals – the ultimate disgrace. **John Dominic Crossan** (1994) proposes that Jesus' body was *"eaten by scavenging dogs."* This is known as the 'Shallow Grave' Theory.

In support of this, it is very improbable that Pilate would have made an exception to Roman practice for Jesus. Joseph of Arimathea is a character never previously mentioned in the Gospels and never mentioned again; 'Arimathea' is an unknown place and may well be fictional.

The earliest reference to Jesus' death and resurrection is from **Paul**, who only states that Jesus was *buried* (**1 Corinthians 15: 4**) but never mentions a tomb. The tomb could have been a fiction composed by **Mark's Gospel** which was then copied by the other Gospels.

The authorities (Jewish or Roman) removed Jesus' body

Morison lumps his 2nd and 3rd explanations together, because the same objections apply to both of them.

Morison thinks it is unlikely that *"a very obstinate man"* such as Pilate would have changed his mind about Jesus' burial once his decision was made. He points out that the records show the priests requesting, not the removal of Jesus' body, but a guard of soldiers to prevent **anyone else** removing the body. However, Morison has a more powerful objection to this idea:

> For if the Priests induced Pilate to change the burial place, or to authorize their doing so, they must have known the ultimate and final resting-place, and in that event they would never have been content with the obviously unsatisfactory and untrue statement that the disciples had stolen the body.

The rumour that the Disciples stole the body of Jesus is mentioned in **Matthew 28: 13** and is repeated by **Celsus** in the 2nd century CE. But if the authorities knew where the body was, there would be no need for such a rumour: they could have announced the true burial place and *"destroyed forever the credibility of anyone asserting the physical resurrection of Jesus."*

> It is the complete failure of anyone to produce the remains, or to point to any tomb, official or otherwise, in which they were said to lie, which ultimately destroys every theory based upon the human removal of the body.

Morison's point is a strong one because we know that the Jewish authorities and later the Roman authorities persecuted Christians for their beliefs, but did not think to disprove them by showing that **they** had removed the body.

Evaluating Morison on the body

Even if the authorities did remove Jesus' body, producing it again to silence Christian claims of the Resurrection would not have been easy. **Luke-Acts** states that the Disciples did not start preaching the Resurrection until after the **Ascension** (p152), which took place 40 days later. This means the body of Jesus would have been at least 7 weeks old – probably no longer recognizable enough to put a stop to the Christian claims.

Furthermore, in order to make this counter-claim, the authorities would have to admit what they had done. For the Jewish authorities, this would be admitting to desecrating a grave, which is very sinful in Judaism. For the Romans, it would have been a huge deviation from their normal procedure for crucifying criminals where the body was left to hang in a public place so that everyone can see the corpse deteriorate – and also graverobbing, which would possibly start a riot (the very thing Pilate wanted to prevent, according to the **political expediency** argument about **Why Jesus Had to Die**, p102).

Jesus did not really die on the cross

This is the 'Swoon Theory' (p178) proposed by **Karl Bahrdt** and **Heinrich Paulus** during the Enlightenment. It also includes the popular Muslim view that Jesus was rescued from the cross or else someone else died in his place.

Morison mentions **Karl Venturini**'s 1800 version of the Swoon Theory: Jesus survived the crucifixion and was rescued by his **Essene** allies, made surreptitious appearances to his followers but finally died a natural death 40 days later, which his Disciples mistook for him 'ascending into heaven'.

Morison sums up the implausibility of this from a medical standpoint:

> It ignores the deadly character of the wounds inflicted upon Jesus, the frightful laceration of the hands and feet, the loss of strength through the ebbing away of blood, the hopelessness of human aid during the critical moments when it would be most needed, the tight-drawn bandages of the grave, the heavy stone.

(Although to be fair, many versions of the Swoon Theory are also conspiracy theories and propose Jesus had help moving the stone and taking off his bandages.)

Morison's refers to the *"death blow to this theory"* from **David Strauss** (1865). Strauss points out that, even if he did survive crucifixion and escape the *sepulchre* (tomb), Jesus would have been

> *a being who had stolen half dead out of the sepulchre, who crept about weak and ill and wanting medical treatment* – **David Strauss**

Somebody in this condition could not have

> *given the disciples the impression that he was a Conqueror over death and the grave, the Prince of Life* – **David Strauss**

Evaluating Morison on the 'swoon'

There are not many defenders today of the Swoon Theory (also known as the Apparent Death Theory or ADT). Morison's (and Strauss') arguments don't have many critics:

> *Anyone who imagines that the survivor of a crucifixion would be in a state to convince anyone that he was the victorious conqueror of death clearly has very little idea what a crucifixion was like. To put the matter mildly, people did not walk away from it –* **Christopher Bryan**

Nonetheless, the best-selling book *Holy Blood, Holy Grail* (1982) speculates that **Pontius Pilate** was bribed to allow Jesus to be rescued before he was dead. The book proposes Jesus went to live in the south of France with his wife, **Mary Magdalene**, and his descendants still exist today.

> *Sounds familiar? Dan Brown lifted the theory for his 2003 hit novel (and 2006 film with Tom Hanks)* 'The Da Vinci Code'. It's a fun story but it's only plausible if you're the sort of person who loves conspiracy theories ...

The Women Made a Mistake

Morison credits this theory to **Prof. Kirsopp Lake** (Lake's book *The Resurrection of Jesus Christ* was published in 1907). Lake argues that, in the darkness before dawn, the women arrived at the wrong tomb (he claims: *"the neighborhood of Jerusalem is full of rock tombs"*) which would be a naturalistic explanation for the account of the tomb (i) being open and (ii) having no body inside.

Mark 16: 5 describes the women finding *"a young man dressed in a white robe"* sitting inside the tomb. The other Gospels represent this person as an angel, but Lake thinks (and Morison agrees) that this was a human being. Lake argues that this was a gardener who tried to tell the women they had come to the wrong place: *"See the place where they laid him"* (**Mark 16: 6**) is the gardener trying to indicate *a different tomb*.

Lake proposes that the women were already running in fear and only half-heard the gardener's instruction and misunderstood the words to refer to the empty ledge in the tomb where a body would be laid.

The obvious criticism of this view is that, as soon as they were notified, the Disciples came to the tomb and checked for themselves (as described by **Luke** and **John's Gospel**): did they also go to the wrong tomb, in broad daylight?

Lake's response is that the other Disciples had *already left* Jerusalem: they had returned home to Galilee. Lake thinks that the Disciples had visions or hallucinations of the Risen Jesus in Galilee *before* they knew anything about the empty tomb. When they returned to Jerusalem, they met the women who told them about Jesus' body 'disappearing'.

Morison makes several criticisms of this theory:

1. The Gospels do not present *all* the Disciples as running away. **Peter** remained in Jerusalem; so perhaps did the 'Beloved Disciple' (who may be **John**). Earlier in his book, Morison argues that the other Disciples only escaped as far as nearby Bethany, not all the way to Galilee.
2. It would be very strange for the Disciples to abandon these women in Jerusalem for weeks, especially since some were their own family and mothers. Morison argues that if a group of women felt safe to visit Jesus' tomb, a group of men would surely have felt safe to stay in hiding in Jerusalem.
3. Why would the gardener have been sitting *inside* an empty tomb?

The final criticism links back to the arguments about someone removing the body:

> Here was the one man who could have spoken with complete and final authority; whose slightest word could have blown the whole flimsy story to the winds.

4. If the Jewish authorities wanted to disprove the Christian claims about the Resurrection, , they could bring in the gardener as a witness to the women's mistake, yet there is no reference to this even as a rumour

Evaluating Morison on the location of the tomb

As you will see when you study **Ian Wilson**'s anthology extract #9 (p38), there are several contenders for the true tomb of Jesus, so it's certainly possible for the women to have gone to the wrong tomb. Nevertheless, **Paul Gwynne** (2000) agrees with Morison: *"the 'mistaken tomb' theory has very few serious supporters these days."*

> *it is difficult to imagine how [a wrong tomb] mistake would not have been quickly corrected* – **C.E.B. Cranfield**

Nevertheless, Morison does agree with Lake on several key points that he develops later in his book:

- Morison agrees with Lake that the women were frightened away by a strange man in the tomb and he shares Lake's view that the other Gospels are fictionalizing when they represent this person as an angel
- Morison also thinks it likely that the women did not understand what the man was trying to tell them
- Morison also agrees with Lake that the women did not at first believe anything supernatural had happened: they just thought Jesus' body had been taken somewhere else

At the end of his book, Morison argues that the man in the tomb was a 'servant of the high priest' who had been in charge of the guards outside the tomb (**Matthew 27: 62-66**). These guards fell asleep at their posts but awoke to find the tomb open and empty. The guards ran back to the city, but high priest's servant stayed behind to investigate.

> *In the closing chapter of his book, Morison offers the charming idea that this 'servant of the high priest' might actually have been the first person to encounter the Risen Jesus.*

The tomb was not visited by the women

This is Morison's final theory. He suggests that it is the only logical alterative to the Resurrection:

> If it could be proved that that grave was not visited on Sunday morning, and that it lay undisturbed and perhaps unthought of for many months afterwards, then the rock upon which all the preceding hypotheses ultimately founder would be removed.

However, in this extract, Morison does not disprove this theory, other than to suggest that it doesn't account for *"what happens afterwards"*.

What does happen afterwards is this: Jesus' disciples become convinced of the Resurrection and go into the streets of Jerusalem, preaching and winning converts. This takes place in a city where:

> *anybody could go and see the tomb between supper and bed-time* – **Frank Morison**

The most prominent Christian apologist today who repeats Morison's arguments is **William Lane Craig**. Craig shares Morison's conclusion that the Disciples would not be able to preach about the Resurrection in Jerusalem if the body was known to be still in the tomb.

Morison concludes that the empty tomb was the one thing the first Christians and their opponents agreed on:

> *We are nowhere told that any responsible person asserted that the body of Jesus was still in the tomb* – **Frank Morison**

He therefore concludes that the women arriving at the correct tomb and found it empty on Easter morning is far more plausible than the idea that the tomb was not visited:

> *However baffling and disconcerting it may seem at first sight, the evidence for the essential accuracy of the women's story is overwhelming in its consistency and strength* – **Frank Morison**

Evaluating Morison's conclusions

A powerful argument that Morison does not consider is that, in the early years of Christianity, there was no interest in visiting Jesus' tomb because the Disciples preached a SPIRITUAL RESURRECTION rather than a bodily Resurrection; i.e. they claimed that Jesus had been raised from the dead as a spiritual being (but his physical body remained dead).

If this is the case, then belief in a bodily Resurrection developed much later, but by then it was too late to track down Jesus' tomb (perhaps because, after 70 CE, the Romans had destroyed it during the siege of Jerusalem).

In support of this, **Paul**'s encounter with the Risen Christ on the road to Damascus (occurring perhaps around 36 CE) seems to be with a spiritual being, not a physical person. The Gospels contain episodes where the Risen Jesus behaves like a spirit (appearing and disappearing, changing his appearance). The examples of the Disciples touching Jesus in **Luke** and **John's Gospel** could have been added in later be the Gospel-writers acting as **redactors** (editors).

There are problems with this interpretation. Jews like the **Pharisees** believed in a bodily Resurrection, whereas Hellenic philosophers supported a spiritual resurrection. You would expect Jesus' earliest followers (who were Jews) to believe in a bodily Resurrection and ideas about spiritual resurrection to creep in over time as more Gentiles join the Church. This is the trend we observe in the **Gospel of Thomas** (introduced in **Topic 3**) and the Gnostic texts, which favour a spiritual resurrection and (probably) date from the 2nd century or later.

Morison can also be accused of CHERRY-PICKING: he harmonises the four Gospels into one narrative by selecting details that support his case and ignoring details that don't. For example, Morison omits the scene in **Matthew 28: 2** where the women see an angel come down and roll away the stone blocking the tomb; Morison also interprets the *young man dressed in a white robe* as a flesh-and-blood human, not an angel. He does this because he is a **rationalist** who (in general) prefers naturalistic interpretations to supernatural ones – he makes an exception for the Resurrection itself, but 'explains away' the other supernatural details.

In this, Morison is following **David Hume**'s idea (p16) that even very improbable naturalistic explanations are more likely than supernatural ones. However, he doesn't follow this to Hume's conclusion, which is that no matter how improbable it might be that someone would move Jesus' body and keep it secret, or that Jesus would recover from crucifixion and escape from his tomb, or that the women would visit the wrong tomb, those explanations are still *more probable* than that a dead man rises back to life.

Does Morison make a persuasive case for the Resurrection as a historical fact?

YES	NO
Morison goes through the naturalistic explanations for the empty tomb, methodically, pointing out what is plausible in them but then analyzing the contradictions that come from them. He shows how they contradict the known early history of the Christian Church or ordinary human nature. He is left with the Resurrection as the only remaining hypothesis.	Like a good lawyer, Morison makes the opposing explanations seem weaker than they really are. If Jesus' body was stolen, it doesn't follow that *all* of the Disciples or the Jewish priests were "in on it". The idea of Jesus 'swooning' on the cross is thoroughly discredited but Morison doesn't take seriously the idea that the early Christians might not have preached a bodily Resurrection at all.
Morison is a **rationalist** who doesn't believe in any and all supernatural events. He rejects the descriptions of angels at the tomb and prefers naturalistic interpretations of the *young man in a white robe*. However, when all naturalistic interpretations fail, he is prepared to accept that a miracle has occurred and this is what he concludes about the empty tomb.	Morison respects Hume's advice that "*a wise man proportions his belief to the evidence*" but doesn't follow it through. He cherry-picks his evidence to produce a naturalistic account but then changes his position at the end by proposing a miraculous Resurrection: even improbable naturalistic explanations are more plausible than miracles.

Ian Wilson, *Did Jesus Really Rise from the Dead?*

> *The Edexcel Anthology includes this passage as extract #9. As with the previous extract, the date is a bit misleading. Wilson's book 'Jesus: The Evidence' was published in 1984 in support of a Channel4 TV series. A new and updated edition was published in 2000.*

Ian Wilson (born 1941) is a writer who specialises in religious and historical mysteries. He was a sceptic in his younger years but converted to (Catholic) Christianity as a result of researching the Turin Shroud.

This curious relic has been kept at the Cathedral of John the Baptist in Turin, Italy since the 14th century CE. Legend claims it is the burial shroud Jesus was wrapped in after crucifixion – the same wrapping found neatly folded in the empty tomb by Peter in **Luke 24: 12** and **John 20: 6**.

The Shroud is a linen cloth bearing the image of a man who is alleged to be Jesus. The image on the shroud is faint sepia (brown) but is much clearer in black-and-white negative – this negative discovered in 1898 by an amateur photographer. Radiocarbon dating suggests the Shroud is from the Middle Ages, not the 1st century, but Wilson and others argue that the Shroud is genuine and preserves the real likeness of Jesus.

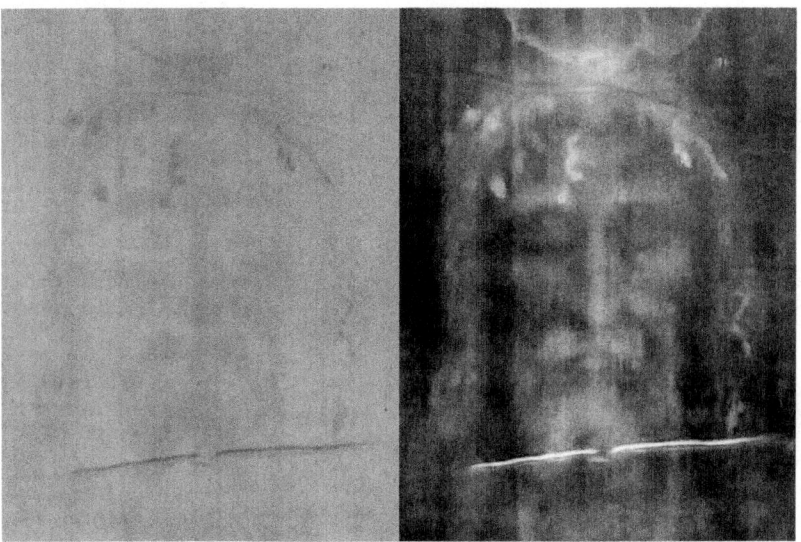

The negative image of the Shroud is striking and shows a man with wounds to his hands and feet, scars on his back and on his brow. No one knows quite how the image was created.

Perhaps because of his association with trying to prove the Shroud of Turin's authenticity, Wilson is not taken very seriously as a New Testament scholar. Wilson doesn't get much praise from conservative Christians either! This seems to be because he's a rationalist who usually prefers naturalistic explanations for the supernatural events in Jesus' life (for example, he speculates that some of Jesus' healings and miracles could be explained if Jesus was a talented hypnotist).

Many of Wilson's religious critics are admiring of **Frank Morison** (p188), despite the fact that both writers have the same rationalist view of the supernatural. The big difference is that Morison is an APOLOGIST: he's defending Christianity and only lines up naturalistic explanations in order to knock them down. Wilson (who wrote his book to accompany a TV documentary) is trying to be fair-minded and balances evidence for the Resurrection with evidence against.

> 'Jesus: The Evidence' *is an attractive 'coffee table' book, full of colour photographs, charts and maps. It takes the reader through the background of Jesus' life and the main arguments. Despite the way 'proper' scholars turn their noses up at it, this book makes a pretty good companion to an A-Level course and students can easily track down second-hand copies for under £3 (including postage).*

Identifying the real tomb

The site of the empty tomb is believed to be the modern-day **Church of the Holy Sepulchre** in Jerusalem. Ian Wilson explains why the current church looks nothing like the original tomb: a pagan temple to the goddess Aphrodite had been built on top of it and the site was re-discovered by Helena, wife of Constantine the Great, in the 4th century CE. A combination of Helena's clumsy excavations, the building of a later church on the site and then centuries of warfare over the city between Christians and Muslims means that nothing is now left of the original rock tomb.

There are other contenders for the site of Jesus' tomb. Wilson claims that there are 60 examples of ancient rock tombs in Jerusalem. The 'Garden Tomb' is a popular site for pilgrims because it is relatively untouched, in beautiful surroundings, outside the Damascus Gate of the Old City.

The 'Garden Tomb'

Wilson points out how unusual it was for Jesus to be buried in an empty tomb in which *no one had ever been laid* (**John 19: 41**) since these rock tombs were typically used by several generations of a Jewish family. The dead body would be laid out on a stone bench and then, once it had decomposed, the bones would be stored in a stone box called an ossuary. The tomb would be sealed with a boulder that could weigh up to 2 tons. This closely matches the description of Jesus' tomb in all four Gospels.

Evaluating Wilson's view of the tomb

There are good reasons for Wilson to be suspicious of the Church of the Holy Sepulchre's claim to be the site of the empty tomb. Its discovery by Helena was a 'publicity stunt' on behalf of her husband, the first Christian Roman Emperor. The fragments of the 'True Cross' and the *'titulum'* (the notice originally fixed to the top of the cross identifying Jesus as 'King of the Jews') are widely thought to be fakes.

However, since the Gospels all describe the tomb as being **outside** the city walls, it's odd that Helena should identify a site **inside** the walls of Jerusalem. What Helena couldn't have known is that the walls had been rebuilt since the 1st century and that the site she selected **would have been outside the walls** in 30 CE when Jesus was crucified. This suggests that Helena didn't pick a site at random: she really was guided by a local tradition that this was indeed the genuine location of the empty tomb.

> There must, therefore, have been something very compelling about the location for Helena to have ignored the gospels' clear descriptions. As archaeologist Dr Kathleen Kenyon discovered in the 1960s, the Church of the Holy Sepulchre site was outside the city walls of Jesus' time, and would seem to have been within a quarry then being used for burials.

On the other hand, the 'Garden Tomb' has been dated back to the 8th century BCE. This means it could not have been a new and unused tomb when Jesus was buried, as **Matthew** and **John's Gospel** both claim. Most archaeologists support Wilson that there's little evidence to connect the 'Garden Tomb' to Jesus, but it is regarded as the true tomb by some religious groups (such as the Church of Latter Days Saints or 'Mormons').

Discrepancies in the Resurrection accounts

Wilson gives a brief account of the circumstances of Jesus' death and burial and the discovery of the empty tomb. Like **Morison** (p188), he produces a harmonized narrative by bringing details from all the Gospels together. Also like Morison, he rejects the earthquake and angel in **Matthew**'s version of the story as *"pious embroideries by an author demonstrably over-fond of the miraculous."*

This is the sort of comment that makes Wilson unpopular with conservative Christians, despite the fact that Morison takes a similar view.

Unlike Morison, Wilson goes on to list the Resurrection appearances themselves, distinguishing those that appear to be spiritual from those that are clearly a bodily resurrection. He also links these appearances to the way the first Christians preached about the Resurrection, as described in the **Book of Acts**.

> *Now I and those with me can witness to everything he did throughout the countryside of Judaea and in Jerusalem itself: and also to the fact that they killed him by hanging him on a tree, yet three days afterwards God raised him to life and allowed him to be seen, not by the whole people, but only by certain witnesses God had chosen beforehand. Now we are those witnesses – we have eaten and drunk with him after his resurrection from the dead ...*
> *(Acts 10: 39–42)*

Wilson dates Paul's belief in the Resurrection to *perhaps as early as 36 AD* [sic] and suggests *"there remains no uncontested rational answer"* to *"the central mystery of the Christian religion"* which is, How did this belief in the Resurrection come about? (Wilson is careful with his words. There is a non-rational answer: the supernatural raising of Jesus from the dead by God.)

Wilson highlights the discrepancies between the Gospel accounts of the Resurrection:

Matthew	Mark	Luke	John
Mary Magdalene is with another Mary	Mary Magdalene is with another Mary and Salome	Mary Magdalene is with another Mary and Joanna	Mary Magdalene arrives alone
An angel opens the tomb	The tomb is open and a young man is inside	The tomb is open and two men/angels appear	The tomb is open is empty
The women tell the Eleven that Jesus has risen and are believed	The women tell no one	The women tell the Eleven that Jesus has risen but are not believed	Mary tells Peter and the 'Beloved Disciple' that the body has been removed
The women meet the Risen Jesus on the way home	The 'longer ending' describes Mary Magdalene meeting the Risen Jesus, but she is not believed by the Eleven	The Risen Jesus appears to two disciples **on the road to Emmaus** but they do not recognise him	Back at the tomb, Mary sees two angels then meets the Risen Jesus, whom she mistakes for a gardener
Jesus appears to the Disciples in Galilee	Jesus appears to the Disciples in Galilee	Jesus appears to the Disciples in Jerusalem	Jesus appears to the Disciples in Jerusalem

Wilson adds two more suspicious details: (1) Mary Magdalene is a poor witness, having been cured of madness by Jesus (she was possessed by 'seven devils'); (2) Paul's account in **1 Corinthians 15: 5-8** has a different order of appearances (with no mention of the women at all).

However, Wilson admits two things in favour of these accounts:

The Risen Jesus appears to Mary Magdalene outside the tomb

1. They possess *"the same quality as the memories of witnesses after a road accident"* which makes them sound like *"personal and highly confused versions of the same story"*

2. If the accounts were invented, why would the Gospel-writers have made women the prime witnesses, especially since *"women's testimony carried a particularly low weight in Jewish Law"*?

Evaluating Wilson on the discrepancies

The speeches in Acts are evidence that the early Christians believed in a bodily Resurrection. However, **Luke-Acts** was not composed until the 70s or 80s CE according to most estimates, so the speeches by **Peter** that are reported may not be authentic (since there are 40-50 years between the original speeches and the Gospel).

Paul's epistles (letters) were written in the 50s CE by someone who knew Peter and the other Disciples personally. They are probably a much better guide to what the first Christians believed, but Paul seems to describe Jesus appearing to him in a vision or as a spirit.

The presence of women as the first witnesses passes the CRITERION OF EMBARRASSMENT since this is not a detail the Gospel-writers would invent if they wanted their story to be believed. Women seem to have been very influential at the beginning of Christianity. Wilson implies that Paul misses out the women from his list of Resurrection appearances out of sheer sexism, but that doesn't fit well with Paul's dealings with Christian women leaders like **Lydia** and **Chloe**; Paul entrusts his Epistle to the Romans to **Phoebe**, who delivers to Rome on his behalf – not the behaviour of someone *"for whom women didn't count."* ✗ Sweeping generalisation to say women don't count.

Frank Morison (p188) suggests a different explanation for these contradictions, which is that the early Christians were accused of stealing Jesus' body themselves. This made it embarrassing for them to admit that the women, Peter and the others had visited the tomb on Easter morning because this would strengthen the accusations that they had carried out a hoax. Therefore, they downplayed the empty tomb and the testimony of the women, which is why, when the Gospel-writers came to record the events years later, the precise details had become confused.

The Six Basic Hypotheses

Just like **Frank Morison** on the empty tomb (p188), Wilson outlines six possible explanations for the Resurrection appearances:

1. **The women went to the wrong tomb**
   Wilson dismisses this in the same way as **Morison** and **Craig**: *"it would have been an easy matter for any sceptic to go to the right location, show the body still there and set the whole matter at rest"*.

2. **Someone removed Jesus' body**
   As pointed out by Morison, Wilson argues that once the Disciples started preaching the Resurrection, *"we might surely have expected someone, some time, to produce it"*.

3. **The disciples removed Jesus' body**
   Wilson doesn't treat the Theft Hypothesis separately, but seems to regard it as inevitable that, if a follower of Jesus had taken the body, that person would at some point have confessed to what they had done (perhaps because of the persecution they faced).

4. **The Risen Jesus was a hallucination**
   Wilson is dubious about hallucinations that could feel so real to so many people but his main argument is that the Hallucination Hypothesis does not explain the empty tomb.

5. **Jesus survived crucifixion**
   Wilson mentions versions of the Swoon Hypothesis by **Hugh Schonfield, D.H. Lawrence** and **Barbara Thiering**, but refutes them all with **David Strauss'** famous comment that *"a being who had stolen half dead out of the sepulchre"* could not have convinced the Disciples that he was really *"the Prince of Life"*.

6. **Jesus really did rise from the dead**
   Wilson suggests this is the most persuasive hypothesis. In support, he describes the transformation of *"the previously denying and demoralized"* Peter into a confident and passionate missionary. He also cites **Edwin Yamauchi** in support of the idea that Paul listing so many witnesses to the Resurrection who were alive at the time he wrote is strong evidence that *"something like [the Resurrection] actually happened."*

> *Wilson maintains a cautious tone, saying only that "something like" the Resurrection happened though we can't know "what exactly happened". This is Wilson being a careful historian and appearing open-minded.*

Wilson offers another criticism, which is that the Gospels were specifically written to counter some of these hypotheses.

1. **Wrong tomb:** The Synoptic Gospels all make a point of mentioning that the women took careful note of where Jesus was buried

2. **Theft of the body:** John's Gospel has Mary Magdalene believing someone has stolen the body

3. **Hoax by the Disciples:** Matthew's Gospel specifically accuses the Jewish leaders of spreading this rumour
4. **Hallucination:** Luke and John's Gospel include scenes where the Disciples are disbelieving until they touch Jesus' hands and feet

If these were standard criticisms leveled at the earliest Christians for their beliefs, then the Gospel-writers might have added these details in purely to answer their critics. This is an example of **Redaction Criticism**: the Gospel-writers edit their material to address problems in their own time rather than to describe what really happened on the first Easter morning.

Wilson concludes by surveying the immense impact of the Resurrection on the lives of the early Christians. He gives the example of Stephen the Martyr and Jesus' own family (such as his brother James) who faced torture and ugly death *"with astonishing cheerfulness, totally confident that what they professed was truth"*:

> What cannot be emphasized enough is that those who made such claims had absolutely no expectation of any material gain for their outspokenness. Their reward instead, as the following decades and centuries would demonstrate, was all too frequently to be faced with some form of violent death, from being stoned, to being torn to pieces by wild animals in a Roman arena, to being crucified in some yet more grotesque and painful manner.

The last remark is a reference to Peter's fate: he was executed in Rome, crucified upside down.

Evaluating Wilson on the Six Basic Hypotheses

Wilson's hypotheses are essentially the same as **Morison**'s (p188, although he adds the Hallucination Theory) and have already been evaluated. His treatment of the Theft Hypothesis is perhaps too brief. When the Disciples started preaching Jesus' Resurrection in public, it was 7 weeks after the Crucifixion according to **Luke-Acts**, which would have made it impossible for anyone to produce a recognisable corpse to refute these claims. It is also at least *possible* that some Disciple died without telling anyone that the Resurrection had been a hoax.

Wilson describes some pretty sensationalist versions of the Swoon Theory – but this is because his book accompanied a TV documentary that tried to catch the viewers' attention with weird ideas. **Barbara Thiering**'s theory is worth a bit more consideration.

Thiering is an Australian scholar whose book *Jesus, The Man* (1992) offers a radical reinterpretation of Jesus' life story. Thiering thinks that Jesus was an **Essene** and that the Gospels are all written in code. According to the way Thiering decodes' the New Testament, Jesus married twice, had four children and died of old age in Rome around 60 CE.

Thiering's ideas are rejected by other scholars but they demonstrate that, with a bit of imagination, the Gospels can be interpreted in *very* unusual ways.

The idea that the transformation of **Peter** and the other Disciples proves that the Resurrection (or *something like it*) happened is a weak argument. We don't know much about what Peter was like *before* the Resurrection, because the Gospels focus more on Jesus than his Disciples' personalities.

Perhaps Peter had always been charismatic and confident and a dazzling public speaker and just needed an opportunity to step out from under Jesus' shadow!

Even if Peter did transform from a cowardly nobody into an amazing preacher, this doesn't prove his Resurrection experience was objectively real, only that Peter and the others **believed** it was real.

It's not unusual for people to 'reinvent' themselves after a breakdown or a life crisis and this might be what happened to Peter, Paul, Stephen and the others. The fact that belief in the Resurrection was psychologically good for Peter and the rest doesn't make it automatically true.

Peter is a spiritual hero to most Christians and Catholics view him as the first Pope

The theory that the Gospel-writers **redacted** details into their accounts to refute criticisms by unbelievers is unprovable. However, it can be shown to be unlikely if there were other naturalistic explanations of the Resurrection which the Gospels do **not** make a point of refuting in this way.

One such hypothesis that Wilson does not consider is the SUBSTITUTION HYPOTHESIS: Jesus was replaced on the cross by a substitute who looked just like him, perhaps even his identical twin brother. This is not a modern idea but is present in 2nd and 3rd century texts like *The Acts of Thomas* (the Disciple Thomas being Jesus' twin, since 'Thomas' is Greek for 'twin').

However, the Gospels don't make a point of refuting the Substitution Hypothesis (e.g. by making it clear Jesus didn't have any twin brothers). The Gospel-writers would surely do this if they were redacting material just to refute all the popular criticisms of the Resurrection that were going around.

Wilson's conclusion is that the rapid spread of Christianity was unusual despite great opposition and *"something very powerful had fired them into such resoluteness of belief."* Wilson is not trying to prove the Resurrection happened so much as encourage his readers to view the matter more open-mindedly before arriving at their own conclusions.

Does Morison make a persuasive case for the Resurrection as a historical fact?

YES	NO
Wilson argues that the **Church of the Holy Sepulchre** probably is the true site of the empty tomb and that the transformation in the lives of **Peter** and other disciples is best explained by the fact of the Resurrection. He demonstrates that naturalistic alternatives to the Resurrection are all flawed.	Wilson makes an equally persuasive case *against* the Resurrection, pointing out that the Gospels were redacted to refute early criticisms of the Resurrection, which makes them poor sources of evidence in favour of it, and that the accounts of the Resurrection are full of discrepancies and contradictions.
Wilson is trying to be fair-minded by presenting arguments for-and-against but his arguments 'for' are stronger. He presents the 'Six Basic Hypotheses' as already refuted by **David Strauss** except for the sixth, which is that the Resurrection happened. The biggest section of the extract concentrates on the transformation of the early Christian believers into fearless martyrs, which is best explained by an experience of Jesus rising from the dead.	Wilson devotes too much time on the weakest of the 'Six Basic Hypotheses' (#5, Swoon Theory) but doesn't give enough serious consideration to the stronger ones (that the body of Jesus was stolen) and gives no consideration at all to the idea that the Disciples originally believed in a spiritual Resurrection, not a bodily one. He is too willing to believe that, because the Disciples were empowered by their belief in the Resurrection, something like it must have happened.

TOPIC 6.2 HOW SHOULD WE LIVE?

Christianity is not just a set of theological beliefs about Jesus and the Resurrection; it is a body of ethical codes for a moral life. Jesus' ministry seems to be a mixture of **eschatological** warnings (about the end of the world, p73) and moral teachings along with **miracles and Signs** (which may have eschatological or ethical hidden meanings).

One of the most distinctive features of Jesus' teachings in the Synoptic Gospels (especially **Luke's Gospel**) is his use of **Parables**. These are short stories, normally rooted in the everyday life of Palestinian farmers but sometimes based on familiar folk tales. Parables have one or more hidden meanings – sometimes eschatological (related to the end of the world or the afterlife), sometimes moral, often both.

Another highlight in Jesus' teaching is the sermon reported in **Matthew** and **Luke's Gospel**. The 'Sermon on the Mount' takes up **Matthew 5-7.** The mountain setting emphasizes Jesus' role as the 'new Moses' in Matthew's Gospel (since **Moses** received the **Law** from God on Mount Sinai). This Sermon includes the famous 'Beatitudes' (blessings) and the 'Lord's Prayer' and is considered to be the core of Christian teachings.

The 'Sermon on the Plain' in **Luke 6** is shorter but contains some similar material and will be considered in detail on p211.

1st century Judaism

Jesus' ethical teaching used to be considered utterly distinctive with its focus on love and forgiveness. However, scholars argue that much of Jesus' preaching is based on Jewish morality contained in the Old Testament.

For example, a central teaching of Jesus is 'love your neighbour' (e.g. **Mark 12: 31**) but this also appears in the Old Testament:

> *You shall not take vengeance, nor bear any grudge against the sons of your people, but you shall love your neighbor as yourself* **– Leviticus 19: 18**

Rather than proposing a brand new moral code, Jesus seems to have taken the traditional Jewish moral code and refocused it:

- Jesus taught that morality should not just be about external behaviour, but internal thoughts and feelings, so that lust is just as bad as adultery
- Jesus was a moral perfectionist, arguing that people should aim for the highest possible standards in their lives; he held particularly high standards on marriage and divorce
- Jesus criticised the Jewish purity laws (such as ceremonial washing and keeping the Sabbath), arguing that moral behaviour was more important than purity

Jesus argued that he did not come to replace the laws in the Old Testament, but to give them their correct interpretation:

> *Do not think that I have come to abolish the Law or the Prophets; I have not come to abolish them but to fulfill them* **– Matthew 5: 17**

As usual with the Gospels, it's hard to tell if Jesus is making an ethical statement (fulfilling the Scriptures through his moral teachings) or an eschatological statement (fulfilling them through dying an atoning death).

Christian codes of living

The early Church took Jesus' teachings and applied them in the light of Hellenic ethical theories like Stoicism. Stoicism (which was the major philosophical system of the Roman Empire) urged people to show self-control and resist passions. Stoic ethics are an influence on Paul' epistles (letters) which became guides for Christians:

> *Let us behave decently, as in the daytime, not in carousing and drunkenness, not in sexual immorality and debauchery, not in dissension and jealousy* **– Romans 13: 13**

This focus on CONTINENCE (controlling the passions and bodily urges) led to a distinctive Christian emphasis on virginity and a powerful sense of sex as being sinful. Christian churches still promote CELIBACY (rejecting sexual relationships) and CHASTITY (restricting sex solely to married partners). Other forms of sex are condemned as the sin of FORNICATION. This pessimistic view of sex is **not** directly based on Jesus' teaching or on Judaism generally (which tends to view sex as a positive thing, although the **Essenes** seem to have taken vows of celibacy).

A related teaching is the condemnation of homosexuality as the sin of SODOMY. This is clearly a teaching adapted from Judaism, since the Old Testament threatens homosexuality with severe punishments.

However, a crucial Christian teaching is stated by **Augustine of Hippo** (354-430 CE): *Cum dilectione hominum et odio vitiorum* is translated as:

Love the sinner and hate the sin – **Augustine**

In other words, although Christians condemn homosexual or promiscuous BEHAVIOUR, they should continue to love and respect the PERSON.

Another distinctive moral teaching among early Christians was the sharing of property (COMMUNAL OWNERSHIP). The **Book of Acts** describes converts to Christianity selling their houses and land and donating the money to the Christian community so that *"there were no needy persons among them."*

No one claimed that any of their possessions was their own, but they shared everything they had – **Acts 4: 32**

This practice seems to have faded from the Church as belief in an imminent *Parousia* ('Second Coming' of Jesus) was replaced by a belief in a delayed *Parousia* (a change in belief that scholars claim is shown in **Luke's Gospel**).

However, a new movement replaced communal ownership, which was MONASTICISM. Christians like **Anthony of Egypt** (251-356 CE) would escape from life in the pagan cities to live as hermits in the desert.

These hermits were known as ANCHORITES and over time they started living together in small communities, taking vows of celibacy and sharing property in common like the first Christians. In Europe, they are known as MONKS and their places of retreat are called monasteries.

St Catherine's monastery, Mount Sinai in Egypt: one of the oldest Christian monasteries in the world (founded in the 6th century CE)

This practice has little in common with Judaism (which encourages Jews to be productive members of society), but the **Essenes** lived in desert monasteries and Jesus advised his followers to give up their possessions:

> *If you want to be perfect, go, sell your possessions and give to the poor, and you will have treasure in heaven* – **Matthew 19: 21**

This advice continues to be divisive, with some Christians believing Jesus commands 'holy poverty' – such as **Francis of Assisi** (1181-1226 CE) who gave up everything he owned.

Other Christians argue for AFFECTIVE POVERTY, which means being detached from caring about wealth but still using wealth to do good in the world.

> *Spelling matters. Affective (with an 'a') means 'emotional'; effective (with an 'e') means having consequences. Effective poverty is literally owning nothing but affective poverty means that money doesn't matter to you emotionally.*

Equality today

A distinctive Christian insight is the **equality** of all people before God:

- God loves all persons equally (*"God does not show favouritism"* – **Romans 2: 13**)
- All persons are equally sinners and all need God's forgiveness and mercy (*"all have sinned and fall short of the glory of God"* – **Romans 3: 23**)

This is linked to the central Christian teaching of mutual love (*agape* in Greek, meaning selfless compassion for all people). Jesus gives this final teaching to his Disciples:

> *A new command I give you: Love one another. As I have loved you, so you must love one another* – **John 13: 34**

An early Christian scholar named **Tertullian** (160-230 CE) quotes the Roman pagans as saying *"See how these Christians love one another!"* because they were so struck by the equality and charity in Christian communities.

However, Christians have often failed to put this EGALITARIANISM (philosophy of equality) into practice

- **Slavery:** Jesus did not comment on slavery in the Roman Empire. **Paul**'s Christian converts included slaves and he advised them to obey their masters (**Ephesians 6: 5**). Paul's epistle (letter) to **Philemon** concerns a runaway slave whom Paul has converted to Christianity; Paul writes to the Christian master asking him to forgive the slave but does not ask him to *free* the slave.

  In the 18th century, Christian abolitionists like the **Quakers** and **Methodists** successfully banned slavery in Britain, but other Christians opposed them at the time with Biblical arguments. Today, all Christian churches oppose slavery.

- **Women:** The first Christian churches seem to have been led by women like Lydia, Priscilla, Chloe and Phoebe who are mentioned in **Acts** and in **Paul's epistles**. Christianity seems to have been popular with women, because it allowed them to preach, it promoted celibacy (which meant women converts didn't have to marry and fall under the authority of a husband) and it opposed the Hellenic practice of abandoning unwanted baby daughters to die.

  However, the Church quickly acquired the sexist gender roles of the Roman Empire and later New Testament texts forbid women to teach or even to speak in church. The **Catholic Church** continues to refuse women priests, although other churches are changing in this regard: the **Church of England** ordained its first female priest in 1994 and first female bishop in 2014.

- **Antisemitism:** Hostility towards the Jews is rooted in the experiences of the 1st century Christians, who blamed the Jewish leaders for the crucifixion of Jesus and experienced some persecution from the Jewish authorities. This hostility is particularly evident in the **Gospel of John**, which lays the foundation for centuries of Christian antisemitism.

  Once Christianity became the main religion in the Roman Empire, Jewish communities suffered attacks and legal restrictions (such as refusal of permission to build or repair their Synagogues).

  In the Middle Ages, European Jews were forbidden to own land and were forced to work as moneylenders; they were subjected to attacks and were expelled from many countries (England in 1290 CE, Spain in 1492 CE, and many others). Jewish communities were forced to live in ghettos, identify themselves with special clothing and were subjected to 'pogroms' (genocides). Many Christian churches today have apologised for supporting these atrocities: the Catholic Church condemned antisemitism in 2015.

In the 21st century, Christianity faces challenges for how the principle of equality should be applied to new groups that have previously been ignored, such as the LGBTQ+ community.

Pluralism today

Pluralism is the idea of many truths – or many approaches to the truth. The early Christians lived in a pluralistic Roman Empire, where people followed a variety of philosophies and worshipped different gods and goddesses without necessarily regarding the others as 'false'. However, Christianity followed the Jewish teaching of their being only one God, with all the other pagan deities being either idols (mere statues with no reality behind them) or else demons.

Christianity made EXCLUSIVE claims right from the start, teaching that salvation *only* comes through accepting Jesus as Lord. The first preaching by **Peter** concerning Jesus claims that "*salvation is found in no one else*" (**Acts 4: 12**); this links to Jesus' own statement:

> *I am the way and the truth and the life. No one comes to the Father except through me –*
> **John 14: 6**

Christianity continued to be an EXCLUSIVIST religion through the Middle Ages, with examples of some people (e.g. the pagan Lithuanians) being forced to convert to Christianity at sword point and heretical movements (such as the Cathars in southern France) targeted by military reprisals.

When Christianity split into Protestant and Catholic factions during the Reformation, these groups maintained exclusivist views and fought against each other in particularly bloody wars through to the 17th century.

However, the sheer brutality of these wars produced a counter-response: the ECUMENICAL MOVEMENT looks for common ground between Catholics and Protestants, focusing on the beliefs they share and encouraging them to worship together.

One response to this was the institution of RELIGIOUS LIBERTY: the freedom of individuals to follow whichever religion they choose without fear of punishment or persecution. This is a particularly important principle in the Constitution of the USA. It is linked to the idea of RELIGIOUS TOLERATION: the obligation on all religions to coexist peacefully with different faiths.

At first, liberty and toleration were ideas applied to different Christian churches, then to Jewish minority populations in Christian countries and atheists. However, mass immigration in the 19th and 20th centuries introduced the demand for the liberty and toleration of non-Judeo-Christian religions, such as Hinduism, Islam and Sikhism.

In the 20th century, many scholars encouraged the idea of RELIGIOUS PLURALISM: that all or most religions **worship the same God** despite expressing themselves with different imagery, myths and terminology. There are broadly two responses to this:

- LIBERAL scholars encourage religious pluralism, which means downplaying or abandoning exclusivist teachings. **John Hick** is a famous Christian pluralist; **Dietrich Bonhoeffer** argues for "*religionless Christianity*" and **Rudolf Bultmann**'s de-mythologized Christianity (p33) is a way of interpreting the Bible for a pluralist society. This approach sees Christianity as just one religious path among many and Jesus as not necessarily superior to other religious founders like the Buddha or Muhammad.

  there is a deep devotion to God, true sainthood, and deep spiritual life within these other religions – **John Hick**

- CONSERVATIVE scholars reject religious pluralism as taking religious liberty and toleration too far. They argue that religious pluralism undermines the essential truth claims of Christianity (e.g. that Jesus is the Son of God and the only way to salvation) and point out that religious pluralism also disrespects other religions too by undermining **their** distinctive truth claims (e.g. that Muhammad is the last and greatest prophet and that the Qur'an is God's definitive revelation).

  it is comforting to pretend that the great religions make up one big, happy family. But this sentiment, however well-intentioned, is neither accurate nor ethically responsible – **Stephen Prothero**

The Sermon on the Plain in Luke 6

Luke describes Jesus' memorable sermon as happening on *a level place* after Jesus has descended from a mountaintop. Scholars debate whether this is the same Sermon that **Matthew's Gospel** describes happening on a mountain (in which case it may be from the **Q-source**) or a different sermon with a similar theme.

A difference between the two sermons is that Matthew's 'Sermon on the Mount' focuses on Jesus' Disciples and teaches them how to live as righteous Jews, Luke's 'Sermon on the Plain' has more of a focus on topics that would interest Gentiles as well as Jews.

Frank J. Matera (p244) argues that Matthew's 'Sermon on the Mount' is *"to show that Jesus did not come to abolish the Law and the Prophets but to fulfil them"* whereas Luke's 'Sermon on the Plain' *"focuses on the need to extend love to all, even to one's enemy"*.

> *It's a bit odd that the Exam Board expects you to know this passage well enough to answer on it, but doesn't include it as an extract in the Anthology.*

The Beatitudes ('Blessings') – Luke 6: 20-23

In both sermons, Jesus blesses his Disciples. Each blessing identifies a particular type of unhappiness *now* and promises a *future* reward or consolation.

> Blessed are you who are poor,
>> for yours is the kingdom of God.
> 21 Blessed are you who hunger now,
>> for you will be satisfied.
> Blessed are you who weep now,
>> for you will laugh.
> 22 Blessed are you when people hate you,
>> when they exclude you and insult you
>> and reject your name as evil,
>>> because of the Son of Man.

There are four blessings here: for the poor, the hungry, the weeping and the persecuted.

1. **The Poor:** This is the idea that poverty is a blessed state. The Christian idea of poverty is rather contradictory: the poor are blessed yet Christians are commanded by Jesus to give their money to the poor to relieve their poverty.

Poverty is blessed because the poor, having nothing else, are able to depend entirely on God, whereas the rich are tempted to cling to the illusory comforts of their possessions. Luke makes the same point in the **Parable of the Sower** (p81) where the *good seed* is choked by *thorns* which represent worldly possessions and commitments.

In Matthew's version this is also the first blessing but Matthew makes this meaning clearer by writing *"blessed are the poor in spirit"* to show that it is the spiritual impact of poverty, rather than the brute fact of having no money, that enables the poor to live within the **Kingdom of God** (p75). This is the basis for affective poverty, which is trying to live *as is* you were poor in order to make room for God in your life.

2. **The Hungry:** Hunger is linked to poverty and Christians are expected to end hunger through charitable giving. However, Jesus' promise that the hungry will be *satisfied* is also an eschatological promise: it refers to the Afterlife or to the Kingdom of God on earth when God rules and everyone is treated fairly.

There is a link here to the **Parable of the Banquet** (p87) and the **Sign of the Feeding of the 5000** (*c.f.* **Topic 2**) as well as Jesus describing himself as the **Bread of Life** (*c.f.* **Topic 2**). When Jesus talks about food, he is often speaking symbolically: the hunger is a spiritual hunger and the food is himself; this spiritual food is received through Jesus' teachings but also in the **Eucharist** ceremony when Christians share bread in memory of Jesus' atoning death.

Once again, Matthew's version of the sermon spiritualizes this blessing, writing *"blessed are those who hunger and thirst for righteousness"* which makes the symbolic meaning clearer.

> *Did the Beatitudes start out as spiritual blessings which Luke has transformed into social morality (literal poverty and hunger) or did they start off as social morality which Matthew then spiritualizes into something more allegorical?*

3. **The Weeping:** Those who *weep* refers to all human misery, but particularly people mourning for the dead. Matthew's version makes this the second blessing and explicitly refers to *"blessed are those who mourn"*.

There is an instruction here to comfort the unhappy people, but there are also links to occasions when Jesus describes the **Kingdom of God** as being like a party, with everybody celebrating; for example, the **Parable of the Banquet** (p87) or the **Sign of Turning Water into Wine** (*c.f.* **Topic 2**). There is an eschatological promise here that the sufferings of this world will come to an end.

On another level, the blessing refers to the **Resurrection**: those who weep are the Disciples themselves, after the Crucifixion, but they will laugh again when Jesus is raised from the dead.

4. **The Persecuted:** Those who are hated, excluded, insulted and rejected are the future Christians (this is the only blessing that does not use the word *now*). Jesus adds that they should *"leap for joy"* when they are persecuted for their faith because it shows that they are his true followers, just like *the prophets* who were also persecuted by the Jews.

Of course, the later Christians **were** persecuted in various ways by the Jewish and Roman authorities (these persecutions were perhaps still happening while Luke's Gospel was being written). Some Christians abandoned their faith, going back to their pagan or Jewish communities. This links to the **Parable of the Sower** (p81) where the good seed that produces a harvest is the one that *perseveres*.

1st century Judaism: There are strong links from the Beatitudes back to the Jewish Scriptures. For example, **Psalm 41** begins with a blessing for those who watch out for the poor and are kind to the weak; **Psalm 107** promises that God will *fill the hungry soul*; **Isaiah 61: 2** promises that God will comfort those who mourn and the Jewish experience of mourning for their lost homeland during the Babylonian Exile (586-538 BCE) gave mourning and weeping a spiritual significance in Judaism too.

Christian codes of living: The Christian duty to give to the poor, feed the hungry, comfort the unhappy and to bear suffering cheerfully is summed up here. In Anthology extract #9, **Ian Wilson** (p197) comments on how the early Christians took the message to heart when they faced martyrdom *"with an astonishing cheerfulness"*. Religious reformers like **Francis of Assisi** have been inspired by the Beatitudes: Francis gave up all his possessions, exchanged his clothes with a beggar's rags and lived entirely dependent on God for food and shelter, living as a 'holy fool'. Francis composed the beautiful *Canticle of the Sun*, in which he praises Brother Sun and Sister Moon even Sister Death, while he was suffering from an eye disease that caused him unspeakable pain and left him nearly blind.

Equality today: The Beatitudes have been criticised by political reformers because they appear to be promising believers 'pie in the sky' as a consolation for putting up with injustice in the world. However, many Christians interpret the Beatitudes as a 'call to arms' instead: poverty, hunger and misery are things that God expects humans to confront and deal with. These Christians see the promise at the end of each blessing as something **we humans** are supposed to achieve in **this** life, not something that God brings about in the Afterlife. Much of the world's poverty, hunger and misery is linked to inequality of wealth and opportunity so Christians follow Jesus' example by challenging the powerful on behalf of the weak and the helpless.

Pluralism today: In 2016, **Pope Francis** preached a sermon on the Beatitudes and offered 6 more to *"recognise and respond to new situations with fresh energy"*:

- Blessed are those who remain faithful while enduring evils inflicted on them by others, and forgive them from their heart
- Blessed are those who look into the eyes of the abandoned and marginalized, and show them their closeness
- Blessed are those who see God in every person, and strive to make others also discover him

- Blessed are those who protect and care for our common home
- Blessed are those who renounce their own comfort in order to help others
- Blessed are those who pray and work for full communion between Christians

The last of Pope Francis' beatitudes is a clear reference to ECUMENISM (the coming together of different Christian churches). The reference to *"those who see God in every person,"* *"who protect and are for our current home"* (the environment) and *"who renounce their own comfort to help others"* also links to RELIGIOUS PLURALISM, because such people do not have to be Catholics or even Christians.

The Four Woes – Luke 6: 24-26

The next section occurs only in Luke's version of the sermon (but similar warnings directed against the **Pharisees** are in **Matthew 23:1–39**). Jesus pronounces four *'woes'* (literally 'sorrows' but here meaning 'warnings') for different groups of people. These *'woes'* are the mirror-image of the Beatitudes, describing people who are happy and contended *now* and threatening dreadful things for them in the future.

> [24] 'But woe to you who are rich,
>
>   for you have already received your comfort.
>
> [25] Woe to you who are well fed now,
>
>   for you will go hungry.
>
> Woe to you who laugh now,
>
>   for you will mourn and weep.
>
> [26] Woe to you when everyone speaks well of you,
>
>   for that is how their ancestors treated the false prophets.

1. **The Rich:** The reference to the rich *receiving their comfort* in the here-and-now is echoed in the **Parable of the Rich Man & Lazarus** (p235), which would make this an eschatological warning about events at the end of the world or in the Afterlife. This also links to **The Rich & The Kingdom of God** (p91) and its simile of a camel going through the eye of a needle (**Luke 18: 18-30**). The underlying idea is that the pleasures of wealth are short-term and fleeting, but the pains of Hell last forever.
2. **The Well-Fed:** These people will *go hungry* in future. This also links to the **Parable of the Rich Man & Lazarus** (p235), suggesting God punishes those who feed themselves rather than caring about the needs of others. *Going hungry* could be another eschatological warning about Hell. However, a symbolic interpretation would be that the *well-fed* are people who do not recognise their spiritual needs and satisfy themselves with worldly pleasures instead: they will *go hungry* because they will be spiritually empty.

3. **The Laughers:** These people will *mourn and weep*. Luke's Gospel describes Jesus being laughed at and mocked by the Jewish rulers, the soldiers and the other crucified thieves. The 'laughers' are also the people who insult and sneer at the future Christians – people like the pagan critic **Celsus** (p172) who describes Christianity as appealing only to *"the silly, and the mean, and the stupid, with slaves, women and children."* This eschatological warning suggests that these critics won't be laughing on Judgement Day! However, more generally, the 'laughers' are people who live only for pleasure and the present moment who, like the rich, have chosen temporary pleasures and an eternity in Hell.

4. **The False Prophets:** These are the people who are *well spoken of* and Jesus compares them to *"false prophets"*. In the later Church, these people are the heretics who attract crowds of fans with distorted versions of the Christian message. Conservative Christians today would link this warning to liberal Christians who produce 'watered down' versions of Christianity that are acceptable to atheists.

1st century Judaism: There is a criticism here of the Jews whose ancestors *spoke well of false prophets* just as they persecuted the true prophets. The prophets the Jews are supposed to have killed are **Isaiah** (sawed in half, according to tradition) and **Jeremiah** (cause of death unknown). The *false prophets* refer the priests of pagan gods like Baal that the Israelites went over to worshiping in the past. By condemning the ancestors of the Jewish leaders, Jesus is condemning the religious traditions of the **Pharisees** and the **Sadducees** as misguided.

Christian codes of living: The condemnation of the 'Laughers' invites later Christians to CENSOR writing and performances that use satirical humour to attack Christian beliefs. Recent examples of this include: *Monty Python's Life of Brian* (1979), which was banned in several cities and countries (Ireland and Norway!), picketed by protesting Christians and accused of blasphemy; *Jerry Springer – The Opera*, which was shown on the BBC in 2005 and drew 55,000 complaints for its representations of Jesus. More recent satirists who have attacked Christianity include Ricky Gervais, Bill Maher and Trey Parker/Matt Stone (creators of *South Park* and the musical *The Book of Mormon*).

Equality today: The 'woes' threatened to the 'Rich' and the 'Well-Fed' inspire Christian activism against powerful and privileged groups. Christian thinkers are also coming to see how these categories represent ***everyone*** in Western countries: we are all, collectively, *wealthy* and *well-fed* compared to the developing economies and therefore are condemned by Jesus too unless we can contribute to making the world a fairer place.

Pluralism today: The concept of *false prophets* has been very divisive in Christianity. Alternative interpretations of Jesus' teachings were treated as HERESIES and some of them were crushed with extreme violence (such as the Cathar heresy in the South of France in the 13th century CE). Later Christians developed the idea of the '**Antichrist**': a servant of the Devil who would lead people astray and persecute true Christians. For centuries, Protestants have viewed the Catholic Pope as 'antichrist' but throughout history the title has been awarded to the Emperor Nero, Napoleon Bonaparte and Barack Obama!

Loving Your Enemies – Luke 6: 27-36

This passage is similar to **Matthew 5: 43-48** but uses different terminology and examples. Jesus sums up his teaching at the start:

> *love your enemies, do good to those who hate you* **– Luke 6: 27**

Jesus gives a series of illustrations of this teaching in action:

- If you are slapped, *turn the other cheek* (so that that cheek can be slapped too)
- If someone takes your coat, give them your shirt too
- Don't ask for something back if someone takes it

These instructions go beyond the normal 'law of reciprocity' (which says, treat other people the way they treat you) and amounts to a sort of radical altruism (treat other people well *regardless* of how they treat you). Jesus sums up again at the end:

> *love your enemies, do good to them, and lend to them without expecting to get anything back* **– Luke 6: 35**

These recommendations are 'counsels of perfection' and are often criticised for being too idealistic and unworldly. However, Jesus shows a shrewd grasp of psychology when he points out that even *sinners* have friends whom they treat well (e.g. Hitler loved his dog!). The fact that you are nice to the people who are nice to you really reveals very little about your character: the mark of a moral person is that you behave well towards the people who are *not* nice to you.

In this passage, Jesus states the 'Golden Rule' of ethics:

> *Do to others as you would have them do to you* **– Luke 6: 31**

Again, this goes beyond the 'law of reciprocity' (which says, treat other people *exactly* the way they treat you) and amounts to something more radical (treat other people the way you'd like to be treated, *regardless* of how they treat you).

Jesus himself lives out this code: during his trial he is slapped by the priests and the soldiers, during the Crucifixion the guards divide his clothes between them, **Luke 23: 34** describes Jesus praying for his enemies from the cross.

> **1st century Judaism:** The Jewish Scriptures also contain instructions to love your enemy so Jesus is not deviating from Jewish ethics here. **Exodus 23: 4-5** contains instructions to return an enemy's livestock and **Proverbs 24: 17-18** advises Jews not to rejoice when their enemies suffer. However, there are also verses that counsel the law of reciprocity, such as the famous *"eye for an eye"* instruction (**Leviticus 24: 20**, known as the *lex talionis* or 'law of retaliation'). Jesus is clarifying the Scriptures and offering a definitive interpretation.
>
> Jesus also goes beyond standard Jewish ethical advice. The famous Jewish teacher **Hillel the Elder** (110 BCE – 10 CE) summed up the ethics in the Torah as: *"What is hateful to you, do not do to your fellow."*

However, this is a NEGATIVE formulation (saying **don't** treat others the way you'd hate to be treated yourself) whereas Jesus' formulation is POSITIVE (**do** treat others the way you'd ideally like to be treated yourself). Jesus' version of the Golden Rule is an ethical advance on previous versions.

Christian codes of living: The first Christians (and perhaps Jesus himself) were APOCALYPTICISTS: they believed in an imminent end of the world. Therefore, incredibly demanding ethical rules about submitting to injustice, not retaliating and giving away your possessions would only have to be followed for a short time. Later Christians came to understand that *Parousia* (Jesus' 'Second Coming') had been delayed and settled into the 'long haul' of history with a less extreme ethical code. For example, **Augustine of Hippo** (410 CE) set out the conditions for a 'Just War' under which Christians were morally allowed to retaliate against their enemies. Nonetheless, Christian martyrs really did follow Jesus' original advice, going to their torture and death without resisting and forgiving their enemies.

Later protestors adapted the tactic of PASSIVE RESISTANCE from Jesus' teachings. For example, **Gandhi** used this technique in India and **Martin Luther King** used it in the USA. Gandhi was a Hindu, but called Jesus *"the most active resister known perhaps to history... non-violence par excellence"* (1948). King explained his non-violent protests against racism: *"the Christian doctrine of love operating through the Gandhian method of nonviolence was one of the most potent weapons available to oppressed people in their struggle for freedom"* (1959).

Equality today: Since every person desires to be treated as an equal by others, the Golden Rule states that we must treat others as equals, even if they are enemies (perhaps, for Christians, **especially** if they are enemies). There are implications here for the 21st century in which homosexual couples demand equal rights to marry and transgender persons demand equal respect as members of their self-identified gender. Conservative Christians who argue that these equal statuses should **not** be granted have to explain why the Golden Rule need not apply in these cases.

For example, in 2014 a family-run bakery in Northern Ireland refused to make a cake with a slogan supporting same-sex marriage because it opposed their religious beliefs about marriage; they were prosecuted by the Equalities Commission and fined for discrimination. Similar cases are being tried in the USA with similar results: equality laws mean that religious principles do not justify discrimination.

Pluralism today: The Golden Rule supports religious liberty and religious toleration, even toleration of religions that some Christians might consider to be their 'enemies'. However, this raises questions about how far tolerance should go, as has been seen in debates about faith schools, religious dress codes and extremist violence.

For example, in 2017 a terrorist bomb outside an Egyptian Cathedral killed 47 Christians celebrating Easter; the widow of one of the victims forgave the ISIS-inspired attacker, saying: *"I'm not angry at the one who did this, I am telling him, may God forgive you."* However, even when individuals choose to react this way, the state still has an obligation to punish terrorists and prevent future attacks. Augustine's argument that circumstances justify Christians using force against enemies could also justify restricting the rights of extremist groups in the interests of protecting people.

Parables About Hypocrisy – Luke 6: 37-49

The 'Sermon on the Plain' finishes with a series of Parables around the theme of HYPOCRISY. Hypocrisy is 'saying one thing but doing the opposite' and someone whose words do not match their behaviour is a HYPOCRITE. *Hypocrisy/hypocrite* occurs 20 times in the Synoptic Gospels (but never in **John's Gospel**, oddly) and is a major theme of Jesus' ethical teaching.

The word comes from the Greek hupokrisis *which means 'to play a part', like an actor in the theatre. Hypocrites are like actors: they are pretending to be better than they really are.*

Warning about judging others – Luke 6: 37-42

Jesus warns about 'judging' other people, specifically condemning them for their faults. He advises people that God will judge them the way they judge others: if you are merciful and forgiving, you will receive mercy and forgiveness from God, but if you are hard-hearted and punish others for their sins, God will punish you for yours.

For with the measure you use, it will be measured to you – **Luke 6: 38**

Frank J. Matera (p244) explains the psychology behind this advice:

Human judgement is flawed because it cannot fully understand the heart and motives of the other. Moreover, those who judge others rarely understand their own motives and faults – **Frank J. Matera**

Jesus illustrates this with two short Parables:

- **The Blind Leading the Blind (Luke 6: 39-40):** This is the image of one blind person pretending to be sighted so he can guide another blind person – but of course *they both fall into a pit*. The hypocrisy here is that the so-called guide is pretending to be wiser and more insightful than he really is.
- **The Log in the Eye (Luke 6: 41-42):** This is the image of someone pointing out that their friend has a *speck of sawdust* in their eye (representing any minor fault or mistake), while the whole time they have a *plank* in their own eye. The hypocrisy here is that the critic is even more guilty than the person they are criticizing.

Both of these short Parables are intended to be funny as well as wise. It's not just John's Gospel that tells jokes!

Jesus clearly addresses this to his Disciples (using the term *brother* for each other). There's also a difference between JUDGEMENTALISM (hypocritically judging others when you have no right to) and MORAL CORRECTION (rightly pointing out when someone has made a mistake or is behaving badly).

The Tree & its Fruit – Luke 6: 43-45

This short Parable uses the symbolism of different types of fruit trees for different types of people. *Figs* and *grapes* are very desirable fruits, but you don't go looking for them in *thornbushes* and *briers*.

The sweet fruits are good actions; the thornbushes and briers are sinful people who don't produce good actions (but like to talk as if they do).

This could be summed up as 'actions speak louder than words' – never mind what people *say* they believe in and care about, what matters is what they *do*.

Hypocrites talk as if they are deeply moral people, but they don't act in a moral way.

This links to other agricultural symbols that Jesus uses:

Tasty figs on a fig tree

- **The Fig Tree:** In the Old Testament, the Fig Tree symbolises the Jewish nation itself. Jesus accuses the Jewish priests of being spiritually dead: this is the lack of fruit on the Fig Tree of Israel. In **Mark 11: 12-14**, Jesus curses a fig tree that has no fruit on it; since he does this immediately before **cleansing the Temple** (p103) we can be confident the fig tree represents the Jewish religion of the 1st century

- **The True Vine:** In **John's Gospel**, Jesus states **"I am the True Vine"** (*c.f.* **Topic 2**) and his Disciples are the *branches that bear fruit* but the Jewish religion is represented by the fruitless branches that God cuts away.

- **The Parable of the Sower** (p81)**:** This Parable also the idea of a harvest growing from a seed that lands in good soil, representing people who listen to Jesus' teachings and genuinely act on them, contrasted with the other seeds that land on bad soil and produce no harvest.

When Jesus is about to be arrested, he compares the suffering ahead of him to drinking a cup of wine (e.g. **Luke 22: 42**) – wine is made from grapes, so suffering is the fruit of the vine too.

Later on, when the early Christians faced persecution and some turned away from their faith, the symbol of the trees bearing fruit took on another meaning: the good trees produce the fruit of suffering and martyrdom whereas the bad trees do not.

Wise & Foolish Builders – Luke 6: 46-49

Jesus compares his teaching to rock foundations for a house: anything built on them will last and survive the *torrent* (flood) that is coming. In contrast, trying to live your life ignoring these foundations is like building a house without solid foundations: when the *torrent* comes, the house is destroyed.

But what is the *house* and what is the coming *torrent*?

The house could be an individual's life. Jesus uses this sort of symbolism in the Parable of the demon **Beelzebub** invading a strong man's house (**Luke 11: 14-28**, p83); the *torrent* would represent setbacks in life, temptations and persecutions, perhaps ultimately death itself. The *wise builder* is a Disciple who will survive all these things and receive Eternal Life because she followed Jesus' teachings. The *foolish builder* is someone following another code in life (such as a pagan religion or a philosophy like Stoicism or atheism). They are overwhelmed by the problems in life and, ultimately, they do not receive Eternal Life.

The house on strong foundations could be the Church and the house without foundations is the Jewish religion. The *torrent* is the events of history still to come: the Jewish War of 67-73 CE, the persecutions by the Romans, and so on through the centuries. Christianity has endured, but the **Pharisees**, **Sadducees**, **Essenes** and **Zealots** have all vanished.

The Parable could have an eschatological meaning, with the *torrent* representing the Apocalypse. Jesus uses similar imagery of some surviving the arrival of the Kingdom of God and others being swept away, for example the **Coming of the Kingdom** (p89).

The link to hypocrisy is in the opening line: people address Jesus as '*Lord*' but they do not follow his teachings. In other words, they pretend to be Christians, but they do not produce the fruits of good actions.

> **1st century Judaism:** The Jewish religion of the 1st century was based around many forms of external behaviour: making sacrifices, washing, wearing certain clothes, avoiding certain foods, keeping the Sabbath regulations. This made it easy to judge, in a superficial way, who was a 'good Jew' and who was not. Jesus criticises this sort of religiosity as HYPOCRITICAL: a person can keep all the outwards requirements of the Jewish religion and still harbour evil thoughts, never going out of their way to do good for other people.
>
> There is scholarly debate about whether this sort of assessment of ancient Judaism is fair. **Form** and **Redaction Criticism** argue it is really an attitude of the early Christians towards the Jews who rejected them, not an attitude that Jesus would have had towards his fellow-Jews.
>
> However, Jesus does seem to reinterpret Jewish morality in a much more personal way, focusing on loving motives and positive altruism. In this way, his teachings are a development on traditional Jewish ethics.

Christian codes of living: The challenge to live authentically, without hypocrisy, is not easy. Christianity became the official religion of the Roman Empire in the 4th century, introducing a social pressure to *appear* to be a pious Christian by attending church, praying, etc.

Reformers rebelled against this sort of hypocritical Christianity, particularly the existentialist philosophers like **Søren Kierkegaard** (who criticised the respectable Christianity of 19th century Denmark). **Existentialism** values authenticity above all else and this is **Rudolf Bultmann**'s reason for de-mythologizing Christianity (p33) to make its existentialist message more accessible to modern people.

Equality today: The warnings abut judging others contribute to the popularity of egalitarian practices. Discrimination usually begins by judging other groups harshly (prejudice), then acting on those judgments to treat members of these groups unfairly.

Augustine's motto of '*love the sinner, hate the sin*' enables some Christians to make harsh judgements about BEHAVIOUR that goes against their Christian principles (such as abortion, euthanasia or same-sex marriage) while still loving and not judging the PERSON who does things.

However, not everyone feels this is a fair distinction to make. For example, saying to someone who is obese '*I love you, it's your fatness I hate*' would be very hurtful: homosexuals similarly feel that their sexuality is part of their identity, not something that can be separated from them and treated as sinful while the non-sexual part of them is 'loved' in some abstract way.

Pluralism today: In the same way, religious liberty and religious tolerance are based on not judging members of other churches or religions. However, the warning about *false prophets* is exclusivist, suggesting that one version of Christianity is the true one and other churches and religions are condemned as false.

However, there is a tension here: Christians are commanded not to judge, but they are also commanded to preach the Gospel. Preaching the Gospel involves criticising immoral or blasphemous behaviour and trying to convert atheists and members of other religions, which goes against the idea of religious pluralism. Christians who **don't** try to convert friends, neighbours and work colleagues can be criticized for HYPOCRISY: they claim to follow Jesus but, like the *foolish builders*, they *don't do what he says*.

Evaluating the Sermon on the Plain

The 'Sermon on the Plain' is less influential than its longer equivalent, the 'Sermon on the Mount' in **Matthew's Gospel**. Matthew's Sermon has specific teachings on matters like murder, adultery, divorce, swearing oaths, prayer, fasting and donating to the poor.

The 'Sermon on the Plain' is less specific, offering broad principles instead. Nevertheless, it's more succinct and contains key Christian teachings such as the Golden Rule and commandments about loving your enemies and not judging others.

The Sermon sets out a clear picture of the Christian ethical life, but perhaps an impractical one. If people who are poor or hungry are 'blessed', is it a priority to reduce poverty and hunger in the world? Just how rich do you have to be to count as one of the well-fed and wealthy? Do these blessings and 'woes' apply only to individuals or to entire societies? For example, the Central African Republic, the Democratic Republic of the Congo and Burundi are the poorest nations on earth. Does that mean they are 'blessed'? Qatar, Luxembourg and Singapore are the richest: should they feel guilty about that?

Similarly, the instruction to love your enemy and not to judge becomes impractical if applied in society: should criminals be set free because, at the end of the day, only God can judge them? Should managers not fire employees who break the rules or underperform because that involves condemning someone? The Sermon is usually understood to apply to people's private lives rather than political or business decisions. However, this can lead to inconsistencies where someone is endlessly forgiving of friends and family, but harsh in their job as a magistrate or boss.

However, **Frank J. Matera** (p244) rejects the idea that the Sermon is impractical or intended to be for only the most dedicated followers:

> *Jesus expects those who hear the sermon to do what he teaches. He is not presenting an impossible ideal. Nor does he intend his sermon for the chosen few* – **Frank J. Matera**

Matera argues that critics who find Jesus' ideals too impractical make the mistake of imagining he is speaking to INDIVIDUALS. People who try to put the sermon into practice as individuals *"will always be frustrated."* Matera believes the Sermon is preached to *"a community of like-minded disciples"* – in other words, a church.

> *Those who live in a community in light of the in-breaking kingdom of God, however, will find the strength to live the ethic Jesus presents here* – **Frank J. Matera**

We are to imagine a Christian community trying to live by this ethic and taking part in the **Kingdom of God** (p75) by doing this. Viewed this way, Jesus' sermon seems more attainable and very attractive.

Does the Sermon on the Plain provide a basis for how to live in the modern world?

YES	NO
The Golden Rule as stated by Jesus has never been improved on as a basis for morality: *do as you would be done by* makes everyone ask themselves how **they** would wish to be treated, then treat others that way. The world would be a more equal and tolerant place if people practiced love towards their enemies and refrained from judging others.	The Sermon only provides broad principles but these collapse as soon as you try to apply them to specific situations. The Golden Rule doesn't answer questions like abortion or euthanasia because we can't imagine how we would like to be treated if we were a foetus or terminally ill. Human rights provide a stronger basis for securing equality and tolerance in society.
The Sermon can be applied to specific situations if further principles are used alongside it, such as **Augustine**'s *love the sinner but hate the sin* or **Aquinas**' Natural Moral Law. The Sermon provides the vision of the Christian moral life: loving, forgiving, non-judgmental and expressing itself in altruism towards other people. The practical details can be worked out separately.	The Sermon describes a moral outlook that is **eschatological** – rooted in the expectation that the world is about to end or in the Afterlife. Modern morality needs to be humanistic, rooted in this world's problems and solutions. The self-denying qualities Jesus recommends are not practical in a secular society where people have to be bosses, magistrates, policemen, soldiers and politicians.

Parable of the Good Samaritan (Luke 10)

> *These three Parables make up the final extract #10 of the Edexcel Anthology for this course*

This is probably Jesus' most famous Parable; being a 'good samaritan' is a popular phrase for being a helpful stranger. The Parable occurs only in Luke's Gospel and beautifully illustrates Luke's major themes of compassion and the ethical use of money.

But before we start...

Who are the Samaritans?

The Samaritans are the inhabitants of **Samaria**, a highland region nestled between the rugged hills and deserts of Judea in the south and the fertile valleys of Galilee in the north.

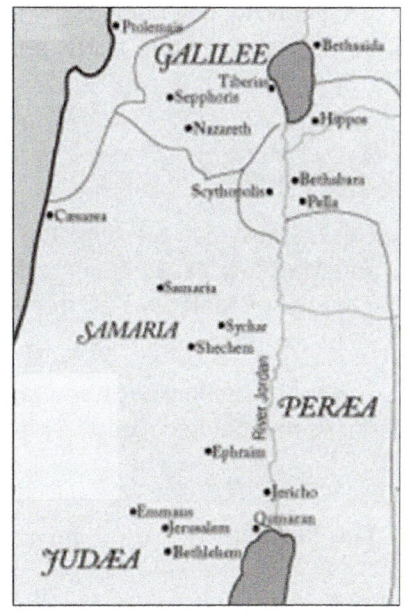

Centuries earlier, Samaria had been the heartland of the Jewish kingdom of Israel which was conquered by the Assyrian Empire in 720 BCE. The ten northern tribes of the Israelites were taken away as slaves and disappear from history, leaving only the Kingdom of Judah in the south to carry on the Israelite lineage and the Jewish religion. The Assyrians resettled pagan tribes in Samaria and their descendants are the current Samaritans.

Or that's how they tell it in Judea. The Samaritans themselves claim to be the surviving descendants of the ancient Israelites. They worship God on Mount Gerizim in Samaria rather than in Jerusalem, they have their own version of the Torah and they claim that **their** religion is the original religion of the Israelites from before the Babylonian Exile. They too wait for a messiah that they call the 'Taheb' (meaning 'Restorer').

> *The Samaritans still exist today in the State of Israel, but they number about 700 and this is shrinking because they only marry within their own group and do not encourage anyone to convert to their religion.*

Needless to say, two groups who both claim to be the original worshippers of the same God are **not** going to get along.

Jewish and Samaritan religious leaders taught that it was wrong to have any contact with the other group. Jews were not supposed to enter Samaritan territory or even speak to Samaritans. The historian **Flavius Josephus** reports battles between Jews and Samaritans in the 1st century and the Romans used Samaritan soldiers to keep order in Judea – so the Roman soldiers who mocked and executed Jesus were probably Samaritans, not Italians from Rome.

Jesus & the Samaritans: Jesus seems to have an unusual amount of contact with the Samaritans and is willing to speak with them. **Luke 9: 51-53** describes Jesus trying to stay overnight at a Samaritan village but being turned away because he is a Jew; however **Luke 17: 11-19** describes Jesus healing 10 lepers but the only one who thanks him is a Samaritan, whom Jesus praises. **John 4: 4-42** describes Jesus stopping in at a well in Samaria, speaking to a Samaritan woman and converting her family. Jesus seems to accept her claim that her people are Israelites too. **Acts 8: 1-25** describes Phillip, Peter and John converting many Samaritans to Christianity.

Raymond E. Brown proposes that the Johannine Community that composed **John's Gospel** contained a mixture of Jewish Christians and Samaritan Christians and that some of John's distinctive ideas and traditions might have come from this Samaritan influence.

The Context of the Parable

Jesus is being questioned by *an expert in the Law* (presumably a **Pharisee**) who wants to know how to achieve **Eternal Life**. Jesus bounces the question back at him and the Pharisee answers:

> "'Love the Lord your God with all your heart and with all your soul and with all your strength and with all your mind; and, 'Love your neighbour as yourself.'"

This is Jesus' own teaching: it is the 'Great Commandment' that Jesus explains in **Mark 12: 28-31** and **Matthew 22: 35-40**. In both cases, Jesus explains the Commandment to a *scribe* (in Mark) or a *lawyer* (in Matthew), so this *expert in the law* might be intended to be the same person that Jesus has previously taught.

This time, the Pharisee has another question: *"Who is my neighbour?"* Jesus, perhaps sensing the Pharisee is being deliberately awkward, answers with the Parable.

The Parable

> "A man was going down from Jerusalem to Jericho, when he was attacked by robbers. They stripped him of his clothes, beat him and went away, leaving him half dead. 31 A priest happened to be going down the same road, and when he saw the man, he passed by on the other side. 32 So too, a Levite, when he came to the place and saw him, passed by on the other side. 33 But a Samaritan, as he travelled, came where the man was; and when he saw him, he took pity on him. 34 He went to him and bandaged his wounds, pouring on oil and wine. Then he put the man on his own donkey, brought him to an inn and took care of him. 35 The next day he took out two denarii and gave them to the innkeeper. 'Look after him,' he said, 'and when I return, I will reimburse you for any extra expense you may have.'

Jerusalem is up in the mountains (2500 feet above sea level) but the ancient city of Jericho to the north is 825 feet *below* sea level which is why the man *goes down* to Jericho.

Although the route connecting the cities is only about 18 miles, it is steep and difficult to travel, dropping from cold mountains into dry desert. Worse than that, the road was known as 'the Way of Blood' because of the number of murders that took place on it, due to gangs of bandits that could lie in wait among the cliffs and crags.

This traveller falls victim to such a gang and is left for dead. Two travellers pass him as he lies near death but refuse to help:

- A **priest** from the Temple in Jerusalem
- A **Levite** (a clan of Jewish monks who assisted with priestly sacrifices)

Although these two men are supposed to embody all the values of the Jewish religion, they show no compassion. This might be because of the danger (the robbers might return) but also because the man appears dead and touching a corpse would make a priest or Levite ritually unclean and they would be unable to perform their duties (so this is putting religious rules ahead of moral duties).

The third traveller **does** help – and in fact goes out of his way to look after the victim, treating him himself then bringing him to an inn and paying the bills to have the man looked after. This compassionate stranger is a Samaritan, someone no sensible Jew would talk to or expect to get help from.

The Conclusion

Jesus asks, which one of the three was the victim's neighbour? The Pharisee, clearly unwilling even to **name** the Samaritan, answers: *"the one who had mercy on him."*

Jesus tells the Pharisee to go and be more like the Samaritan in future!

Interpreting the Parable

The Parable puts Jesus' teachings about *love your enemy* (from the **Sermon on the Plain**) into action: Samaritans and Jews are supposed to be enemies, yet the Samaritan shows compassion for his enemy and goes to personal expense to see that his enemy is cared for.

The moral is that we should treat all our enemies this way. In answer to the Pharisee's question *"Who is my neighbour?"* the answer is: *Anyone in need of help or compassion*!

The Pharisee's prejudices have also been challenged: he thought he understood the 'Great Commandment' but Jesus has used this Parable to reveal what *loving your neighbour* really means – and it's something the Pharisee is uncomfortable with.

The Parable also illustrates the **Kingdom of God** coming about in surprising ways, which is an important theme in Luke's Gospel.

Christian scholars like **Irenaeus** and **Origen** interpreted the Parable **allegorically**:

- The road from Jerusalem to Jericho is the descent from Paradise/the Garden of Eden to the Fallen world of sin (i.e. all human history)
- The traveller is the soul of every human being
- The robbers are the forces of evil and the traveller's wounds are sins
- The Priest and Levite represent the **Law**, which is powerless to help people
- The Samaritan is Christ who comes as a **Saviour**
- The donkey that bears the wounded man is Christ's body, which takes on the burden of human sins by his atoning death on the Cross
- The inn represents the Church, which does Christ's work on earth
- The Samaritan promises to return, which is *Parousia* (the 'Second Coming')

This allegorical interpretation is also a good illustration of the concept of **salvation-history** in Luke's Gospel (p77).

1ˢᵗ century Judaism: Jesus' 'Great Commandment' is based on Jewish Scriptures. **Deuteronomy 6:5** commands Jews to *"love the Lord your God with all your heart and with all your soul and with all your might"* and this forms part of the *Shema*, a daily prayer offered by Jews to this day. **Leviticus 19: 18** contains the instruction to *"love your neighbour as yourself."*

What Jesus does is place these two together, making the authentic love of God **the same thing** as the love of your neighbour, so that you can't properly do one without the other. Jesus also UNIVERSALISES the instruction to *love your neighbour*, by making *neighbour* mean **anyone** rather than just fellow-Jews.

Christian codes of living: This Parable profoundly influenced Christian ethics, leading to the founding of hospitals, charities and other institutions to care for the needy.

In 1953, the **Rev. Chad Varah** founded a new charity, staffed by volunteers, who would support depressed and suicidal people through a free telephone helpline (tel: 116 123). He named this organisation 'the Samaritans' to show his debt to Jesus' Parable and ethic of compassion. Varah was motivated to do this by the funeral of a 14 year old girl who had committed suicide, fearing she had contracted a STD; in fact, she had started menstruating but had no one she could talk to about her problems.

The Parable also illustrates the ethical use of money to help others (and as an alternative to the belief that Christians must live in 'holy poverty').

The UK Prime Minister **Margaret Thatcher** used the Parable to illustrate this positive view of wealth in 1980 when she told a TV interview:

*No one would remember the Good Samaritan if he'd only had good intentions; he had money as well – **Margaret Thatcher***

However, critics argue that this distorts the message of the Parable, since the only person in the story motivated solely by money is the innkeeper (who must be paid to care for the wounded man), but the point of the Parable is that we should be like the Samaritan rather than the Innkeeper.

Equality today: The Parable offers a powerful message of equality, showing that differences of race, nationality and culture are meaningless compared to the duty to show compassion to fellow human beings.

Matt Broomfield, writing in *The Spectator* (2017) argues that we should all give unconditionally to street beggars, even if we suspect they're drug addicts:

If your money funds the final hit, accept that the person would rather be dead. If your act of kindness makes him wake up the next morning and decide to change his life, that's nice but not your business either **– Matt Broomfield**

Not many Christians would be comfortable with the thought of an addict overdosing using their donation, but Broomfield's argument that giving to the needy should be unconditional and direct, without making moral judgments about why they are in that position, is very close to the spirit of the Parable and to the **Sermon on the Plain**.

Pluralism today: The clearest message of the Parable is one of religious pluralism: the Jews and the Samaritans worship the ***same God*** who wants them to love each other as he loves them. Religious distinctions (like the religious rituals of the priest and the Levite) are distractions from the true duty to love God through loving your neighbour.

This interpretation has not been emphasized over the centuries (and the allegorical interpretation of the Samaritan as Christ perhaps distracts from this meaning). Christians were inspired by the Parable to build hospitals and orphanages, but not to reconcile with Jews (whom they accused of 'deicide' – the murder of God).

However, in the 1960s the **Second Vatican Council** changed the Catholic Church's position on many things, including rejecting the concept of Jewish 'deicide' and focusing on the '*shared patrimony*' (inheritance) of Christians and Jews.

Parables of the Lost (Luke 15)

These three Parables emphasize the qualities of compassion and God's mercy that are particularly important in **Luke's Gospel**.

The context is important. The **Pharisees** are *muttering* that Jesus associates with *sinners* and *eats with them*. The *sinners* are publicans (like the tax collector **Matthew/Levi** who becomes one of Jesus' Disciples and **Zacchaeus** who repented after Jesus dined with him). These people are sinners because they collaborate with the **Roman occupation** and swindle their fellow Jews. However, Jesus associates with other *sinners* too:

- **Prostitutes**, like the woman who anoints Jesus' feet (**Luke 7: 36-50**) and also (arguably the same person) the woman caught in adultery (**John 8: 1-11**)
- The **diseased**, like the lepers (**Luke 17: 11-19**} or the man who was blind from birth (**John 9: 1-3**), whose illness was regarded by 1st century Jews (but not by Jesus) as a punishment for sin
- **Samaritans**, like the Samaritan woman at the well (**John 4: 27** – even Jesus' Disciples are surprised by this)

The criticism of Jesus is not just that he associates with these people without judging them, but also that he makes himself ritually unclean (according to 1st century Jewish purity laws) by coming into contact with them.

The Lost Sheep

This is Jesus' immediate reply to the criticism that he associates with *sinners*:

> [4] "Suppose one of you has a hundred sheep and loses one of them. Doesn't he leave the ninety-nine in the open country and go after the lost sheep until he finds it? [5] And when he finds it, he joyfully puts it on his shoulders [6] and goes home. Then he calls his friends and neighbours together and says, 'Rejoice with me; I have found my lost sheep.' [7] I tell you that in the same way there will be more rejoicing in heaven over one sinner who repents than over ninety-nine righteous persons who do not need to repent.

Jesus' point is simple: his mission is to people who are 'lost' in sin, not to people who are already *righteous*. This links to Jesus' statement **"I Am the Good Shepherd"** (*c.f.* **Topic 2.2 Titles of Jesus**).

There is also the image here of the celebratory banquet, which Jesus uses to represent the **Kingdom of God** (p75). The *sinners*, who know that they are sinners, have the opportunity to repent and enter the Kingdom of God; the Pharisees, who mistakenly believe themselves to be *righteous*, will not repent and will be excluded.

The Lost Coin

Jesus moves on to a more comedic response that makes a similar point:

> 8 "Or suppose a woman has ten silver coins and loses one. Doesn't she light a lamp, sweep the house and search carefully until she finds it? 9 And when she finds it, she calls her friends and neighbours together and says, 'Rejoice with me; I have found my lost coin.' 10 In the same way, I tell you, there is rejoicing in the presence of the angels of God over one sinner who repents."

Here, the woman searching for her coin represents God, searching for the lost souls. This represents the activity of God throughout human history, sending his prophets and ultimately sending Jesus himself (which may be the symbolism of the woman *lighting a lamp* – **John's Prologue** describes Jesus as the *Light that shines in the Darkness*).

As with the previous Parable (p230), there is celebration when the lost soul is found.

However, this Parable is more surprising, since God is depicted as a woman. More than that, the image of a Jewish woman obsessively turning the house upside down in the middle of the night over a single misplaced coin plays into a lot of comedy stereotypes about Jewish mothers.

> *Is Jesus making his audience laugh here with distinctively Jewish humour? It's interesting that the NARRATOR of John's Gospel is often witty, but in the Synoptic Gospels Jesus himself is frequently witty. Although the Gospels present Jesus as crying, they never state that he laughed – but I think he certainly made his audiences laugh!*

The Lost Son

This Parable is often called the 'Prodigal Son' ('prodigal' meaning 'careless with money'). It is second only to the **Parable of the Good Samaritan** (p225) in terms of its influence in Christian thought. It represents a complete illustration of Jesus' teaching about lost souls and the **Kingdom of God** (p75).

The story concerns a farmer with two sons. Rather than wait for his inheritance, the younger son wants the money up-front, so his father *divides his estate* (presumably selling off land to raise money for the younger son). The younger son shows no gratitude or respect:

> 13 "Not long after that, the younger son got together all he had, set off for a distant country and there squandered his wealth in wild living. 14 After he had spent everything, there was a severe famine in that whole country, and he began to be in need. 15 So he went and hired himself out to a citizen of that country, who sent him to his fields to feed pigs. 16 He longed to fill his stomach with the pods that the pigs were eating, but no one gave him anything.

The younger son is 'prodigal' by spending everything in *wild living* (with *prostitutes*, we later learn). It's worth noticing that the prodigal son is living among Gentiles: he has gone to *a distant country* and ends up *feeding pigs* (no Jewish farmer would keep pigs).

The prodigal son is thoroughly degraded. He is cut off from his people and his religion. He lives among Gentiles and is ritually polluted by working with pigs. In other words, his position is exactly the same as the publicans and other *sinners* that Jesus associates with.

The prodigal son has hit rock bottom but *no one gave him anything* – he's not even allowed to eat pig swill! This represents the way publicans and other *sinners* are ostracised by respectable Jews. Of course, 1st century publicans weren't living in poverty: working for the Romans made them well-off. However, they were spiritually poor, because they were cut off from worshiping God – and the prostitutes and lepers were probably poor in wealth as well.

The prodigal son decides to go back to his father. He's too ashamed to ask for forgiveness. He intends to ask for a job as a labourer on his father's farm. He feels he has lost forever the right to be called his father's son. This represents his sincere repentance.

> "But while he was still a long way off, his father saw him and was filled with compassion for him; he ran to his son, threw his arms around him and kissed him.
>
> 21 "The son said to him, 'Father, I have sinned against heaven and against you. I am no longer worthy to be called your son.'
>
> 22 "But the father said to his servants, 'Quick! Bring the best robe and put it on him. Put a ring on his finger and sandals on his feet. 23 Bring the fattened calf and kill it. Let's have a feast and celebrate. 24 For this son of mine was dead and is alive again; he was lost and is found.' So they began to celebrate.

This passage makes the same point as the previous Parables. The father is God and the prodigal son is a soul lost to sin. When the sinner repents, God rejoices and there is a celebration and a banquet. The sinner's sins are utterly forgiven: *he was lost and is found*.

However, the Parable does not end here. Jesus explores the implications of repentance in greater depth by considering the **other** son who stayed at home and did his duty. This son is resentful towards his younger brother and the celebration over his return:

> 28 "The older brother became angry and refused to go in. So his father went out and pleaded with him. 29 But he answered his father, 'Look! All these years I've been slaving for you and never disobeyed your orders. Yet you never gave me even a young goat so I could celebrate with my friends. 30 But when this son of yours who has squandered your property with prostitutes comes home, you kill the fattened calf for him!'
>
> 31 "'My son,' the father said, 'you are always with me, and everything I have is yours. 32 But we had to celebrate and be glad, because this brother of yours was dead and is alive again; he was lost and is found.'"

The older son represents the Pharisees who keep the Jewish **Law**. There is something self-righteous about him: he is proud but he works for his father out of hope of reward rather than love. He sees himself as a *slave* rather than a son.

Many critics detect insolence in the older son's words. He says *"Look…"* to his father rather than addressing him as *"Father"* – and of course Jesus teaches his Disciples to address God as their *Father in Heaven*.

It's significant that the older son cannot name his own brother, calling him *"this son of yours"* (rather like the Pharisee in the **Parable of the Good Samaritan** (p225) who cannot bring himself to name the Samaritan). By contrast, Jesus encourages his Disciples to call each other 'brother'.

The father's response, like God's, is painstaking and compassionate. He does not get angry. He assures the brother that *you are always with me and everything I have is yours*. There is a gentle irony in the way he refers to the prodigal son as *this brother of yours* – echoing the older son's hard-hearted words to bring him to his senses and reminding readers that **all** unfortunate people who suffer hardship and ostracism are really their *brothers*.

The Parable ends there, unresolved. Will the older son soften his heart and be reconciled with his brother? Or will he stay out in the fields, angry and self-righteous, while the party goes on back at the house? This is a question the Pharisees must answer for themselves: will they enter the **Kingdom of Heaven** (p75) alongside the repentant publicans, prostitutes, lepers and Samaritans – or be left out like the ungrateful guests in the **Parable of the Great Banquet** (p87)?

---

*It's odd that this Parable is known as the **Parable of the Prodigal Son**, when really it's not about him at all. The truly 'lost son' is not the prodigal but the one who stayed behind but never learned to love his father. Really, it should be the 'Parable of the Dutiful Son'.*

1st century Judaism: Many of the details here must be contextualised: the ritual pollution from working with pigs or socialising with Gentiles. This Parable emphasises the hard-hearted nature of **Phariseeism** (which calculates how much God owes us for our good deeds rather than loving God in a humble spirit). Scholars are divided over whether this is a fair representation of what Pharisees were actually like, but it's certainly what later Christians **thought** they were like, so **Form Critics** would treat this story is a *pericope* expressing the attitudes of 1st century Christians (who saw themselves as the prodigal son and the Jews as the hard-hearted older brother).

Christian codes of living: The key theme for Christians is REPENTANCE and the importance of second chances. Christians are supposed to be like the father (delighted when somebody repents) rather than the older son (still angry about the sins they have repented). However, Christians did not find this code easy to live by.

For one thing, sexual misconduct troubled early Christians and led to lapsed members being expelled from churches and not forgiven. It is interesting that the prodigal son's sins included fornication, because this was rarely tolerated by the early Church.

Another problem was what to do with former-Christians who denied their faith during persecutions then wanted to return to the Church when the persecutions ended.

The Church soon developed the institution of confessing sins and asking for forgiveness – and divided sins into VENAL sins (which could be forgiven by your fellow-Christians) and MORTAL sins (which could only be forgiven by God).

The Catholic Church continues the practice of EXCOMMUNICATING members who commit mortal sins. Excommunicants cannot receive the Church's sacraments (including the Eucharist). Throughout history, excommunication was used to control people (including kings and queens) with the threat of damnation after death.

Equality today: The Parable's message of repentance and forgiveness is still important for individuals but also takes on a social dimension in the 21st century. There are historic crimes (such as slavery, colonialism, genocide and environmental damage) of which entire societies are responsible. This is COLLECTIVE GUILT and the need for NATIONAL REPENTANCE.

One country that has taken on this message is post-war Germany, which has engaged in national repentance over the Holocaust and other Nazi atrocities. Similarly, in 2007, the UK Government apologized for its historic role in the slave trade.

However, it's one thing to apologise but another to REPENT. People in Western societies continue to benefit from the crimes committed by their ancestors (for example, by the wealth taken from former-colonies or generated by slave labour). Some argue that equality demands that victims are COMPENSATED for historic crimes. For example, Germany makes reparations to the State of Israel to compensate Holocaust survivors and the families of victims. However, Western nations have not offered reparation to countries in Africa or Asia for mistreatment in the past, despite huge inequalities in wealth that continue to exist.

Pluralism today: Many religious divisions are based on historic grievances. Christian antisemitism has occurred for centuries, but the Crusades that began in the 11th century CE created historic grievances between Christians and Muslims. The Reformation and the European Wars of Religion that followed in the 16th-17th centuries have left behind mistrust and bitterness between Catholics and Protestants that continue to this day in places like Northern Ireland. Such hostility makes religious tolerance difficult.

There have been moves towards greater religious tolerance. In 2000, the Catholic Church formally apologised for sins committed against Jews, heretics, Gypsies and native peoples. Many religious groups are in the position of the older son rather than his prodigal younger brother: it's hard for them to admit their role in historic evils because they see themselves as righteous and acting in accordance with divinely-inspired teachings. The words of the father are a reassurance from God to repent: *you are always with me and everything I have is yours.*

Parable of the Rich Man and Lazarus (Luke 16)

There has been a debate over the years about whether this story is a Parable at all or a description of actual events. **Luke's Gospel** does not introduce this as a Parable and it's unusual for Parables to give the main characters names (usually they are just 'a traveller', 'a man who had two sons' or 'a sower'). On the other hand, the story functions like a Parable. **I. Howard Marshall** (p243) argues it is a Middle Eastern (possibly Egyptian) folk tale, which Jesus has adapted by giving the characters new names:

> the background to the teaching is more probably found in non-biblical sources – **I. Howard Marshall**

> The 'Lazarus' in the story is not the same Lazarus who is raised from the dead in **John's Gospel**. The Rich Man is sometimes named 'Dives'. This is based on misreading the Latin text ('dives' just means 'wealthy') but Dives is as good a name as any so I'll use it in this analysis.

In context, Jesus has been telling Parables about money to the **Pharisees** "who loved money ... and were sneering at Jesus". Jesus warns them that they cannot serve two masters:

> You cannot serve both God and money – **Luke 16: 13**

The Parable follows on from this, illustrating Jesus' attitude to wealth and to the Pharisees.

The Parable

Dives is a rich man who lives in luxury; Lazarus is a beggar covered in sores who lives in the street. When the two men die, they go to different Afterlife destinations:

- Dives goes to *Hades*, a place of fiery suffering
- Lazarus goes to *Abraham's side*, in paradise where he is welcomed by Abraham, the founder of the Jewish race and religion

Dives begs Abraham for help: will he send Lazarus down to place a drop of water on Dives' tongue? Abraham declines, saying:

> 'Son, remember that in your lifetime you received your good things, while Lazarus received bad things, but now he is comforted here and you are in agony. [26] And besides all this, between us and you a great chasm has been set in place, so that those who want to go from here to you cannot, nor can anyone cross over from there to us.'

When Abraham says that Dives has already *received his good things*, this echoes Jesus' teaching in the **Sermon on the Plain** (p212), that the rich have *already received their comfort* but the poor will *receive the Kingdom of God*.

There is a debate among Christians about who Lazarus and Dives are supposed to be and where they end up.

- Some see Dives as a purely symbolic figure for 'wealthy people. Others think he represents the **Pharisees** (whom Jesus is addressing in context**). Johann Sepp** (1864) suggests that the description of Dives wearing the *purple robes* and *living in luxury* suggests a **Sadducee** rather than a Pharisee.
- Lazarus represents all poor people. His *sores* suggest he is a leper and 1st century Judaism regarded leprosy as a punishment for sin. This links to the **Parables of the Lost** (p230) because Lazarus would be one of the *sinners* that Jesus associates with and this Parable also rejects the belief that there is a link between sickness and sin.

The description of the Afterlife also poses problems for Christian interpretation:

- Lazarus is in some sort of paradise, but is this supposed to be Heaven? Since Jesus has not yet died his atoning death, how could Lazarus go to Heaven? Lazarus seems to be in the 'Bosom of Abraham', a belief of the **Pharisees** that the righteous dead would go to a comfortable Afterlife to wait for Judgement Day.
- Dives is in a state of torment. Conservative Christians take this Parable as evidence of the literal existence of Hell as a place of eternal punishment. Others point out that the term *Hades* is a Greek translation of the Hebrew *SHEOL* which just means "the grave"; for them, Dives is frightened of his ***future*** suffering on Judgement Day.

Many Christian scholars, such as **Martin Luther** (1483-1546), regard the afterlife details in this Parable as purely **symbolic**: what matters is just that Lazarus and Dives have SWAPPED ROLES, just as Jesus warned in his Beatitudes and Woes during the **Sermon on the Plain** (p212).

It's interesting that the Afterlife in this Parable doesn't match with Jesus' own eschatological predictions. Rather than 'the Bosom of Abraham', Jesus preaches about the Kingdom of God as something happening on Earth; the people who enter the Kingdom are repentant sinners but those who are shut out have rejected the Kingdom: the Kingdom hasn't rejected them.

One interpretation is that, in this Parable, Jesus is describing the Pharisees' ***own*** religious beliefs about the Afterlife rather than his own teachings. His point is that the Pharisees stand to be condemned even in terms of their ***own*** beliefs because they do not *love their neighbours*.

Dives' servants tell Lazarus to leave

The punch-line of the Parable is probably more important than the details about the Afterlife:

'Then I beg you, father, send Lazarus to my family, [28] for I have five brothers. Let him warn them, so that they will not also come to this place of torment.'

[29] "Abraham replied, 'They have Moses and the Prophets; let them listen to them.'

[30] "'No, father Abraham,' he said, 'but if someone from the dead goes to them, they will repent.'

[31] "He said to him, 'If they do not listen to Moses and the Prophets, they will not be convinced even if someone rises from the dead.'"

The Parable shows that God's demand for fairness and charity is well-attested in *Moses and the Prophets* (i.e. the Written Torah and the Oral Law of the Pharisees), but that the Pharisees themselves ignore what the **Law** says.

The prediction that people who ignore the Scriptures won't be convinced by a man rising from the dead looks ahead to Jesus' **Resurrection**. The Pharisees will continue to dismiss Jesus' teachings even after the Resurrection. Furthermore, in Luke's account of the Resurrection, people only *believe* after Jesus has *opened their minds* to the true meaning of the Scriptures, which all refer to his atoning sacrifice (p149).

1st century Judaism: This Parable is strongly rooted in 1st century Jewish beliefs about the afterlife, specifically the **Pharisees'** beliefs. The ideas of the 'Bosom of Abraham' for the righteous dead, *SHEOL* (the Grave) for everyone else, and a Judgment Day when the dead are resurrected to be punished or rewarded: these are all Jewish beliefs from the time period. Similarly, the moral commandment to care for the poor and give your wealth to the needy is part of Judaism too. Jesus' critique is that these beliefs don't ***motivate*** people to live righteously.

Christian codes of living: This Parable reinforces Christian codes about the ethical use of wealth established in the **Sermon on the Plain** (p53) and illustrated in the **Parable of the Good Samaritan** (p225). It reinforces Jesus' teaching that those who fail to show love and mercy in ***this*** life will not receive it from God in the Afterlife. However, Christians believe that their faith in Jesus' atoning death means that their sins will be forgiven if they fail to live up to the high standard God expects, so long as they sincerely tried.

Equality today: This Parable contains a powerful message concerning economic inequality. There is a tendency for Christians to over-emphasize sexual sins (such as the prodigal son and his prostitutes), but Jesus has far more to say about wealth than about sex. This Parable follows Jesus' warning that people *cannot serve two masters*: they must choose between God and money. A 2018 report by Oxfam shows the widening gap between the world's super-rich and everyone else, with 82% of wealth generated in the previous year going to the richest 1% of the population. The CEO of a big fashion retailer earns in 4 days what a Bangladeshi textile worker earns in an entire lifetime.

Pluralism today: If Jesus (or at any rate, Luke) really did adapt an Egyptian folk tale to represent Pharisee beliefs about the Afterlife (as **I. Howard Marshall** suggests) then this is a good example of religious pluralism, because it suggests that we can learn things from other religions too. For example, **David Burrell** (2014) argues Christians can learn from Islam, saying that *"the attraction of Islam can most often be traced to the palpable sense of community"* because Islam preserves a community spirit that Christianity has lost sight of. Jewish rabbi **Jonathan Sacks** (2002) argues for 'religious diversity', saying, *"no one civilization encompasses all the spiritual, ethical and artistic expressions of mankind"* and therefore all religions can learn from each other.

Do Luke's Parables provide a basis for how to live in the modern world?

YES	NO
The Parables show how the teachings from the Sermon on the Plain must be put into practice: the Good Samaritan illustrates loving your enemy, the Lost Son illustrates weeping turning to joy through repentance, the Rich Man & Lazarus shows the dangers of wealth and the blessings for the poor and hungry.	The Parables are too rooted in the world of the 1st century to guide people today: ethnic conflicts between Jews and Samaritans, Jewish purity laws, the politics of a Roman occupation and ancient mythologies about the afterlife. The 21st century is beset by complex problems of global inequality, environmental destruction and terrorism not covered by these.
The Parables have guided Christians for centuries, long after the original contexts were forgotten: it's not important who Samaritans were or what happens after we die, because the Parables illustrate loving *any* enemy and caring for *all* the poor in this life The Parable of the Lost Son invites religious people to examine their consciences even if they consider themselves to be good people and recognise every 'lost soul' as their brother, no matter what that person might have done in the past.	The Parables fly in the face of normal morality. While it's nice to 'love your enemy', you also have an obligation to look after your family and friends and protect your country; it's good to see bad people turn themselves around, but we should still reward good people for doing the right thing; giving to the needy is admirable, but people have also got a right to enjoy the wealth they have earned. No one seriously tries to act on the values in these Parables and society wouldn't work if they did.

Evaluating How We Should Live

If you also study **Unit 2 (Religion & Ethics)** then there is a lot of crossover with this topic, especially when it comes to answering the 'synoptic' essay question in Section C of either paper. With that in mind, let's look at two ethical theories from Religion & Ethics in the light of Luke's **Sermon on the Plain** (p212) and **Parables** (p224).

Natural Moral Law

Natural Moral Law (NML) was first expounded by **Aristotle** in the 4th century BCE and developed by **Thomas Aquinas** (1225-1274); it is the ethical system favoured by the Catholic Church today.

NML argues that there is a moral code that humans are naturally inclined towards. Aristotle starts by looking at the purpose (or '*telos*') of human life and concludes the natural human life is a rational life. Aristotle argues that, as rational creatures, we have an obligation to keep ourselves alive, to reproduce, and to live in an ordered society. Giving in to non-rational desires enslaves and degrades the individual, threatening our security and the security of our society.

Thomas Aquinas merged Aristotelian ideas with Christianity and he brings a strong religious dimension to this, saying that you cannot think about the purpose behind human life without considering the Afterlife and God: our ultimate *telos* is to enjoy communion with God forever.

The problem is that people choose "apparent goods" that make them happy in the short term (like drunkenness or fornication) rather than "actual goods" that secure them long term happiness (like sobriety or chastity). We can tell the difference between these apparent and actual goods by using "right reason".

For Aquinas, we do not invent morals, we discover them. God makes portions of his Eternal Law obvious to us through revelation, such as Jesus' teachings: this is the Divine Law. The Eternal Law can be worked out through observing nature, because God is the Creator of the universe: this is the Natural Law. So, for example, you don't need to be a Christian or read the Bible to work out that a life of drunkenness and casual sex will not, in the long run, make anyone happy or fulfilled. Humans then set up their own laws and social conventions, based on Natural Law, maybe mixed with bits of Divine Law: this is Positive Law, which is a human creation and therefore imperfect. For example, in the past Positive Law discriminated against women but over the centuries clearer thinking about Natural Law and interpreting Divine Law has led to greater equality for women.

Evaluating NML with reference to Jesus' teaching

On the face of it, NML seems a long way away from Jesus' ethical teaching. NML is all about laws that must be followed without exception (i.e. it is DEONTOLOGICAL). Jesus' ethics are all about the exceptions: love and forgive your enemy, don't judge other people, celebrate the repentant sinner more than the righteous person.

NML also contradicts the eschatological element of Jesus' teaching. It's a very this-worldly ethical system. It assumes that people want to work in jobs, raise a family, grow old and die peacefully. Jesus praises people who abandon their jobs and family to seek the Kingdom of God (**Luke 14: 26**) and warns about an Apocalypse that will end society as we know it; the earliest Christians did not expect to grow old, since Jesus predicted the *Parousia* ('Second Coming') before they died in **Luke 21: 32**.

This is why Aquinas' contribution to NML is important. Aquinas introduces the importance of the Afterlife and the idea of Divine Law (from the Bible) supplementing Natural Law (from common sense):

- Natural Law tells us that we don't want to have a huge gap between the rich and the poor because that leads to crime and revolution in society; Divine Law goes further with Jesus' teachings to give to the poor unselfishly
- Natural Law tells us to show some restraint in the way we punish enemies, otherwise society falls apart because of feuds and vendettas; Divine Law goes further with Jesus' teachings to forgive enemies unconditionally

In many ways, the strict rules of NML remain a 'bad fit' for Jesus' teachings, but Aquinas shows how Jesus' ethics supplement and complete an ethical code we can work out for ourselves.

Situation Ethics

Situation Ethics (SE) was first developed by **Joseph Fletcher** (1905-1991); it is an ethical system favoured by liberal Christians today.

Fletcher claimed he was inspired by a St Louis cab driver who said to him: *"Sometimes you've gotta put your principles to one side and do the right thing"*. Fletcher argues for the importance of the Christian idea of **agápē** (loving compassion) as the thing that makes our behaviour moral. We act out of love for others, trying to do the best for other people rather than ourselves.

SE states that decision-making should be based upon the circumstances of a particular situation, and not upon some fixed law or rule (LEGALISM). Fletcher founded his ethics upon **1 John 4: 8**: *"God is love."* The only absolute is Love. Love should be the motive behind every decision. As long as Love is your intention, the end justifies the means.

So a person who practises SE approaches ethical problems with some general moral principles rather than a complete set of ethical laws and is prepared to give up even those principles if doing so will lead to a greater good. Since *"circumstances alter cases"*, what in some times and places we call right is in other times and places wrong.

For example, lying is ordinarily not in the best interest of people and relationships, but is justifiable in certain situations (such as encouraging an ageing relative to believe that all is well in your troubled marriage).

Evaluating SE with reference to Jesus' teaching

On the face of it, SE seems a good fit with Jesus' ethics. The **Sermon on the Plain** (p212) boils down to a commandment to *love your neighbour* and this is illustrated in the **Parable of the Good Samaritan** (p225), where the Priest and the Levite's religious rules get in the way of their showing *agape*-love but the Samaritan breaks all the rules to show love to someone in need. The punishment of Dives in *Hades* can be interpreted as a condemnation of his failure to show love to Lazarus (because Fletcher says "*justice is love distributed*").

However, conservative Christians have been reluctant to embrace SE. Jesus says he comes *not to abolish the Law but to fulfill it* (**Matthew 5: 17**) and SE sounds very much like it is abolishing the laws of morality. Jesus also warns against *false prophets* who will be popular but whose ethical teachings are like a *house built without a foundation*.

The conservative evangelical **William Barclay** (1971) opposes SE with this argument:

> *it is much easier to agree that extraordinary situations need extraordinary measures than to think that there are no laws for ordinary, everyday life* – **William Barclay**

Possibly, Fletcher only ever meant to argue that *extraordinary situations need extraordinary measures* and this might be all Jesus is saying too: the **Parable of the Good Samaritan** and the **Lost Son** both describe *extraordinary situations*. However, scholars like **I. Howard Marshall** (p243) do not accept SE as the best ethical interpretation of Jesus' teachings. Marshall recognises Fletcher's point that Biblical teachings have to be reinterpreted for the modern world but doesn't think we can just ignore 'difficult' teachings (e.g. about homosexuality being sinful).

Case Study: Westboro Baptist Church

The Westboro Baptist Church (WBC) is a church with less than 40 members, mostly the children of its founder, Fred Phelps (1929-2014). The congregation lives and worships together in a compound of houses in Topeka, Kansas. Many of the family are qualified lawyers and run a law firm that helps support the WBC's activities. Over the years, several family members have left the church to pursue normal American lives; these people are completely rejected by the WBC and can have no further contact with their parents, brothers and sisters.

In many ways, the WBC has beliefs that are quite typical of American evangelical churches. They believe humanity is living in the "End Times" and *Parousia* will happen soon, with Christ re-appearing on Earth to judge people for their sins.

However, in other ways the members of the WBC are extremists. They believe that they alone follow the true Christian faith so people who are atheists or follow other religions (e.g. Jews, Muslims, Hindus) will go to Hell and so will other Christians with different beliefs (e.g. Catholics, Anglicans, Methodists). Phelps argues that churches which preach about God's love are misleading people because he believes that the Bible makes it clear that God also hates; if you visit the WBC website, the first message you will see is the slogan 'God Hates You'.

However, the WBC attracts the most controversy for its stance on homosexuality. Most evangelical churches claim that homosexual sex is against the will of God, but they argue that although God hates the sin, he still loves the sinners. The WBC rejects this and claims America is under God's curse for tolerating homosexuality and all Americans who die in foreign wars or as victims of terrorism or disasters are being punished by God for America's sins. Members of the church picket outside military funerals with placards saying 'God Hates America'. This causes great distress to the families of the dead but the WBC believe they are doing God's will, arguing like this:

WBC picket in 2008 (photo: David Shankbone)

> *You think our job is to win souls to Christ? All we do, by getting in their face ... is make what's already in their heart come out of their mouth* – **Shirley Phelps-Roper**

Making what's already in their hearts come out of their mouths links to Jesus' teaching about trees producing good and bad fruit. In other words, the WBC has no interest in making converts; they just want to make a clear distinction between people who ignore Biblical rules and people (like themselves) who condemn homosexuality, in preparation for Judgment Day.

Evaluating the WBC with reference to Jesus' teaching

The WBC's teachings and actions seem far-removed from Jesus' ethics. Jesus taught his Disciples to love their neighbours, forgive their enemies and not to judge, whereas the WBC deliberately causes distress to neighbours, is unforgiving of its opponents and behaves very judgmentally. Most ordinary Christians (including evangelicals) view Pastor Phelps is a *false preacher* who has led his congregation astray. However, the WBC's eschatological teaching about the End Times being imminent **does** link to Jesus' teaching and, from their view point, it is the ordinary Christians who have been led astray by *false preachers*.

Although the WBC's behaviour is completely out of line with Christian thought, it does illustrate a problem with applying Jesus' ethical teachings. The Bible **does** contain teachings that condemn homosexuality and other religions as sinful. If the WBC is 'cherry picking' by focusing on these hostile teachings and ignoring the loving ones, liberal Christians are also focusing on the loving teachings and ignoring the hostile ones. How can mainstream Christians justify doing this?

Key scholar **I. Howard Marshall** (p243) sets out to show how the Bible can be interpreted for today without falling into the extremes of fundamentalism (like the WBC) or liberalism (like Situation Ethics). **Frank J. Matera** (p244) also explores the unified voice of the Bible (he calls it the "*master story*") that puts its hostile teachings into a positive context.

KEY SCHOLARS

I. Howard Marshall

Topic: 6.2 How Should We Live?

I. Howard Marshall is a Scottish professor of theology. He is a Methodist (like **Morna Hooker**) but leans towards a conservative position. His area of specialism is **Luke's Gospel** and the **Book of Acts**. He is also a key scholar for **Topic: 5.1 The Kingdom of God in Luke** and **Topic 5.3 Crucifixion & Resurrection Narratives in Luke**.

Marshall is an evangelical Christian – he believes that the Bible should be taken literally as far as possible, he does not discount miracles and he thinks that, even though it is the product of many authors, it speaks with one voice in revealing God.

In **Beyond the Bible** (2004), Marshall explains that the task of Biblical interpretation is:

> *how we discover the message of the Bible for today, both for our fellow believers and for our non-Christian neighbours* – **I. Howard Marshall**

Marshall argues that the Gospel-writers and Paul were inspired but still could not *"foresee the world of which we are a part"* and therefore modern people have to interpret the Bible to work out how it should apply. Marshall points out that there are modern ethical problems where there is *"nothing closely analogous in Scripture"* and gives the examples of fertility treatment, genetic engineering and medical euthanasia.

Marshal argues for a balance between liberal and fundamentalist approaches: not ignoring parts of the Bible that contradict scientific understanding (e.g. the way **Rudolf Bultmann** does, p33) but not rejecting scientific thinking either. Marshall talks about 'broadening horizons'. For example, the Old Testament often claims violence and genocide can solve moral problems, but in the New Testament that is a commandment to love your enemy. This broadens the ethical horizon and forces us to reinterpret the Old Testament rather than taking it at face value.

> *we do recognize that we are to listen to it in a different way from the original hearers* – **I. Howard Marshall**

Marshall applies this to the New Testament too. There are passages in the Gospels and in the Epistles that have a *"limited horizon"* because they represent 1st century values: slavery, women as second-class citizens and homosexuality as sinful are examples he considers.

> *we have to go beyond biblical teaching expressed in a specific cultural setting, for example in recognizing that slavery ... is fundamentally at variance with the biblical understanding of man* – **I. Howard Marshall**

In going *beyond the Bible*, Marshall is prepared to admit the liberal argument that 'times have changed' but he still insists *"the Bible must be free to speak its prophetic and critical word to the practices and beliefs of our world."* He admits that this creates a *tension* that has no easy answer for Christians trying to work out an ethical response to issues like homosexuality.

Frank J. Matera

Topic 6.2 How Should We Live?

> *Is F. Matera the right scholar for this topic? Earlier versions of the Specification identify "L. Matera" but the recent editions confirm that Frank J. Matera is the intended scholar.*

Frank J. Matera is an American Catholic priest and professor of theology. Like **I. Howard Marshall**, he leans towards a conservative position but, as a Catholic, he feels free to interpret the Bible more liberally. He is also a key scholar for **Topic 5.3 Crucifixion & Resurrection Narratives in Luke**.

In ***New Testament Ethics: The Legacies of Jesus & Paul*** (1996), Matera acknowledges (rather like Marshall), that neither Jesus nor Paul left a complete ethical system behind, so modern readers have to interpret what they wrote and apply it to new situations that didn't exist in the 1st century. Matera distinguishes between **diachronic interpretation** (recognizing there are many authors in the New Testament and they all have different views) and **synchronic interpretation** (the idea that all these authors speak with one underlying voice – this is Marshall's position as well).

Matera resembles Marshall in that he tries to explore a 'middle way' between these approaches: he examines the teachings of each Gospel then harmonises them into a single ethical vision of how we should live today. For example, Matera looks at what is distinctive about Luke's Gospel:

> *The Gospel of Luke addresses a new situation in which Gentiles play a dominant role in the Church* – **Frank J. Matera**

Marshal argues this Gentile audience shapes Luke's ethical concerns, in which the **Law** and Jewish concepts of 'righteousness' become less important and there is more focus on universal ethical principles for ordinary people all over the Roman Empire. This can be seen in Luke's short **Sermon on the Plain** (p212) and the focus on social issues like poverty in his Parables.

However, as well as specific concerns, there is a unity to the New Testament:

> *The unity of New Testament theology is grounded in the implied master story ... Humanity finds itself in a predicament of its own making from which it cannot extricate itself* – **Frank J. Matera**

Matera argues that this *master-story* is timeless and therefore true today, even though our cultural situation has changed since the 1st century: we are still in a *predicament of our own making*, which includes our social inequality, sexual and ethnic conflicts and attitudes to money. Therefore, the Bible continues to offer us ethical advice.

Matera denies this ethical standard is too idealistic or impractical for modern people. He argues Christians must be *'"doers of the word rather than mere hearers,"* referring to **Luke 6: 46** where Jesus condemns those who call him '*Lord*' but *"do not do what I say."*

GLOSSARY OF TERMS

Abraham: Ancestor of the Jewish race and founder of Judaism (lived perhaps 2000 BCE)

Acts: Fifth book of the New Testament describing the growth of the Christian religion guided by **Peter** and **Paul**; written by the same author as Luke's Gospel

Agape: Greek word for 'love' in the sense of 'selfless compassion' or 'altruism' rather than 'romance'; sometimes translated as 'charity'

Allegory: A text with a hidden or secondary meaning where the key features stand for something else

Anachronism: A person, object, action or idea represented in a time period that would be historically impossible (like a telephone in 1st century Palestine)

Apocalypticism: Belief in the coming end of the world

Apologetic: A text defending a religion; someone who defends their religion with arguments is an apologist

Ascension: Mysterious event when the Risen Jesus leaves this world and returns to his Heavenly Father

Atoning Death: A death that makes up for sins

Barabbas: Prisoner whom **Pontius Pilate** releases instead of Jesus; referred to as a revolutionary in some Gospels

Beatitude: Blessing; there are four blessings described in the **Sermon on the Plain**

Beelzebub: A name for the Devil

Bet Din: A religious court in Judaism

Blasphemy: A crime against God

Bosom of Abraham: 1st century Jewish belief in a paradise after death for the souls of righteous people

Caiaphas: Joseph Caiaphas was the High Priest who condemned Jesus to death

Cathar Heresy: Christian sect popular in the South of France in the Middle Ages; brutally suppressed by the Catholic Church and the Frankish nobility in the 12th-13th centuries

Celsus: Greek philosopher of the 2nd century CE who criticised Christianity

Cephas: Named used for **Peter** in **Paul**'s epistles (it is Aramaic for 'Rock', which is what 'Peter' means in Greek)

Cherry-picking: Selecting only details from a text that support a theory while ignoring those that don't

Christology: Theory about the status of Christ, from an **exalted** human (low Christology) to an **incarnated** divine being (high Christology)

Christophany: Vision of the Risen Christ revealed to **Paul** on the road to Damascus

Conservatism: Christian trend opposed to **liberalism** and trying to conserve Biblical truths; see **traditionalism**

Criterion of Embarrassment: Suggestion that a Biblical event may be historical since it contains details that go against early Christian beliefs

Deism: Popular religion of the **Enlightenment** that worships a non-interventionist God; rejects miracles and organized worship

De-mythologizing: Rudolf Bultmann's project to strip away mythological details from the Bible to reveal its timeless *kerygma* or preaching

Dictation Theory: Theory that the Bible was inspired directly by God, word-for-word, with the authors passively recording

Dualism: Belief in **Hellenic** philosophy that there is a physical world and a (superior) spiritual world

Eisegesis: Faulty **exegesis** that imposes the reader's own meanings on the text

Emmaus: Town where two disciples share a meal with the Risen Jesus; not identified and may be symbolic

Empiricism: Knowledge that comes through experience and the 5 senses

Empty Tomb: Mystery of the tomb of Jesus being discovered with no body inside; reported in all the Gospels

Enlightenment, The: Period from mid 17th to late 18th century when European scholars pioneered a new scientific outlook

Eschatology: Beliefs about the end of the world and the afterlife

Eternal Life: Spiritually transformed life, either after death or in the present

Eucharist: Christian act of worship involving shared bread and wine representing Jesus' body and blood

Evangelical: A type of **conservative** Christianity that focuses on being 'Born Again' and interprets the Bible as literally as possible

Exaltation: Promotion of a human to a divine rank

Exclusivism: Belief that only your own religion is true and all other religions (and atheists) will go to Hell

Exegesis: Analysing Bible passages for their meaning

Existentialism: Philosophy that proposes the meaning of an authentic life in a world where God does not intervene and there is no afterlife

Exorcism: Driving out demons or evil spirits that possess a person

Form Criticism: Interpretation of the Bible based on its origins as *pericopae* circulating among the first Christian communities

Fourth Gospel: Another term for John's Gospel

Futurist: Belief that **prophecy** or **eschatology** refers to the far future, not the present (**preterism**)

Galilee: Region to the north of **Judea** consisting of wooded hills and farmland surrounding Lake Galilee; an agricultural community with a mixture of Jews and **Gentiles**

Gentile: Someone who isn't Jewish by birth

Golden Rule: Moral code of reciprocity: treat others the way you want to be treated

Golgotha: Hill outside Jerusalem where Jesus was crucified (means 'place of the skull')

Great Commandment: Love God and love your neighbour as yourself

Great Commission: Instruction by the Risen Jesus for his Disciples to go and spread his message to all people, including **Gentiles**

Hallucination Theory: Theory that the appearances of the Risen Jesus to his Disciples were hallucinations brought on by stress, grief or guilt

Hegelianism: Philosophy of historical progress through the conflict between conflicting ideas

Hellenism: The Greek culture of the Roman Empire, especially its pagan religion, philosophy and art

Hermeneutics: Technique for interpreting the Bible

Herodian: The Jewish dynasty descended from Herod the Great (73-4 BCE)

Hillel the Elder: Jewish philosopher who lived in the 1st century BCE and claimed the Old Testament all boiled down to the **Golden Rule**

Historical Approach: Hermeneutic approach that tries to uncover the historical forces or events behind the Bible text

Hypocrisy: Sin of pretending to be good but acting sinfully; someone guilty of this is a hypocrite

I Am: The sacred Name of God in Hebrew, revealed to **Moses** by God and claimed by Jesus in John's Gospel

Idolatry: Worshiping something other than God or mistaking something man-made for God

Incarnation: Arrival of a divine being in physical form

Inerrancy: 'Without error'; belief that every word of the Bible is true

Inspired: Coming from God; a text containing God's wisdom and purposes

Johannine Community: Community of Jewish and Samaritan Christians who were expelled from the Synagogues, perhaps in Antioch c. 90 CE; composed John's Gospel

John the Baptist: Figure mentioned in all the Gospels who preceded Jesus and baptized many followers but was executed by Herod Antipas

Joseph of Arimathea: Wealthy man who takes down Jesus' body and provides an empty and unused tomb for it to rest in

Judea: Kingdom of Herod (including **Galilee**); after his death a smaller province (not including Galilee) ruled by a Roman governor

Kerygma: Greek for 'preaching'; the original Christian message of Jesus and his Apostles

Kingdom of God: rule of God over human life; may be a literal kingdom or a spiritual kingdom; may be experienced in the present or **eschatologically** (at the end of the world or after death)

Last Supper: A **seder** meal shared by Jesus and his Twelve Disciples on **Passover**; the basis for the **Eucharist**

Law: The religious rules of Judaism passed from God to Moses and written in the Torah; **Pharisees** believed in applying these rules to every aspect of life

Liberal Christianity: Christian trend opposed to **conservatism** and freely interpreting the Bible to new circumstances

Literalism: Interpreting the Bible in a straightforward factual way

Literary Approach: Hermeneutic approach that interprets the Bible as poetry or myth; see **narrative theology**

Luke-Acts: Luke's Gospel and Acts treated as a single book (since they have the same author)

Mary Magdalene: Female follower of Jesus; the first witness to the Resurrection in some Gospels

Messiah: The Anointed One; predicted saviour or king in Judaism (*Christos* in Greek)

Modernism: Christian trend opposed to **traditionalism** that redefines Christian teachings for the modern world

Moral Influence: Theory that atonement is brought about by **repentance** inspired by Jesus' perfect example

Moses: Greatest prophet and lawgiver in Judaism; received the **Law** from God (lived perhaps 1400 BCE)

Myth: (1) A story that may not be factually true but which contains a deeper meaning; (2) a pre-scientific way of expressing truths about the world

Mythicist Hypothesis: Theory that pagan or Jewish myths were attributed to Jesus after his death, producing stories of a Resurrection believed to be real

Narrative: A story, as opposed to a **proposition**

Narrative Theology: Hermeneutic approach that interprets the Bible as a story and resists attempts to reduce it to **propositions**

Nicodemus: Senior **Pharisee** who defends Jesus at his trial and helps to bury Jesus' body

Oral Tradition: Accounts of Jesus memorized and passed on by word-of-mouth

Origen: Greek-Egyptian philosopher of the 3rd century CE who defended Christianity against **Celsus**

Parable: Story told by Jesus, usually with peasant characters but containing a spiritual message; there are several in the **Synoptic Gospels**, especially Luke

Parousia: The 'Second Coming' of Christ to judge the world

Paschal Lamb: Animal sacrifice carried out in the Temple by the High Priest on the eve of **Passover**

Passover: Jewish festival celebrating the liberation of the Israelites from slavery in Egypt by **Moses**

Paul: A Christian missionary who converted after persecuting the early Christians; previously known as Saul

Penitent Thief: Crucified convict who defends Jesus, repents and is promised **Eternal Life**; tradition names him Dismas

Pericope: In **Form Criticism**, a textual unit that was originally a memory of Jesus passed on by word of mouth before the Gospels were written (plural *pericopae*)

Peter: The leader of the Twelve Disciples; also called Simon and **Cephas**

Pharisees: Jewish sect concerned with obeying the Law in every aspect of life; represented as in conflict with the first Christians

Pluralism: Arrangement where religions coexist and respect each other; also the belief that there is spiritual truth in all religions

Pontius Pilate: Roman *prefect* who governed **Judea** and sentenced Jesus to death

Preterist: Belief that **prophecy** or **eschatology** refers to the present not the future; can be **immediate** (right now) or **imminent** (not yet but soon)

Prophecy: A statement (often in the form of poetry) that reveals the will of God to humans

Proposition: A statement of truth, such as a definition, law or instruction (as opposed to a **narrative**)

Q-Source: Theoretical source for material common to Matthew and Luke that is not shared by Mark

Rational Approach: Hermeneutic approach that rejects the supernatural and historical elements in the Bible in favour of a rational Deist interpretation

Rationalism: Knowledge that comes from logical reasoning

Redaction Criticism: Interpretation of the Bible based on the idea of a redactor editing earlier material to address issues going on in the church in his time

Repentance: Feeling guilty for your sins and resolving to make amends to God; first stage of **atonement**

Sabbath: The 7th day of the week; Jewish Sabbath regulations forbid many types of work

Salvation-history: The idea that God has a plan for saving humans that is laid out in the Jewish Scriptures, begins to be fulfilled in the life, death and Resurrection of Jesus and is completely fulfilled in the future in the afterlife

Samaria: Hilly region between **Galilee** and **Judea**; homeland of the **Samaritans**

Samaritan: A religious group hated by 1st century Jews because of their different traditions about how to worship God

Sanhedrin: (1) A religious council of Jewish leaders; (2) According to Ellis Rivkin, a privy-council serving the High Priest and dealing with political threats

Scepticism: Doubting any knowledge without convincing evidence or argument; alternatively, disbelief in the possibility of certainty in knowledge

Seder: Ritual meal of lamb, bread and wine that is the highlight of the **Passover**

Sermon on the Plain: Sermon delivered by Jesus in Luke's Gospel, featuring teachings about loving your enemy and not judging each other

Sheol: Hebrew for 'the Grave'; word used for the Afterlife in the Old Testament; translated as *Hades* in New Testament Greek

Simon of Cyrene: Bystander forced by the Romans to carry Jesus' cross to **Golgotha**; may have been a Christian convert known to the author of Mark's Gospel

Sociological Approach: Hermeneutic approach that interprets the Bible as an example of a religious myth

Son of Man: Title Jesus adopted for himself based on prophecies in the Old Testament

Source Criticism: Interpretation of the Bible based on the different sources each Gospel is composed of

Swoon Theory: The idea that Jesus did not die on the cross and instead recovered later in the tomb

Synoptic Gospel: Matthew, Mark and Luke; from the Greek 'seen together' because of the shared content and structure of these Gospels

Theft Hypothesis: Theory that Jesus' body was stolen from the tomb (by his Disciples or by the Jewish authorities)

Traditionalism: Christian trend opposed to **modernism** that resists redefining Christian teachings for the modern world

Tropology: Interpreting the Bible as a moral **allegory**

Vision Theory: The theory that the appearances of the Risen Jesus were visions sent by God rather than a bodily resurrection

Woe: A curse or warning; thee are four Woes described in the **Sermon on the Plain**

Zealots: Jewish sect that believed in armed revolt against the Roman occupation

TOPIC 6 IN THE EXAM

A-Level Paper 3 (New Testament)

Section A

1   Explore the key ideas of Karl Barth on the ways of interpreting Scripture. **(8 marks)**

> *"Explore" questions award marks for AO1 (knowledge & understanding). You don't need to evaluate any of these ideas – just describe them. This question is pretty specific but it could be phrased more broadly, such as "explore the ways of interpreting Scripture".*

2   Assess the significance of rational approach to interpreting Scripture. **(12 marks)**

> *"Assess" questions award some marks for AO1 (4 marks in this question) but more for AO2 (evaluation – 8 marks in this question). You need to describe a bit about the content of this topic (such as Deism and the idea of the historical Jesus), but more about the debates concerning how it should be interpreted (are Christian moral ideas more important that supernatural beliefs? was Reimarus right about Jesus?).*

Section B

The Rich Man and Lazarus

[19] "There was a rich man who was dressed in purple and fine linen and lived in luxury every day. [20] At his gate was laid a beggar named Lazarus, covered with sores [21] and longing to eat what fell from the rich man's table. Even the dogs came and licked his sores.

[22] "The time came when the beggar died and the angels carried him to Abraham's side. The rich man also died and was buried. [23] In Hades, where he was in torment, he looked up and saw Abraham far away, with Lazarus by his side. [24] So he called to him, 'Father Abraham, have pity on me and send Lazarus to dip the tip of his finger in water and cool my tongue, because I am in agony in this fire.'

[25] "But Abraham replied, 'Son, remember that in your lifetime you received your good things, while Lazarus received bad things, but now he is comforted here and you are in agony. [26] And besides all this, between us and you a great chasm has been set in place, so that those who want to go from here to you cannot, nor can anyone cross over from there to us.'

[27] "He answered, 'Then I beg you, father, send Lazarus to my family, [28] for I have five brothers. Let him warn them, so that they will not also come to this place of torment.'

[29] "Abraham replied, 'They have Moses and the Prophets; let them listen to them.'

30 "'No, father Abraham,' he said, 'but if someone from the dead goes to them, they will repent.'

31 "He said to him, 'If they do not listen to Moses and the Prophets, they will not be convinced even if someone rises from the dead.'"

Quote from New International Translation, Luke 16: 19-31

3   (a) Clarify the ideas illustrated in this passage about the ethical teaching of Jesus. *You must refer to the passage in your response.* **(10 marks)**

> *"Clarify" questions only award marks for AO1 (knowledge & understanding), so all that is required is description. There is no need to evaluate whether this is a Parable or not – just discuss the ethical message about poverty, wealth, death and the Jewish prophets.*

(b) Analyse the claim that Jesus' ethical teachings are impractical. **(20 marks)**

> *This "Analyse" question awards some marks for AO1 (5 marks in this question), but mostly for AO2 (15 marks in this question). You need to describe a bit about the content (such as forgiving enemies and loving neighbours), but more about whether it is practical or not (are these teaching idealistic? how do we run into problems if we try to live by them?).*

Section C

4   Evaluate the view that Jesus was executed for blasphemy. In your response to this question, you must include how developments in New Testament Studies have been influenced by one of the following:

- Philosophy of Religion
- Religion and Ethics
- the study of a religion (other than Christianity)   **(30 marks)**

> *This "Evaluate" question awards some marks for AO1 (5 marks in this question), but mostly for AO2 (25 marks). You need to describe a bit about the content (such as Jesus' claims to be God), but more about whether this s the reason Jesus had to die (e.g. rather then political expediency). In order to attain beyond the top of level 4 (i.e. score 25+) you must link to another area of the course (such as religious language or religion & morality).*

Total = 90 marks

> *In these examples, all the questions are drawn from Topic 4-6. A real A-Level exam might draw from Topics 1-3 as well.*

LOOKING BACK OVER YEAR 2...

If you are studying for the A-Level exam, you have reached the end of the New Testament Studies course. When revising this course, it is helpful to 'work backwards'.

Start off by reflecting on the link between the **Resurrection** and **Jesus' ethical teaching**. This raises the question, *What IS Christianity?* Is it a belief in a world-changing supernatural event that happened on Easter morning 2000 years ago – and perhaps a world-ending Apocalypse that could occur in the imminent future? Or is it a set of moral teachings to love and forgive and be generous? Can you stop believing in the Resurrection as a physical event in history and still be a Christian? Or is believing in the Resurrection part of the life-changing transformation (called being 'Born Again' in **John's Gospel**) that goes beyond just following moral rules?

- Are Christians moral people following the wise teachings of a man who died 2000 years ago?
- Or are they people who have been transformed by their faith in Christ who still lives and guides them?

Reflecting on this will help you decide whether the **Kingdom of God** in **Topic 5** is supposed to be an event in future history, a spiritual change that comes over people today or a description of the Afterlife.

- Did Jesus teach a spiritual message of transformation and love that was misunderstood by his literal-minded followers?
- Or did Jesus predict a literal Apocalypse that never occurred – with his later followers salvaging a message of love and goodness from the failure of his 'Kingdom' to materialise?

This will help you look again at Jesus' **conflicts with authority**, his **trial** and **crucifixion** in **Topic 5**.

- Was Jesus trying to tell people something they were too blind or bigoted to hear? If so, his message might still be relevant today, even though the people of his own time misunderstood him.
- Or was he an innocent pawn caught up in the political intrigue of the Jewish priests and the Roman Empire? If so, he's a tragic loser and later Christians misunderstood him.

This theme of 'misunderstanding' runs through our analysis of the Gospels. **John's Gospel** frequently represents people misunderstanding Jesus, but a lot of Biblical criticism suggests that it may be the later Christians who have misunderstood things – and that the historical Jesus might have been nothing like the 'Christ of faith'.

With this is mind you can look again at the conflict between **Barth** and **Bultmann** in **Topic 4**. Bultmann assumes Jesus and his message have been massively misunderstood by Christians and atheists. He wants to 'wipe the slate clean' and look at Jesus again with fresh eyes so we can all take a new message from the Gospels. Barth thinks any attempt to interpret the Bible with philosophy will only lead to misunderstanding. He thinks that the Bible is our only witness to the Word of God in Jesus – and we have to read it as if it's speaking to us personally.

ABOUT THE AUTHOR

Jonathan Rowe is a teacher of Religious Studies, Psychology and Sociology at Spalding Grammar School and he creates and maintains the **www.psychologywizard.net** site for Edexcel A-Level Psychology and **www.philosophydungeon.weebly.com** for Religious Studies. He has worked as an examiner for various Exam Boards but is not affiliated with Edexcel. This series of books grew out of the resources he created for his students. Jonathan also writes novels and creates resources for his hobby of fantasy wargaming. He likes warm beer and smooth jazz.

Printed in Great Britain
by Amazon

16484694R00147